Guillermo del Toro

Guillermo del Toro

Film as Alchemic Art

Keith McDonald and Roger Clark

Bloomsbury Academic
An imprint of Bloomsbury Publishing Plc

B L O O M S B U R Y
NEW YORK • LONDON • NEW DELHI • SYDNEY

Bloomsbury Academic
An imprint of Bloomsbury Publishing Inc

1385 Broadway	50 Bedford Square
New York	London
NY 10018	WC1B 3DP
USA	UK

www.bloomsbury.com

**BLOOMSBURY and the Diana logo are trademarks of
Bloomsbury Publishing Plc**

First published 2014
Paperback edition first published 2015

Library of Congress Cataloging-in-Publication Data
McDonald, Keith.
Guillermo del Toro: film as alchemic art/Keith McDonald and Roger Clark.
pages cm
Includes bibliographical references and index.
Includes fi lmography.
ISBN 978-1-4411-2449-4 (hardback: alk. paper) 1. Toro, Guillermo del, 1964–Criticism
and interpretation. I. Clark, Roger, 1950- II. Title.
PN1998.3.T583M34 2014
791.4302'33092 – dc23
2013045230

ISBN: HB: 978-1-4411-2449-4
PB: 978-1-5013-0861-1
ePDF: 978-1-4411-8402-3
ePUB: 978-1-6235-6013-3

Typeset by Integra Software Service Pvt. Ltd.

For Kelly and Lesley

Contents

Acknowledgements

We would like to thank York St John University (YSJU) for their support and encouragement during this project; the Faculty of Arts at YSJU has been an excellent environment in which to research and write. The help and expertise of the staff at the British Library (Boston Spa) have also been invaluable to this book. Bobby Kuehl at Syracuse University, Madrid, has provided expert advice on Hispanic cinema, and we wish to thank him for his valuable observations. Lesley Clark's proofreading skills have been a tremendous help, and Katie Gallof's editorial advice and guidance has helped make the production of this book a pleasure. Finally, we would like to thank our students, whose passion for the study of cinema has invigorated our work.

Introduction

The title of this study of Guillermo del Toro's films was decided upon early on in the project. The alchemic metaphor is one that he himself employs from the very start of his film-making career and has been cited elsewhere as being applicable to an artist whose work is composed of so many diverse elements. For example, in a recent study of the Gothic, Victoria Nelson avers that '[m]ore than any other element of the Old Goth worldview ... the imagery of alchemy permeates del Toro's films' (2012: 229). His first major film *Cronos* (1993) begins with a voice-over account of the sixteenth-century alchemist Fulcanelli's flight from Europe to Mexico, an uncanny reverse image of del Toro's own journey as a director from Mexico to Spain for two of his most critically lauded films, *The Devil's Backbone* (*El Espinazo del Diablo*) (2001) and *Pan's Labyrinth* (*El Laberinto del Fauno*) (2006). Given the centrality of the alchemic analogy to del Toro's approach to film, this study attempts to unpick its implications and relate them to a number of broader issues in contemporary cinema. It is plain that alchemy's obsession with transformation pervades del Toro's oeuvre, from the vampiric metamorphosis in *Cronos* (1993) to the human/machine interfaces in his most recent *Pacific Rim* (2013), which was premiered just before this book's completion. As director/alchemist he takes often disparate generic elements and transmutes them into new and startling forms, a process of filmic chemistry certainly not unique in the annals of cinema, as demonstrated in the careers of earlier figures such as Orson Welles and del Toro's own acknowledged master Alfred Hitchcock, as well as in the cinema of more recent directors such as David Cronenberg and David Lynch. Like these film-makers, del Toro is a committed illusionist and in being so has one fundamental trick up his sleeve. Alchemists are famed for taking base metals and through a process of transmutation producing precious materials. Del Toro's alchemic art is bound together by the fact that although others may see his base texts as *base*, as trash (B-movies, comic books, horror), he himself clearly values them as treasured commodities with rich creative potential. Born in 1964, del Toro is still in mid-career, but we feel that the body of work he has produced thus far is sufficient in its distinctiveness and importance to warrant an analysis, albeit interim. His peculiar brand of alchemy has its own very identifiable features. Rather like the exiled magus figure of Prospero in Shakespeare's *The Tempest*, his films conjure fantastic spirits and acknowledge the power and significance of monsters whilst exploring, through this intersection of fantasy and reality, the tensions and conflicts of human history and politics. Alchemy's interest in hybridity and the consequent loosening of apparently inviolable borderlines, cultural and generic, provides a clue to del Toro's modus operandi, since his art is predicated on similar motifs and tropes. This applies to both the content and the form of his films, as well as to his presence as an influential figure within contemporary cinema. As Antonio Lázaro-Reboll observes in a recent study of Spanish Horror, 'Many cultural commentators describe del Toro as fan, connoisseur, craftsman, cinephile and auteur, since he is equally comfortable talking about films in Cannes as he is discussing them in front of fans at comic conventions' (2012: 255). Ultimately, it is his ability to traverse such extraordinarily varied cultural domains with a kind of egalitarian fascination and wonder that imbues his films with such alchemic originality. Del Toro's engagement with fandom and popular culture and the impact of his extraordinarily wide-ranging and near-obsessive connoisseurship of film, literature and art on his own cinematic craft are considered in this study. We also locate his work within other theoretic and thematic contexts and spaces that help to define contemporary cinema, in particular transnationalism and the relationship between film, cultural memory and trauma.

Charles Derry appropriately describes del Toro's methodology as 'eclectically postmodern'; however, we should not assume that this eclectic approach involves only intertextual reference to other fictions, although such referents are vast (2009: 316). Moreover, the eclecticism in his oeuvre is present at almost every level – narrative, visual, generic and technical. Perhaps paradoxically, it is the eclectic, alchemic nature of the work which holds it together as a remarkably coherent body rather than the smörgåsbord it may initially appear to be. It is our argument that a number of central thematics and approaches synthesize his work in a remarkable fashion and that del Toro has exhibited a consistent cinematic project unusual in a film-maker who has worked in various industrial contexts.

Central to this mode is hybridity which emerges from appropriation, re-contextualization and re-presentation: existing texts transformed into a new entity made up of their various components – now as a coherent whole. Del

Toro's obsession is the obsession of Victor Frankenstein, compelled to create from used, discarded and diverse sources, with monstrous results. All of del Toro's films feature the fantastical and supernatural, yet all are set on Earth and in clear socio-historic settings. All of his films portray children or adults arrested in childlike states and portray broken families and the search for kinship with others who are similarly disenfranchised from the nuclear family unit. All of his films portray human beings coming into contact with other supernatural species (vampires, ghosts, insectoids, demons, reptilian monsters). All contain monsters, but they are equally ambiguous about assigning binary moral statuses on what is monstrous and what is evil. Often, the real moral void in the films is to be found in the human characters, whereas the monsters themselves are misunderstood and alienated by the human population, much like Victor Frankenstein's creation.

This hybridity is fuelled by three cinematic legacies: genre cinema, transnational cinema and Queer cinema. Guillermo del Toro is an extremely vocal champion of horror; indeed, it unifies all of his work (often hybridized with science-fiction, adventure, fairy tale and the political narrative) and in some sense it provides a narrative and thematic philosophy. Robin Wood writes, 'Central to the effect and fascination of horror films is their fulfilment of our nightmare wish to smash the norms that oppress us and which our moral conditioning teaches us to revere' (Wood in Jancovich 2002: 28). This nightmare wish typifies del Toro's oeuvre, which consistently undermines rule and order (Fascistic rule, logic, binaries of good and evil) in terms of dark chaos, disorder and madness. This is further fuelled by his Lovecraftian sensibility. Victoria Nelson notes that the typical Lovecraft story portrays a descent into madness and/or a transformation into monstrosity, and in all cases, the by-product of knowledge is chaos and discord, highlighting a familiar narrative trope in del Toro's work (Nelson 2012: 59–60). In all cases, we have an unusually brief (for mainstream cinema) period of equilibrium which is quickly disrupted; chaos ensues, and although our protagonists may prevail, this is never a Hollywood happy ending involving the restoration of order (Ofelia dies in *Pan's Labyrinth*, the orphanage burns to the ground in *The Devil's Backbone*, Hellboy's group is exiled in *Hellboy II: The Golden Army* (2008)). This ambiguity around closure is also at the core of the horror genre and its central disavowal of civilization. Wood continues, 'One might say that the true subject of the horror genre is the struggle for recognition of all that our civilization represses or oppresses: its re-emergence dramatized, as in our nightmares, as an object of horror, a matter for terror, and the "happy ending" (when it exists) typically signifying the restoration of repression' (2002: 28). It's illuminating, when considering the centrality of horror in del Toro's oeuvre, to compare the work of Steven Spielberg. There are clear similarities between del Toro and Spielberg in terms of the subject matter they explore. For instance, both are interested in the figure of the child as a cipher witness figure. Charles Derry uses the term 'wide-eyed child protagonist' to describe the character trope in del Toro's oeuvre (following on from Victor Erice's *The Spirit of the Beehive* (*El Espíritu de la Colmena*) (1973) as a template text), and this is famously evident in Spielberg's body of work. Both directors have perpetuated and re-invigorated the monster movie as serious cinema; both have tackled Fascism and its legacies; both have re-interpreted fairy tale for adult audiences (*A.I. Artificial Intelligence.* (2001) mines *Pinocchio* as *Pan's Labyrinth* riffs on *Alice's Adventures in Wonderland*). However, in terms of tone and resolution, del Toro and Spielberg differ dramatically. Peter Kramer provides a succinct overview of Spielberg's cinematic project:

> At the heart of Spielberg's filmmaking are his overwhelming desire and exceptional ability to move audiences [that is, to provide them with sensual thrills and emotional stimulation]. He focuses strongly on families both on and off screen, telling stories about problem-ridden relationships between parents and children to multigenerational audiences. He is driven by a belief in cinema's potential to engage people with important developments in American and indeed world history, to offer models of moral behaviour, and even its ability to provide spiritual comfort. (2006: 167)

Even more succinct is Derry's summation of del Toro's work, which he describes as cinema of 'exceptional brutality and fantasy' (318). This level of brutality in relation to Spielberg's output is referenced by del Toro himself, who has said when discussing his decision to kill off two 'wide-eyed' child characters in his monster movie *Mimic* (1997):

> It is something that I really take very seriously when I make the movies. I feel that there is so much more danger in showing kids in a movie about giant dinosaurs and claiming that the dinosaurs won't eat them. In reality, they would. I think it's best to show that should a child ever encounter danger they should act cautiously. (Wood 2006b: 36)

Not only is there more inherent danger in the dark adventures of del Toro, but the endings of the films are far bleaker or at least ambivalent towards neat, optimistic closure which is informed by a belief in a manifest destiny mentality. Spielberg's tendency for last-act depictions of the triumph of good over evil and closure is well documented (McDonald 2002), and for some this is a weakness in an otherwise phenomenal ability to tell stories. As Williams et al. confirm, Spielberg's project also focuses on American culture, history and its place in the wider world and cosmos. It is here that another key contrast can be found in relation to del Toro. This is not simply in terms of the fact that Spielberg places America in context whereas del Toro includes Hispanic and non-US perspectives even in his US-funded projects (as is the case in the *Hellboy* series and *Pacific Rim*). It is more so the case that whereas Spielberg looks from American soil to the stars in the case of much of his sci-fi work (*E.T. The Extra Terrestrial* (1982), *Close Encounters of the Third Kind* (1977) and *War of the Worlds* (2005)), del Toro looks from more transnational locations to the underworld, where it is not the cosmic but the occult which manifests itself (*Cronos, Pan's Labyrinth, Blade II* (2002), *Hellboy* (2004) and *Hellboy II: The Golden Army* (2008)). This fascination with darker territory (such as in the character of Hellboy, who is borne out of a Nazi occultist programme) and refusal of many Hollywood conventions situates del Toro as an alternative to mainstream cinema as epitomized by Spielberg. In this sense, del Toro does not make anti-Spielbergian cinema, as in many ways both directors draw from the same wells, but does make alter-Spielbergian cinema, where the subversive triumphs over the satisfying. Consider, for example, this comparison. Both directors deal with the Second World War and its legacies and both directors re-interpret and represent fairy tale. However, whereas for the most part Spielberg has carved out two outstanding oeuvres, one realist (*Schindler's List* (1993), *Saving Private Ryan* (1998) *and Munich* (2005)) and one fantastical (*Hook* (1991), *Jurassic Park* (1993) and *Minority Report* (2002)), del Toro's filmic alchemy portrays the blending together of real-world historic trauma with supernatural phenomena (*The Devil's Backbone, Pan's Labyrinth* and *Hellboy*). Notably, the horrors of the historic trauma in *Pan's Labyrinth* and *The Devil's Backbone* are not diminished by the fantastical elements. In fact, the violence and trauma of war, such as the executions and attacks depicted in these films, are seen by netherworld beings, bearing witness to the brutality of these strange humans and their greed for money and power. Interestingly, the only occasion where Spielberg blends historic trauma with the supernatural is in the Indiana Jones series, which the opening scene in *Hellboy* closely resembles (although del Toro has been critical of Spielberg's representations of non-US characters in this franchise (Wood 2006b: 36)).

This alternative alchemic process along with other factors situates Guillermo del Toro as an outsider compared to the perennial insider status of Spielberg, who as film-maker, producer and icon has had more effect on modern Hollywood cinema than anyone else. Another key element which sets del Toro apart is his (unfixed) position as transnational and exilic film-maker. Transnational film scholar Hamid Naficy employs the term 'accented cinema' in relation to the output of exilic and diasporic film-making, and this is entirely relevant to del Toro's position and oeuvre (2001). As a man in exile from Mexico as a result of his father's kidnapping in 1998, del Toro has worked in Spain and the US as well as spending several years in New Zealand on *The Hobbit* (1937) adaptation. It may be no coincidence then that all of his films feature outcasts, exiles and displaced individuals with tenuous yet vital links to their homelands. This is, for instance, as important a factor in the *Hellboy* franchise, whose protagonist is cast out of the netherworld, as it is to Ofelia in *Pan's Labyrinth*, orphaned in a turbulent world and perhaps originating out of a mystical monarchy. Although Naficy arguably underestimates the complexity of some Hollywood output, he draws clear differences between contemporary US and accented transnational cinema:

> Applied to cinema, the standard, neutral, value-free accent maps onto the dominant cinema produced by the society's reigning modes of production. This typifies the classical and the new Hollywood cinemas, whose films are realistic and intended for entertainment only, and thus free from ideology and accent. By that definition, all alternative cinemas are accented, but each is accented in certain specific ways that distinguish it. (23)

In this context, as an outsider working within Hollywood, del Toro remains alternative, no matter how 'mainstream' the films may at first appear. This disrupts the notion that del Toro produces art-house films and popcorn entertainment in mutually exclusive strands. Charles Derry dismisses del Toro's English-language output as inferior to the Spanish-language works which he sees as 'more artful and so allow for the clearer expression of Del Toro's personal obsessions – particularly those relating to politics, children, and the central role of fantasy in our lives' (2009: 317). Others see value in the English-language work and accept that the bolder, bigger canvas of the US output (and in particular the *Hellboy* films) suits a film-maker who himself is a champion of popular fiction. Del Toro contends that his two favourite films are *The Devil's Backbone* and *Hellboy*, which contradicts the prevalent opinion that *Pan's Labyrinth* is the zenith of this part of his career (Wood 2006b: 45). What is clear though is that even when directing in Hollywood, del Toro still works against the grain and offers another accent to the mainstream dialogue. Consider for instance *Mimic*, his first English-language film which at first glance appears to be a standard B-movie monster picture. On close inspection though, the prickly, bizarre nature of the film emerges. This includes the infanticide plague which starts the film, the refusal to allow safe passage to the child characters and the surreal, Goya-esque insectoid creatures which have been read by some as cross-dressing serial killers. Other paradoxes are also apparent in his US films. For example, on a certain level, in making a superhero franchise such as *Hellboy* (and contributing to the *Blade* series), del Toro could be said to participate in a prevalent popular trend of the last 15 years, the adaptation and evolution of the US superhero movie. However, noteworthy is the point that the comic books from which he takes inspiration are not from the dominant publishing houses of DC and Marvel. *Hellboy*, for instance, emerges out of Dark Horse comics, a company specifically set up to offer an alternative to the 'big two' and cultivate darker, adult-orientated alternatives to the mainstream. Similarly, *Pacific Rim* appears initially to be made as a part of the commercial appeal of the *Transformers* (2007–) franchise (produced by Steven Spielberg from a toy range co-produced by Japanese Tomy and US Hasbro) with its mega-tech action adventure contents. Del Toro, though, has countered this impression in interview and in a veiled reference to *Transformers* rejects the claim and attests to the Gothic nature of *Pacific Rim*:

> [what you see] is not a sleek, fluorescent lit super-cool recruitment video for the army, it's very very rusty and fucked up and emotional and romantic. We fetishize the tech in a different way, I love tech that has gone through a lot of battle, it's really really damaged and romantic and beautiful in that way. (http://www.youtube.com/watch?v=HhellFhEcU8)

Furthermore, it's worth noting that *Pacific Rim* reinstates the East Asian element to the mega-tech genre and his interpretation of the Kaiju monster genre creates in essence a transnational blockbuster.

In addition to the accented transnational qualities evident in del Toro's methodology and output, there is a concurrent strand of Queer cinema at play. In some ways, situating Guillermo del Toro in the realm of Queer cinema might appear incongruous. Certainly, on a surface level, del Toro seems remarkably coy in relation to sexual content (in both heteronormative and alternative contexts) in his output hitherto. True, many of his films are generally aimed towards a mature audience, but it is in the macabre, twisted and often violent content where this adult material is most evident. In comparison to one of del Toro's mentors, Pedro Almodóvar, the sexual content of del Toro's work seems positively tame. Of course, Queer cinema is much more than the inclusion of gay and queer-identified characters and 'LGBT' issues. Using suitably Gothic language, Sue-Ellen Case sums up Queer as a stylistic phenomenon. She writes:

> The queer is the taboo-breaker, the monstrous, the uncanny. Like the Phantom of the Opera, the queer dwells underground, below the operatic overtones of the dominant, frightening to look at, desiring, as it plays its own organ, producing its own music. (Case 1993: 3)

This assessment of the Queer is entirely applicable to del Toro and his entire project is at once inspired by art (both visual and literary) and artefacts that are bizarre and beautiful and a commitment to turning that which is established and sterilized into that which is dangerous and 'down and dirty' (Clark and McDonald 2010: 60). Yingjin Zhang contends that Queer cinema disavows 'fixed identity, and mainstream acceptance' and instead 'thrives on provocation, ambiguity and strangeness' (2012: 519). In this context, although del Toro is not a gay-identified director like many of the New Queer Cinema film-makers (Pedro Almodóvar, Gus Van Sant, Todd Haynes), nevertheless his work has what has been described as a 'queer appeal' because it challenges conventions of gender and sexuality. Here then, del Toro can be considered alongside non-Hollywood directors who produce accented cinema that is also Queer in nature. Directors such as David Cronenberg, Luc Besson and Baz Luhrmann operate in transnational contexts and all provide counter-discourse perspectives to heteronormative, straight narratives. Other factors that are key in relation to Queer cinema and del Toro, such as the Gothic dimensions of his films and the outsider status that both defines and stratifies his subjects, will be discussed later in this book.

One aspect which provides a clear bridge between the accented and Queer elements on del Toro, a potent mix in his alchemic cinema, is genre hybridity and appropriation. One of the defining features of New Queer Cinema is the re-interpretation of canonical or familiar stories whilst simultaneously 'queering' them in order to highlight alternative scripts and counter-discourses. This can be seen, for example, in the work of Derek Jarman, who takes Shakespearian and other canonical, mythical narratives and applies to them uncustomary formations. David Hawkes contends that in his 'treatments' of established

Renaissance texts by the likes of Marlowe and Shakespeare, in which gay subjectivity is highlighted as a disruptive force, Jarman also provides a critique of classical cinema. He writes:

> In Jarman's films, the spectacle re-emerges from the underground to disrupt and to complicate the assumptions of narrative realism, and, in doing so, it challenges the definitions of sexuality and gender roles which have defined classical cinema. (Lippard 1996: 105)

Similar treatments of the like can be seen in Gus Van Sant's *My Own Private Idaho* (1991), which provides a version of *Henry IV* as a homosexual romance, and Baz Luhrmann's *Romeo and Juliet* (1996), which colourfully situates the transgressive nature of the central romance in an environment where sexual alternatives and Queer attitudes thrive. More closely linked to the work of del Toro, New Queer Cinema also resulted in an invigorated vampire cinema. The influence of the AIDS epidemic on New Queer Cinema is well documented, and Kathryn Bigelow's *Near Dark* (1987), Neil Jordan's *Interview with the Vampire* (1994), Abel Ferrara's *The Addiction* (1995) and Francis Ford Coppola's *Bram Stoker's Dracula* (1992) all incorporate the notion of infected blood into a recognizable thematic subtext (Benshoff and Griffin 2004). Considering this in relation to del Toro's oeuvre, *Cronos* also works in this manner, not least in a scene where Jesús licks blood from a public toilet floor. Del Toro has drawn attention to the power of this scene, influenced by the social paranoia associated with the HIV virus which added a sinister danger to the notion of public intercourse in a post-AIDS world:

> The character in the film is a very prissy antiquarian that lives an incredibly secluded life. I wanted him to be alive only after he dies. Here, we see the first symptoms of vampirism in him … To me this scene is incredibly erotic but it's absolutely perverse. And the idea was, how do I prove that this guy needed the blood like an addiction? If you're going to suck Winona Ryder, I'm up for it. Everybody would have their hand up. Or if you're going to have Brad Pitt suck you, I'm sure a lot of people would raise their hands. So I wanted to do the most vile thing to show he really needed the blood. So it's an addiction scene. (Kermode 2006b)

Here the spectre of AIDS (associated with many New Queer Cinema narratives) is also given a transnational, accented dimension as the HIV epidemic in Mexico during the 1980s was spread largely due to intravenous drug use, and so the addiction scene in the film is a hybrid of New Queer Cinema and accented thematics.

Hybridity is also a central effect of del Toro's alchemy. Drawing from the rich lineage of hybridity in genre film (in, for instance, *La Belle and la bête* (1946), *Alien* (1979) and *Spirit of the Beehive* (1973)), which most frequently includes elements of horror, del Toro has thus far made a modern-day fable vampire film, a bildungsroman ghost story, a political horror/fairy tale, Gothic superhero movies and a wartime adventure monster movie. Hybridity itself is a part of both Queer and accented cinema. For example, Ira Jaffe contends that '[h]ybrid cinema … emerges as a vehicle for exploring hybrid dimensions of human identity' (2008: 27). In the context of Queer Cinema, hybridity brings to the fore the nature of gender as a performance and the ways in which re-contextualization through appropriation illuminate this performance in, for instance, hybrids of westerns and romances, such as *My Own Private Idaho*, *Thelma and Louise* (1991) and *Brokeback Mountain* (2005). Darren Elliott argues that appropriation is inherently subversive in relation to sexuality and gender, in that it disrupts hegemonic scripts, noting that '[t]he very act of appropriating imagery and the iconography from mainstream and cult film works to reconfigure gendered subjectivities that are imposed upon subjects via ideological (and often heteronormative) narratives' (2010).

Elliott and others note that hybrid transnational cinema tends to be more critical of mainstream given that it acts as a counterpoint to received codes and conventions. Jaffe contends that hybrid cinema has the potential to 'jolt' our consciousness because of its fundamental incongruity and that the convergences of transnational cinema draw upon artistic fascinations with the surreal (Jaffe 2008: 154). Considering this, Hispanic cinema with its direct line to the founders of Surrealism, its allegiance to surrealistic film-makers such as Buñuel and its discourse of subliminal coded imagery is a perfect wellspring for hybridity. This also has its roots in the cinema of the Franco regime, where real threats to direct political critique in art resulted in layered, symbolic and suggestive discourse. Antonio Monegal points out that under Franco, Spanish cinema enacted a 'remarkable tendency to disguise its message by means of a highly codified symbolic discourse' (1998: 203). Monegal uses the example of Carlos Saura's *The Hunt* (*La Caza*) (1966), where a day of hunting rabbits acts as a motif of national conflict, a symbolic note that is echoed in *Pan's Labyrinth*.

In terms of the wider cinematic project that del Toro is undertaking, the symbolic, enigmatic and intricate puzzle is a key motif. Be it the complex, mystical device in *Cronos*, the virus to be cured in *Mimic* or the labyrinth which hides the pathway to the future in *Pan's Labyrinth*, the centrality of the puzzle provides a key narrative driver. Del Toro has described his work as academic and has engaged in scholarly publishing in the past. This deeply layered cinema filled with ancient lore and mythology, complex and arcane references to fiction, art and intertextual pop-cultural artefacts is labyrinthal in itself and has something of the academic about it. Lindsey Steenberg describes del Toro's films as 'explicitly philosophical', and this in turn relates to the genres he is drawn to, where the centrality of the secret is key to Gothic narratives and the inquisitive 'what if' nature of science-fiction rules. In addition, it's also worth noting that scholars and scientists play key roles in his films. A mysterious alchemist creates the Cronos device, *Mimic's* protagonist is a scientist and the Hellboy's mentor is an academic occult historian. This yet again ties in with the motifs of Gothic and science fiction. Dr Frankenstein, Stoker's Dr "Jack" Seward and many protagonists from the fiction of Lovecraft are driven by scientific and academic enquiry, and the narratives of seminal science-fiction texts from the likes of H.G. Wells and Jules Verne are propelled by keen academic minds. The complex rubrics of the works and workings of Guillermo del Toro follow in this tradition and are dedicated to decoding the network of complexities and mythologies of past art and artefacts but are also equally dedicated to re-coding complex and potent new mythologies from what has come before.

The structure of this book

This book is broadly structured into two parts, each with separate components which explore key features of del Toro's creative output and mode of operation. The first part deals with key contexts in which the film-maker operates and the second explores in more detail the films and projects on which he has worked.

Chapter 1 investigates a range of influences on del Toro's work from the worlds of Film, Literature and Art. Others have noted that attempts to fully document the gargantuan set of intertextual references and the enormous web of symbolic, iconic and thematic interplays which del Toro employs are doomed to failure. If intertextual exchanges are to be equated with a kind of filmic theology or worship, then del Toro is a true pantheist, drawing from the full range of art modes and genres, and these intertextual exchanges will be charted many times in this book. What is absolutely apparent is a threefold intertextual strategy. First, there is a temporal span which sees del Toro reference and play with texts from ancient cultures to twenty-first century zeitgeist. Iconography from ancient Greece is spliced with video game or Manga motifs (such as in

Pacific Rim) to create playful yet resonant new formations. Second, del Toro is genuinely blind to the merit distinctions between 'high' and 'low' culture. Goya is mined as an inspiration alongside 1970s slasher B-movies with no distinction between cultural worth (as in *Mimic*), and del Toro's absolute belief in the power of pop is a key driving force to his cinematic project. Third, the whole notion of intertextual reference is destabilized because hybridity and interpretation are always present. Rather than simply include reference to another text as an intertextual nod, del Toro almost always alters, blends or upturns his referent in order to produce new meaning and re-contextualization. His film-making is an example of cinematic bricolage of reconfiguration and translation.

The first section of Chapter 1 deals with filmic influences. Canonized auteurs of cinema such as Hitchcock and Buñuel are explored as is the creative dialogue which del Toro engages in across his work. Key here is the notion that del Toro's films, whether they are lower budget films which some have considered 'art house' or Hollywood action adventure films, are all engaged in this dialogue with some of the world's most celebrated film-makers. This section also takes into account some of the more obscure filmic intertextual exchanges and suggests that he engages with B-movie and lesser celebrated film-makers as well as recognized auteur figures.

The second section considers literary influences and exchanges. Similar to the huge array of film sources which del Toro draws from and responds to, the library from which del Toro borrows is vast and, unlike Borges's labyrinthine Babel, extraordinarily fertile. However key genres and movements can be identified. Del Toro's films are all inspired by Gothic literature in one way or another and some are very specifically engaged with the Victorian Gothic tradition, as will be explored. His interplay with key Gothic writers such as Mary Shelley and Bram Stoker is relatively well documented and the influence of underrated writers such as H.P. Lovecraft is clear. However, we also explore other Gothic influences and argue that canonically familiar English authors such as Charles Dickens act as a fruitful source from which he draws inspiration. We also discuss the importance of fairy tale and magic realism as a fundamental part of del Toro's creative DNA.

The third section of Chapter 1 investigates the influence of visual art forms; and the plural is important here. Del Toro is influenced by key painters ranging from Hieronymus Bosch to Goya to late nineteenth-century Symbolists. Equally though, photography plays a more significant than hitherto documented role in his filmic compositions and styles. This involves a potent mix of social realism photography from the likes of Robert Capa and Henri Cartier-Bresson with experimental and surrealist photography from artists such as Man Ray and Joel-Peter Witkin. In keeping with his commitment to pop-cultural forms as wellsprings for creative engagement, del Toro is also heavily influenced by children's illustrators such as Arthur Rackham, book cover illustrators such as Frank Frazetta and of course comic book artists and video-game creators. Most notably, del Toro's collaboration with comic book writer and illustrator Mike Mignola is significant and we explore the role of Dark Horse Comics as a creative hub of which del Toro is a significant part.

Chapter 2 situates del Toro's oeuvre in relation to two movements in screen studies: transnationalism and Queer film. More specifically, we contend that del Toro's particular brand of cinema is a blend of transnational film-making and Queer cinema and that this blending is present across his entire body of work. In many ways del Toro typifies the transnational film-maker. Not only do his films take place in transnational locations (Mexico, Spain, North America, the South Pacific, etc.), but they come from inter-continental production sources. In addition, del Toro is committed to bringing Hispanic cinema to a wider audience and has championed the films of, amongst others, Alfonso Cuarón, Juan Antonio Bayona and Andrés Muschietti. As a film-maker in exile, del Toro not only exemplifies the role of the director working with the aid of the outsider's eye but crucially incorporates exilic narratives into his body of work, which can be described as accented. This section of the chapter then explores key thematic transnational elements which are literally and figuratively present in his oeuvre. These are the use of language in the films, border-crossing and kinship.

The second half of this chapter takes into account del Toro's relation to Queer cinema. Central to this is his Gothic sensibility and the ways in which the Queer uncanny fuels all of his work to date. We chart some of the history of the Queer Gothic and the ways in which artists in the genre have crafted transgressive narratives. We explore the nature of sex and sexuality in his films, and in particular the ways in which del Toro destabilizes heteronormative relationships in movies which have been described as 'gleefully impure'. In addition, we explore some of del Toro's work in relation to New Queer Cinema and the ways in which vampire mythology took on new significance in the wake of AIDS. Finally, we argue that a distinct level of 'queering' takes place in del Toro's work, particularly the ways in which he presents a perverse religion which works in the context of the Queer Gothic.

Chapter 3 explores fandom in the work of del Toro and his position in the renaissance of 'geek' culture which currently dominates Western cinema and television. Del Toro is a film-maker who has an incredibly open and active engagement with fans of cult culture and is a self-confessed uber-geek. If there is a direct polar opposite to the reclusive film-maker figure of the likes of Terrence Malick, it is Guillermo del Toro, and he has garnered an extremely loyal fan base in the blogging community. We explore the nature of fandom, and explicitly the ways in which fan communities adhere to a value system which celebrates 'low' cultural forms and how this sensibility pervades del Toro's output. Following in the footsteps of Forrest Ackerman, one of the founders of science-fiction fandom, del Toro is not only an avid collector of genre paraphernalia and paratextual film material but also acts as a kind of cultural ambassador of the fan community and as a curator of what we describe as 'geek' couture.

This chapter also focuses on the ways in which fandom is present in the narratives of del Toro's cinema, and we argue that the power of fandom and the ability of pop culture to draw together individuals are key moral drivers in his films. For example, obsessive individuals can often be found in del Toro's work, and this obsession with cultural artefacts often leads to salvation; indeed obsessive behaviour is presented in del Toro's films as a positively admirable trait. Finally, this chapter looks at the ways in which recent changes to the modes of production, distribution and communication of film have allowed del Toro to inhabit his persona of fan as film-maker and that technological developments such as the advent of the Internet and the DVD/Blu-ray commentary have functioned as highly suitable channels for del Toro's willing voice.

The second part of this book looks more closely at the films themselves; these chapters discuss several films at a time in sections which are linked thematically, following a loosely chronological order.

Chapter 4 considers the ways in which del Toro twists genre conventions and produces bizarre and transgressive genre films, focusing on the strange hybrid texts in *Cronos* and *Mimic*. *Cronos* provides an early example of del Toro's intertextual mode of film-making. Drawing from the vast annals of Gothic fiction, del Toro creates a film which is engaged in a complex dialogue with canonical Gothic texts such as *Frankenstein* (1818) and *Dracula* (1897), and blended along with a huge array of other texts in what amounts to a paradoxically coherent if bizarre take on the genre. Many of the key tropes of del Toro's movies (the wide-eyed child protagonist, the beautiful monstrous, the activated uncanny device) can be found in *Cronos*, which in some ways functions as a blueprint text for much of his subsequent work.

Mimic is a critically underappreciated film, and in some ways this is because del Toro himself has stated that the restrictions which he experienced in his first encounter with film-making in the Hollywood system scuppered the end product. Regardless of this, we find *Mimic* to be a brutal, curious and at times beautiful film which further illustrates del Toro's dense and complex intertextual process. Drawing from Goya as inspiration for the creatures in this reincarnation of the B-movie, del Toro creates a dystopian vision of New York which is host to monsters which seek symbolical retribution for human arrogance, in what can be read as an ecological allegory. We explore the film's engagement with a host of B-movies and the ways in which del Toro enters into a kind of directorial exchange with two pivotal film-makers, namely Ridley Scott and Steven Spielberg.

Chapter 5 discusses del Toro's treatment of trauma, childhood and testimony in del Toro's two political horror films, *The Devil's Backbone* and *Pan's Labyrinth*. These films have been described as partner pieces and use ghost story and fairytale conventions as a means of interrogating the wartime experience and its powerful legacies. *The Devil's Backbone* features a child protagonist and insists on a child's eye view of horror, continuing a tradition of children-as-witness narratives, and we situate the film in this cinematic context. The film provides a highly symbolic discourse and we explore the ways in which a symbolic order, seen through the eyes of a child encountering mortality, is used as a cipher for a discussion of Civil War and political strife. We explore *The Devil's Backbone* in the context of Spanish cinema, where the representation of the Civil War and its enormous consequences have fundamentally steered film. *Pan's Labyrinth* sees another child protagonist thrust into perilous situations due to the violence of a war-torn Spain in what is del Toro's most critically acclaimed film. Premiered at the Cannes Film Festival in 2006, *Pan's Labyrinth* established del Toro's international reputation as one of the leading directors of his generation and garnered numerous awards. We continue our discussion of Spanish cinema in our exploration of the film and the ways in which del Toro blends Spanish cinematic conventions with the traditions of Victorian literary fairy tale. We also explore gender in the film and consider the relevance of the heroine figure in the context of the bildungsroman narrative.

Chapter 6 concerns del Toro's foray into the superhero genre in *Blade II* and the *Hellboy* franchise. The superhero genre has seen an extraordinary proliferation in the twenty-first century and dominates current Hollywood output. Del Toro engages with this genre, employing his typically idiosyncratic sensibility which results in a Gothic-inflected take on the superhero narrative. *Blade II* sees del Toro return to the vampire film for the first time since *Cronos*, and in this case the vampire mythology is filtered through heavy metal Gothic sensibility. We consider *Blade II* as a pop-cultural interpretation of vampire mythology which nonetheless is steeped in the lore of vampire. We explore the treatment of black masculinity in action adventure narratives which we argue acts as a conduit for a wider exploration of race and identity within the film. We also discuss the presence of desire and fetishization in the film, which includes many of the fetish objects and perverse symbols which are familiar in del Toro's wider body of work. In a typically confessional statement which further strengthens del Toro's message that there need be no distinction between 'art house' and Hollywood fare the director has said that *Hellboy* is his most personal project and that the character is a fictional embodiment of himself. Considering the bombastic nature of the *Hellboy* films as big budget cinema, one might be surprised that these films are fundamentally about the search for identity, tender romantic and fraternal relationships and a need for a social conscience in a harsh world. We explore the nature of identity quests in superhero narratives and situate the *Hellboy* films in the current boom of superhero narratives. In addition, we argue that the *Hellboy* franchise provides a critical deconstruction of the family unit and challenges hegemonic pressures which claim normative status.

The concluding chapter of this book explores del Toro's career post *Hellboy II: The Golden Army* and ends with an analysis of *Pacific Rim*. The first section of this final chapter charts two main projects which del Toro developed in pre-production, both of which did not come to fruition with him as director. Del Toro's creative and intellectual colloquy with H.P. Lovecraft is explicit and discussed elsewhere in this book; it is no surprise then that he has aspirations to develop one of Lovecraft's tales for the screen, and *At the Mountains of Madness* (1931) is a natural extension of such interchange. We explore the pre-production process and del Toro's ambitions for this adaptation. Del Toro had flirted with the idea of working on tent-pole franchises before and engaged in discussions for adaptations of the Harry Potter novels and *The Lion, the Witch, and the Wardrobe* (1950) in the past. The development of J.R.R. Tolkien's *The Hobbit* (1937) was the only one of these projects to come close to fulfilment. He worked extensively on this endeavour before finally withdrawing. In addition, we look at some of del Toro's activity as producer of animated films and live action horror films.

On a certain level del Toro's creative output was a largely frustrated endeavour during this five-year period, but true to his prolific form, he co-wrote *The Strain* (2009–2011) trilogy of novels. These books see del Toro turn again to the vampire mythos and we discuss the ways in which the series act as intertexts which interweave classic Gothic fiction and elements of his own oeuvre in a dystopian epic that can be interpreted as a post-9/11 allegory.

Finally, we turn our attention to *Pacific Rim*, a film which continues to develop his creative and stylistic obsessions in his most action-orientated and science-fictional work to date. We consider the film in a pseudo-Lovecraftian context, where the nihilistic vision of the writer is filtered through a blockbuster sensibility and inverted into what is fundamentally an optimistic film about the redemptive power of human collaboration. We explore the two source genres which *Pacific Rim* blends, the Kaiju and Mecha traditions, and position his engagement with these in post-colonial and transnational contexts. We also consider the film as a war narrative and discuss the monster movie as a World War Two apologue. As well as paying homage to Ishirō Honda and Ray Harryhausen, *Pacific Rim* also continues del Toro's creative response to the work of Ridley Scott and Steven Spielberg and we explore this exchange. In addition to being a thoroughly transnational narrative, *Pacific Rim* also features a good deal of the Queer uncanny and we conduct a psycho-sexual reading of the film in what is a significantly Queer take on the action adventure movie.

Part One

Contexts and Audiences

1

Influences and Intertexts

This chapter represents an attempt to document some of the enormously varied filmic, literary and visual material that has contributed to the evolution of del Toro's art. This evolving process might be dubbed (pace Harold Bloom) the *ecstasy* of influence, since del Toro's eclecticism stems from an excitedly egalitarian fascination with high and popular culture that deliberately collapses critical and cultural boundaries. Inevitably, a considerable degree of selectivity was necessary in order to prioritize those figures and forms that seem, at this stage in his career, to be most significant.

Director as film historian

In 2012 Guillermo del Toro was asked to contribute to two significant film polls, despite his considerable reservations about the exercise. Criterion Films asked him to nominate his top ten films from their very distinguished collection list – a task del Toro bemoaned as the 'unfair, arbitrary, and sadistic top ten practice' (del Toro 2012c). The choice was obviously limited by the nature of the Criterion catalogue, but in response he produced a fascinating longer list of 'thematic/ authorial pairings' which represented an eclectic and revealing range of films by classic directors such as Kurosawa, Bergman, Cocteau, Lean, Dreyer and Sturges, as well as more recent movies by Stanley Kubrick, Kaneto Shindō, Victor Erice, Terry Gilliam, George A. Romero and Ridley Scott amongst many others. For the 2012 BFI/*Sight and Sound* poll of the greatest films, he produced a contrasting list that included only one film made in the last 40 years – Martin Scorsese's *Goodfellas* (1990). Perhaps more predictably, other choices included films by Hitchcock, Buñuel, Murnau as well as James Whale and Tod Browning – all key figures in the development of del Toro's film vocabulary (for the full list of del Toro's choices, see Bell 2012). Such exercises are notoriously random affairs, as del Toro seems to think, but his list does help to make more explicit the major influences that have shaped his work. To give a complete account of these would almost require a separate volume, since in the many interviews he has given he has mentioned an extraordinary array of contrasting and diverse films that have had a significant impact on the development of his art. Of the titles that are included in these lists a number do, however, stand out as having a particular significance for multiple reasons: these include Erice's oblique commentary on the legacy of Francoism and the Spanish Civil War *Spirit of the Beehive* (1973), Buñuel's most successful Mexican film *Los Olvidados* (1950) and Hitchcock's first American classic *Shadow of a Doubt* (1943).

Formations

Before considering any of these filmic precursors it is worth contextualizing them in del Toro's early experience of movies and also other formative influences. His early youth seems to have been saturated by the experience of film, both making and viewing. When he was eight he began making movies with his father's camera, impeded only by the expensive cost of film. His teenage experiments with Super 8 and his time spent in the projection rooms of cinema clubs in Guadalajara, not to mention his early career in special effects through his experience with SFX artist Dick Smith and his own company Necropia, all fed into the melting-pot aesthetic that in part characterizes his approach to cinema. Childhood experiences watching repeats of TV shows that dealt in science fiction and fantasy/horror, such as *The Outer Limits* (1963–1965) and Rod Sterling's *The Night Gallery* (1970–1973), not only gave the hyper-imaginative young del Toro repeatedly ghoulish nightmares but also inspired a fascination with horror as a genre. Before embarking on feature films, del Toro directed five episodes of a fantasy/horror Mexican TV series, *La Hora Marcada* (1986–1990), where he worked with other aspiring film-makers such as Alfonso Cuarón and his brother Carlos, as well as cinematographer Emmanuel Lubezki, now renowned for his work with Terence Malick and the Coen Brothers amongst others. *Hora Marcada* was a cheaply made simulacrum of *The Twilight Zone*, which del Toro and Alfonso Cuarón apparently nicknamed 'The Toilet Zone' because of the low budgets involved (Kehr 2006). However, it provided an invaluable opportunity to exchange ideas, narratives and techniques – in fact del Toro has described how Alfonso Cuarón told him one of his stories: 'It was called "About Ogres" but it was actually "Pan's Labyrinth". He made it bigger, better and with more substance, but it's exactly the same story'

(Kehr 2006). Cuarón has spoken himself about his long friendship with del Toro and the way in which their early experiences were translated into art:

> Guillermo was always the lonely child. There's a lot of him in the lonely little girls and boys he always portrays in his films. His stories are always about innocence, and he has an innocence that is very contagious, and helps you reconnect with your own. But at the same time it's a kind of innocence that is almost perverse. (Kehr 2006)

Growing up in Guadalajara, Mexico's second most populous city, also provided del Toro with contextual and circumstantial experiences that fed into his imaginative engagement with horror and fantasy. In a further interview with Jason Wood, he talks about images of brutality and violence that impacted upon him, including, at the age of four, the sight of mutilated corpses in a car crash (Wood 2006b: 30). He also cites the 'gory' religious imagery that he found in Mexican Catholicism, not only in the iconography and rituals of the Church but also in his grandmother's alarmingly graphic accounts of the perils of purgatory and hell (her influence is affectionately acknowledged in the dedication of *Cronos* to her memory). He has talked, perhaps with a characteristically dark sense of humour, of spending a significant amount of his childhood worrying about the horrors of purgatory and hell: 'I was a tortured soul ... I suffered from the guilt of Catholic mythology' – guilt fuelled apparently by his grandmother's oppressive piety (Laezman 2002: 38). Despite the jokiness with which he describes it, this concern with purgatorial states is a key element in the del Toro canon, as numerous characters in his films seem to exist in a limbo-like, interstitial state of being that blurs the borders between life and death, light and darkness, redemption and loss, being and nothingness. Del Toro's fondness for locating his narratives underground or in crepuscular spaces haunted by seen or unseen monsters is prefigured in this early immersion in the language, ritual and imagery of judgement and potential damnation.

Del Toro seems to have had a sophisticated taste in film as a child – in his commentary on the Criterion list he talks of having seen the two classic Kaneto Shindō shockers *Onibaba* (1964) and *Kuroneko* (1968) when aged ten years old, with the result that 'they did some serious damage to my psyche' (del Toro 2012c). He describes Shindō's films as a 'perverse, sweaty double bill', and their melding of Japanese folklore with a modern sensibility rooted in violence and destructive desire embodies a dynamic that re-emerges in films such as *The Devil's Backbone* and *Pan's Labyrinth*, with their interweaving of fantasy and twentieth-century savagery (2012c). Rather more conventionally perhaps, Disney films such as *Fantasia* (1940) and *Sleeping Beauty* (1959) provided an early exposure to the power of fairy-tale narrative and, in particular, the obsessive and perverse appeal of monsters. Chernabog, the black demon who appears in the 'Night on the Bald Mountain' sequence of the earlier film, is named by del Toro as one of his favourite film creatures, along with the dragon that the evil fairy Maleficent from *Sleeping Beauty* morphs into at the end of the film. (He has collected statues and concept sketches of Chernabog for his 'Man Cave' collection of curiosities.) His first favourite actors were the undisputed stars of classic horror from the early to mid-twentieth century: Lon Chaney, Boris Karloff, Vincent Price and Peter Cushing. This fascination with the icons of classic horror later translated into del Toro's assimilation of stylistic and thematic features from the Universal classics of Whale and Browning, the Poe adaptations of Roger Corman and the Hammer-produced films of Terence Fisher. Karloff's extraordinary capacity for physical transformation is echoed in his repeated use of Doug Jones in roles that require similarly extraordinary metamorphoses. Del Toro's boldly symbolic use of colour and light in particular seems to be heavily influenced by the latter two directors and was further enhanced by his love for the Italian 'giallo' horror movies of the 1960s and 1970s, in particular the work of directors such as Mario Bava (especially *Black Sunday* (1960) and *Black Sabbath* (1963)) and Dario Argento (especially *Deep Red* (1975) and *Suspiria* (1977)). The latter film clearly displayed Argento's increased prioritizing of often extreme images at the expense of plot, surely an influence on del Toro's own aesthetic given his stated preference for the visual over the verbal. Argento's methodology is underpinned by the use of extreme colour contrasts (he used Eastman colour and an outdated Technicolor printing process in order to achieve maximum effect). As L. Andrew Cooper notes of *Suspiria*, 'Jarring sounds, jagged shapes and jolting colors come together in compositions that suggest madness and horror. Their exquisite workmanship makes the film both sublime and beautiful, repellent and hypnotic. It telegraphs the unreality of the diegetic world' (Cooper 2012: 86).

In general, del Toro's account of his early life seems to suggest an extreme level of precocity in terms of taste and interests as well as an intense engagement with the potentially disturbing world of the imagination which also manifested itself in writing and drawing stories:

> I started drawing at a very young age ... I drew monster stories, but I would draw the illustrations and then I would never write the story – 20 illustrations for a

> novel and then never write the novel. I would write one chapter or half a chapter. Because the images were there, I wasn't driven to tell the story anymore. I was too happy with the images by themselves. (Kehr 2006)

This capacity to imagine in elaborate visual images transcribed to paper has remained a vital feature of del Toro's creative process, as evidenced in the extensive notebooks that he prepares for his films – images from these are collected in *Guillermo del Toro Cabinet of Curiosities* (2013, forthcoming) as well as in the Spanish publication of the screenplay for *Pan's Labyrinth* (del Toro 2006). Similarly, the 'Art of the Movie' books published in conjunction with both *Hellboy* films and *Pacific Rim* contain extensive examples of his sketchbooks.

Del Toro's 'seed-time' was indeed 'fostered alike by beauty and by fear' although in ways that differ radically from Wordsworth's; it seems to have been a somewhat haunted space and he has spoken of being old before his time – seventy when he was seven – and is only now really able to be a child. This personal association of childhood with fear and haunting was to become recurrent trope in del Toro's mature film-making and producing. His on-screen children are rarely portrayed in straightforward Romanticist terms of innocence and purity – rather they are witnesses and victims, fully engaged as agents within narratives dealing with power and struggle, identity and death:

> A perfect child is not very interesting to me … I want the children in my movies to be empathetic. When I see children who are smart, cute, and spouting brilliant one-liners, like the kids in *Jurassic Park*, I know that the tyrannosaurus is not going to eat them. They are too perfect and perfection is not human. It is not the norm. (Laezman 2002)

The reference to Steven Spielberg here is significant in that the somewhat idealistic and sentimental view of childhood that emerges in Spielberg's oeuvre could be seen as a reverse image of del Toro's own position.

Another important artistic colloquy can be found in comparing the tone and sensibilities of del Toro's work with that of his friend James Cameron. Both Cameron and del Toro have taken the baton from Ridley Scott and Steven Spielberg, who along with George Lucas, John Carpenter, Joe Dante and John Landis took genre and monster film-making out of its B-movie status and placed it at the centre of American popular cinema. Del Toro and Cameron are closely linked by key thematics and fascinations with Asian pop culture too. For example, strong ecological issues are to be found in both directors' movies.

Where Cameron provides us with a utopian science-fictional eco-tale in *The Abyss* (1989), del Toro's take on the aquatic eco-narrative is more dystopian and Gothic and his alien visitors are intent on vicious destruction rather than spiritual enlightenment. Both del Toro and Cameron also re-present Japanese pop-cultural staples to Western audiences. For example, Cameron introduced the Mecha genre to his audience in *Terminator* (1984), refined this to a boy and his robot adventure in *Terminator 2: Judgement Day* (1991) and also included Mecha versus alien battles in *Aliens* (1986) and later *Avatar* (2009) – a concept that del Toro would later amp up in *Pacific Rim*.

As well as this dialogic relationship with his directorial contemporaries, del Toro is more directly involved with other filmic craftsmen, most notably the cinematographer Guillermo Navarro, comic book writer and artist Mike Mignola and actor Ron Perlman. Navarro has worked on all but two of del Toro's films to date as well as with other intertextualists such as Quentin Tarantino and Robert Rodriguez. The rich, warm, colourful Gothic palette we associate with del Toro's films is no doubt down to the collaborative coupling with Navarro. Indeed, the tonal through line which unifies del Toro's work and which he is largely celebrated for is visually reinforced by Navarro's cinematographic style which has been described as 'elegance-amid-sensory-chaos' (Anderson 2013). Del Toro has found another visual soulmate in Mike Mignola, whose characteristic surreal and Gothic stylistics, honed in his creation of *Hellboy*, provide a comic book counterpart to del Toro's Queer Gothic visuals, as will be discussed later in this chapter. Describing his early collaboration with del Toro on *Cronos*, Ron Perlman has said the following:

> It was this like instant family – just add water and stir. The moment I met Guillermo, within 15 minutes, it was as if it was 15 years, and we had an immediate shorthand, an immediate kind of recognition. We both worshipped at the same shrines, we both had the same heroes … there was something about the way Guillermo kind of fashioned characters that fit into what he saw as my skill set. So he's provided me with the best acting opportunities I've ever been given – or among the best. (Gilchrist 2013)

Perlman's larger-than-life cinematic persona (including baritone voice and comic-book hero-sized jaw) has an almost uniquely fitting place in del Toro's bombastic, hectic cineverse, and just as Johnny Depp has acted as a muse-cum-cipher for Tim Burton's characteristic sensibilities, Perlman is the performance conduit for del Toro's particular worldview.

The big two

In his early twenties del Toro published a full-length study of Hitchcock, described by the author in a 2008 prologue as 'una cápsula de tiempo en la que un joven intenta articular lo que Hitchcock representa para él en particular. Este libro es la plegaria de un cineasta elevada al Olimpo más inasible en busca de inspiración' (a time capsule in which a young man tries to articulate what Hitchcock means for him in particular. This book is the prayer of a film-maker raised to the most unreachable Olympus in search of inspiration) (del Toro 2008b: 15). It is still available in Spanish, although elsewhere in this prologue he critiques his own youthful judgements:

> Las discrepancias entre mi opinión a los 43 años y las que este joven expresa serían numerosas: hay demasiada certeza e impiedad en la evaluación de ciertas cintas que con el tiempo he llegado a valorar más y más – Marnie, la ladrona (Marnie, 1964) – y alguna socarronería que me molesta de cara a lo aprendido en el quehacer cinematográfico. (del Toro 2008b: 1)
>
> (The discrepancies between my opinion at 43 years old and the ones this young man expresses would be many: there is too much certainty and impiety in the evaluation of certain films that I have come to value more and more with time – Marnie – and some sarcastic comments that bother me because of what I have learned in the cinematic activity.)

Of perhaps more general import is his disavowal of the auteurist approaches he employed in his monograph, which he describes as a 'Una absoluta validación de la teoría 'autoral' que me parece ahora inexacta y peligrosa' (An absolute validation of the 'auteurist' theory that I now find inaccurate and dangerous) (del Toro 2008b: 14–15).

Much later in 2012 he published a short article in *Sight and Sound* which focused specifically on the influence that Hitchcock's films have had on his own work. He also gave public master classes at the 2012 Toronto Film Festival on four of the director's films. In the *Sight and Sound* article, his opening remarks acknowledge his debt to Hitchcock, 'I revisit Hitchcock's films more than I do those of any other filmmaker, except perhaps Buñuel (del Toro 2012b: 38), but he then affirms that he doesn't attempt any imitation of Hitchcock 'either thematically or visually', suggesting that the only things he shares with his great predecessor are Catholic guilt and physical girth, despite occasionally borrowing some trademark visual effects such as the keyhole shot which reappears at a particularly frightening moment in *The Devil's Backbone* where the ghostly Santi peers through the keyhole at Carlos:

> In order to get our shot we made an oversized keyhole. I used to call it the Hitchcock keyhole because it was like one of the oversized props that Hitchcock used to get depth of field in films such as *Dial M for Murder* (1953) or the glass of milk that Ingrid Bergman drinks in *Notorious* (1946). It is certainly a Hitcockian/Buñuelian moment and I dreamt for so long about this sequence and I wanted so much for it to be successful. When I finally made it I was filled with a childish sense of glee at being a little closer to my bastion of heroes. (Wood 2006b: 43)

Del Toro focused mainly on Hitchcock's American films and has insightful things to say about *Shadow of a Doubt* amongst others, but he doesn't mention the earlier work, particularly Hitchcock's apprenticeship in Germany in the 1920s where he was profoundly influenced by the expressionist cinema of the Weimar period. As Sidney Gottlieb suggests, 'Throughout his career Hitchcock explored what might be called the guilt of innocence and the innocence of guilt, and this is a recurrent theme of the German films of the 1920s' (Gottlieb 2002: 38). Gottlieb also points to the stylistic impact of expressionism on Hitchcock's technique:

> Cinematic expressionism also calls to mind a particular ensemble of images and camera techniques that Hitchcock adopted. Shadows, night-time settings and so-called chiaroscuro lighting effects help to establish a mood of unfathomable mystery; stairs often lead to places of horror; mirrors heighten the sense that characters are split and relentlessly and painfully self-conscious. (38)

There are parallels here with del Toro's own visual palette, which draws on his own response to the expressionist movies of Murnau and Dreyer as well as on Hitchcock's re-situating of expressionist aesthetics in a narrative context that focuses on the horrors of the everyday rather than on vampires or other manifestations of monstrosity. A del Toro film will characteristically take the viewer beneath external daylight levels of reality into sometimes recognizable, sometimes fantastic underground spaces, whether it be the New York subway system in *Mimic*, the sewer systems of Prague in *Blade II* or the subterranean mazes of *Pan's Labyrinth*. Dynamic contrasts in visual texture, colour juxtaposition and chiaroscuro effects are used to enhance meaning and in particular to destabilize borders between actuality and imagination, human and other.

Hitchcock's manipulation and interrogation of conventional notions of innocence and guilt also provided del Toro with a context for his own meditations on innocence, particularly in relation to childhood. Like Hitchcock he wants to disturb the innocent/guilty binary but unlike him del Toro repeatedly explores the figure of the child in a hostile world. Similarly, Hitchcock's focus on social reality as a starting point for an exploration of the darkness within the human, in del Toro's terms '[the bringing of a] noir sensibility to bear on the quintessential small town' (del Toro 2012b: 38) in films such as *Shadow of a Doubt* and *Psycho* (1960), is replayed by del Toro on a broader and more explicit historical and cultural scale, whether it be Mexican/US relations in the 1990s or the legacy of the Spanish Civil War. Here again there are illuminating contrasts between the two directors. In Hitchcock's *North by Northwest* (1959), for example, the founding fathers of American democracy enshrined in stone on Mount Rushmore look on impassively at the film's climactic struggle between 'hero' and 'villain', suggesting an ironic disconnect between a mythologized past and a devalued present. (There's a hint of this scene in the struggle between Angel and Jesús at the top of the La Guardia factory in *Cronos*.) For del Toro, the borderlines between past and present are permeable and unstable and in contrasting ways all the films explore a notion of past that is sometimes ancient and mythic, informed by a Lovecraftian sensibility of the ancient impinging dangerously on the present (*Hellboy*, *Pacific Rim*), sometimes relatively recent (*The Devil's Backbone*), and sometimes both (*Cronos, Pan's Labyrinth*). The past is ever spectrally present – whether it is the aftermath of the Spanish Civil War or the violent death of a small child. The representation of landscape in particular plays a key role in his exploration of personal and historical memory. This is exemplified in the contrasting landscapes of *The Devil's Backbone* and *Pan's Labyrinth* – the former characterized by the vast, empty plain within which the orphanage is stranded, a fragile Republican outpost in the Fascist desert as well as a theatre for the playing out of submerged desires and revenge. The latter is dominated by the verdant, enveloping, perhaps enchanted forest, which offers Ofelia an emotional and psychic landscape in which to discover her identity and the Republican Maquis an opportunity and context for guerrilla resistance. These landscapes simultaneously embody the mindscapes of the central characters, given their isolation and apparent dislocation from the outside world of history and culture, but also carry the imprint of historical memory. As Ann Davies has suggested:

[T]he landscapes of *El espinazo* and *El laberinto* offer an imbrication between personal and genre-specific histories derived from horror and fantasy and a wider historical background within which Spanish history takes place. Personal memories and stories are, after all, never *just* about national history. (2012: 29)

These land/mindscapes sit also within a Gothic tradition that intimately connects the physical world with labyrinthine territories of the psyche – a tradition that Hitchcock drew on extensively. Interestingly, del Toro gives particular prominence to early and late Hitchcock, eschewing the mid-period masterpieces such as *Rear Window* (1954) and *Vertigo* (1958) for the less fêted or rated *Shadow of a Doubt* (1943) and *Frenzy* (1972). He suggests that the 1940s film 'in many ways marks the death of innocence in American cinematic fiction' (del Toro 2012b: 38) and prefigures much later 'subversive' works such as David Lynch's *Blue Velvet* (1986). It is productive to explore further del Toro's take on *Shadow of a Doubt* as a thoroughly Gothic movie which deconstructs the outwardly placid and stable exterior of the American bourgeois family to reveal layers of disturbance within, as Hitchcock's representation of this doubled and split society connects with his own thematic interests. The central character of *Shadow of a Doubt*, the reassuringly named Uncle Charlie, emerges in the film as a quasi-vampiric figure, albeit one that is fully located within a realistic context, the apparently secure and predictable boundaries of small-town America (in this case Santa Rosa, California). In his broadly Freudian reading of the film, James McLaughlin in his essay 'All in the Family' explores the way in which the film hints at, amongst other things, incest, the repression of the active 'phallic' woman (the Uncle's young female namesake, Charlie), the destabilizing of notions of fixed identity and doubling and bifurcation within the individual – all manifestations of the worm within the bud of the Hitchcockian family. Particularly interesting, given del Toro's fascination for the subject, is McLaughlin's reading of the vampiric in the film – in particular Uncle Charlie's resemblance to Dracula. 'Like Dracula, Uncle Charlie comes from "the East"'. Like Dracula he possesses a fearsome grip – Charlie twice complains that he hurts her when he grabs her. Like Dracula, he is associated with the dead and the dark' (McLaughlin 2009: 146). Charlie also mysteriously and rapidly disappears on a number of occasions when pursued by detectives, echoing a similar capacity in Bram Stoker's creation. He is also characterized by a kind of *weltschmerz*, an almost existential malaise that renders money a thing to be disposed of casually. Of course he preys on women – in this case wealthy widows – and at the beginning of the film his niece feels she has some form of telepathic link with him (see Mina in *Dracula*) as she wills him to come to Santa Rosa and relieve the stultifying boredom she feels like a sickness. There is even a passing reference to Stoker's novel late in the film just to reinforce the link. It is easy to see why del Toro might find this film a rich source of inspiration –

particularly for his Spanish-language films. The cracking façade of the bourgeois family is essentially the starting point for *Cronos*, and although it would be absurd to represent the relationship between grandfather and granddaughter in that film as having any incestuous overtones, there is a sense in which the relationship operates outside 'normal' parameters – there are strong hints of Aurora's jealousy towards her grandmother from the opening breakfast table scene. Indeed, what is perhaps the key scene in *Shadow of a Doubt* takes place around the dinner table as Uncle Charlie's mask begins to slip when he talks (in extreme close-up) of the women upon whom he preys; the effect is to intermingle the apparently reassuring rituals of the family meal, produced by the dutiful housewife and mother, with altogether darker images of consumption and predation. Hitchcock's film makes continued use of chiaroscuro effects to evoke a sense of pervasive darkness within the home and hearth and the progressive implication of the young and idealistic woman in the attractive yet destructive and damaged figure of the 'Merry Widow' murderer, Uncle Charlie. 'For Alfred Hitchcock, family relationships are a source of endless provocation. The family, in the course of its normal and natural existence produces the most oppressive of tensions and the calm matter-of-factness with which it does so is what makes it so frightening' (McLaughlin 2009: 153). In a splendidly ripe piece of cinematic irony, the film ends with the undiscovered murderer given a hero's funeral by the town for his apparent philanthropy – Middle America portrayed as an easy dupe, like the women Uncle Charlie has murdered. For del Toro there is little that is ironic or hidden about the family, as his films regularly centre on an outsider/misfit figure for whom the family unit is overtly associated with disturbance or trauma. Indeed, there are rarely, if ever, complete nuclear families in his films, and often the family units that are constructed consist of figures who are exiled or outcast from 'normality', such as at the end of *Hellboy II: The Golden Army*. Gaps and absences predominate. It's also the case that places which are meant to protect such as orphanages and new family homes are sources of danger and disturbance.

If Hitchcock films embody one key strand in del Toro's imaginative genetic make-up, then the other is the cinematic oeuvre of Luis Buñuel. This is hardly a surprising pairing given their stature as arguably the two most influential directors of the twentieth century, with comparable if contrasted roots in, amongst other things, Surrealism, Freudianism and (rejected) Catholicism. For del Toro, there is clearly a powerful cultural linkage and lineage with his own identity as a film-maker given Buñuel's long period of working in Mexico from

1946 to 1965 and the Spanish-born director's adoption of Mexican citizenship, although it's perhaps ironic that del Toro has made a reverse journey away from Mexico to Spain and the US. Del Toro believes that the films that Buñuel made in Mexico are his best (Wood 2006a: 4), although in general they have received less critical attention than his earlier and later work – a trend that is challenged in more recent studies such as Ernesto Acevedo-Muñoz's *Buñuel and Mexico: The Crisis of National Cinema* (2003). In a 2004 *Daily Telegraph* interview del Toro described his first encounters with Buñuel:

> I remember when and where I first saw every Buñuel film … I saw *Nazarin* when I was about 14, in what was then very common where I grew up, a cinema club. It was projected on a piece of cloth from a 16mm film, in Guadalajara, and they introduced the movie, screened it, and then we had a discussion afterwards … This happened a lot in the 1970s and still in the 1980s … It was a great period of my life, because I was a projectionist in that club, so I would spool the film, and I would see an average of four films over a weekend. (Monahan 2004)

Del Toro expresses particular admiration for the way in which Buñuel allows character to emerge through action rather than dialogue: ' … people now expect screenplays to explain characters, not to show them. But it's a paradigm I think of what is a great screenplay, which is, you let the character be defined by his actions.' There is a clear parallel here with del Toro's own wariness of excessively dialogue-driven narrative, something he rejects in favour of image-laden film-making that can itself occasionally feel overstated. In fact del Toro has intimated in interview that '[m]y ideal movie would have no dialogue; it would just be a camera implicating the viewer in the action' (Wood 2006a: 156). It is another of Buñuel's Mexican films, *Los Olvidados* (*The Forgotten*) (1950), that offers the clearest indication of his importance for del Toro. This is the film with which Buñuel re-established his reputation in Europe, winning best director at Cannes, and which represents his very individual take on one of the dominant cinematic modes of the period, neo-realism. The film begins with a voice-over (also a favourite opener for del Toro) and appears to inaugurate a documentary approach to its subject matter, the daily life of a group of delinquents on the streets of Mexico City. But the film resists and subverts the conventions of neo-realist objectivity, shifting at times into dream and fantasy as well as drawing direct attention to the constructedness of realism; for example, when one of the characters, Pedro, throws an egg directly at the camera lens. Buñuel never sentimentalizes his subjects, who are almost all children. As Robert Philip Kolker says, 'Buñuel's children are no more innocent than his adults, perhaps less so. His adults are merely dulled into insensibility by the brutality of their world. The children take an active and gleeful part in promoting that brutality' (Kolker 2009: 69). Casual but vicious brutality that is uncoupled from any sense of causality is a reiterated trope in del Toro's work, and like Buñuel he uses it to explore not only the relationship between identity and environment but also the disturbingly innate human capacity for violence. Many of his films have a central figure who could be seen as a reworking of Buñuel's apparently irredeemable character Jaibo, who is the central malign presence in *Los Olvidados* – amongst others such figures as Angel in *Cronos*, Jacinto in *The Devil's Backbone*, Vidal in *Pan's Labyrinth* all exist outside any kind of identifiable moral dimension. Jaibo eventually murders the other key child figure in *Los Olvidados*, Pedro, who leads an adult life but from within a child's body. Clearly, *The Devil's Backbone* has the most obvious links to *Los Olvidados*, given its focus on a group of boys and their relationships – boys who have been shaped by trauma, in this case the effect of war rather than urban alienation. Del Toro has compared Buñuel's film to the fiction of Charles Dickens, in particular *Oliver Twist*:

> When I saw on the screen somebody that was doing Charles Dickens, hardcore, because, ultimately, *Los Olvidados* is taken from Oliver Twist, I understood. All of a sudden it was as if all the Dickens I had read as a kid was there in cinematic form. I was watching it 30 years after it was made but it was today's kids. It was incredibly cathartic. (Applebaum 2006)

The 'hardcore' narrative of *Los Olvidados* rather lacks the reassuring ending of Dickens's novel: the film ends shockingly with the central figure Pedro's dead body being tossed on to a rubbish dump. Ernesto Acevedo-Munoz (2003) discusses the film in relation to the writing of the great Mexican poet and writer Octavio Paz, whose influential collection of essays *El Laberinto de la Soledad* (*The Labyrinth of Solitude*) (1950) offers a comparable critique of contemporary Mexican society and nationalist notions of identity. Paz reviewed the film very favourably when it was shown at Cannes, unlike other Mexican critics, many of whom felt *Los Olvidados* was a slur on the international reputation of Mexico. Solitude is indeed the essential state of being of Buñuel's young characters, despite their involvement in the group, and his adults are likewise alienated, desensitized or nostalgic for some mythologized past. Ultimately, though, it is the unflinching and unsentimental centrality given to childhood that defines Buñuel's originality. His figures have complex inner and dream lives that are hinted at in two key fantasy/dream sequences: Pedro's sinister slow-motion dream where desire for mother-love and guilt at witnessing a murder combine when he dreams that the battered corpse is beneath his bed and his hitherto unloving mother floats strangely above him, handing him the meat she has denied him earlier. Similarly, Jaibo's demise is immediately preceded by his vision of a 'mangy dog' approaching him like a harbinger of darkness, accompanied by the disembodied voices of his victims as he imagines falling into the 'black hole' of sleep and death. These moments may be exceptions to the film's dominant objectivity, where monstrosity is seen to be internal to the human condition, and where the dividing line between animality and humanity is an ambiguous one, but they display how a shifting narrative dynamic can open up and subvert generic conventions: the kind of narrative and generic boundary crossing that becomes for del Toro a centrally informing aesthetic.

In *The Spirit of the Beehive*

'*The Spirit of the Beehive* is a seminal movie for me. I even modelled the girl in *Cronos* exactly on Ana Torrent. That movie, along with the films of Buñuel and the films of Hitchcock, is almost a part of my genetic makeup, buried deep in my DNA' (Wood 2006a: 112).

Buñuel's film was made during the apex of neo-realism in mid-twentieth-century film-making. Victor Erice's 1973 *The Spirit of the Beehive* (*El Espíritu de la Colmena*) was made after the decline of its influence, but, initially at least, still seems to exhibit some of the familiar features of the genre – a focus on a small group of figures located in a bleakly realistic context, grainy film textures, a central role given to non-professional actors (in this case children). *The Spirit of the Beehive* remains one of the key Spanish film texts of the twentieth century – in his commentary posted on the Criterion Collection website, Paul Julian Smith suggests that this is a film that has 'left an indelible mark on cinema in Spain and beyond' (Smith 2006). It has a particularly prominent role in del Toro's movie pantheon.

Erice's film was made in the final years of Franco's rule in Spain but is set at the very beginning of his dictatorship in 1940 (the year of the director's birth). Its subject matter – the aftermath of the Civil War, the child's gaze and imaginative potentialities, the haunting of the present by the past, the intertextual links with classic horror (here James Whale's *Frankenstein* of 1931) as well as classic Spanish art and literature – are all elements that are reworked in del Toro's *oeuvre*, albeit metamorphosed and alchemized. *Los Olvidados* locates the idea of horror firmly within a visible contemporary world which juxtaposes superficial modernity (hinted at in the skeletal skyscrapers that provide the backdrop for a number of scenes) with the derelict slums and street corners that the children inhabit. The film's title translates as 'the forgotten ones' and evokes not only the lost children but a lost nation, exiled from itself. Erice's film is set in an equally bleak but very different context – a remote and run-down village on the Castillian plain – *un lugar de la meseta castellana*, with its echoes of the setting of *Don Quixote*. Like the orphanage in *The Devil's Backbone* this is both somewhere in time and place (the credits tell us it is 'hacia 1940' and we see the name of the village Hoyuelos with the Falangist symbol of the yoke and arrow on the wall of a building) and nowhere, as the repeated long-distance shots remind us of its isolation and desolation. As Chris Perriam has noted:

> *El Espíritu de la Colmena* is not only replete with memory referents but is a major part of Spanish cultural heritage as well as forming part of the ensemble of forms that students of Spanish culture take as access points to more or less nuanced readings of its relation to the socio-political realities of the period 1939–1975. It stands as a dynamic memorial. (2008: 72)

Landscape (the windswept and seemingly horizon-less plains of La Mancha, which prefigure the desolate landscapes of *The Devil's Backbone*) and place (the echoing, empty family house, austere village streets, makeshift cinema and school) underline the sense that survival is the best that can be hoped for; Teresa, the mother, says as much in a letter she writes to an unknown lover. However, the distinctiveness of the film and its importance for del Toro stems from its meta-textual storytelling elements. The phrase 'Érase una vez' (once upon a time) appears in the last of the children's drawings that accompany the opening credits and speaks of the fabular narrative that is to follow, which moves between the harsh objective reality of post–Civil War Spain, the imaginary world of film (the film begins with the showing *of Frankenstein* in the village hall) and the subjective interiority of a young child, Ana, played with extraordinary presence by Ana Torrent. This recognition of the power of stories and storytelling informs the world of Ofelia in *Pan's Labyrinth*, who seems enveloped in stories within stories and textuality. She, like Ana who ends the film asserting her own name in the uncanny moonlight 'Soy Ana, Soy Ana', engages in the creative act of making her own stories from the often disturbing material that surrounds her in order to assert her own sense of agency in a world that denies her any power. Del Toro, like Erice, completely avoids any sentimentalizing of childhood. In *The Spirit of the Beehive* children are not subject to physical violence but are seen as victims of powerful cultural, political and societal influences within both family and community. Del Toro has readily acknowledged the significance of this:

> To me 'Spirit of the Beehive' was incredibly beautiful and almost intangible and spiritual in the way it approached fantasy. It was very tenuous and delicate and I have a will to make fantasy actually, almost material, much more tangible, and I think that it only can happen in a universe populated by children. I don't idealize childhood, as you can see in 'Pan's Labyrinth' or even 'Cronos,' but I do think that it's the time where emotions are sort of unfiltered and impulses are unfiltered, including faith and belief and love, for example. In 'Cronos' the granddaughter loves her grandfather even in spite of him falling apart, rotting away. I think these things can only happen in childhood stories, and that brings me very close to the spirit of fairy tales, in which brutal things and brutal rites of passage occur to little. (Keough 2007)

Erice's film proceeds with a kind of intense and uncanny stillness, accentuated by camera positions that are often static and sometime relentless in their gaze; as a number of commentators have noted, Erice's film gazes repeatedly on village walls whose textures are pock-marked and ravaged by time and the memory of trauma. This aura of gradual ruination is also found in the faces of the older protagonists, which evoke a human landscape of loss and disillusion. *The Spirit of the Beehive* was made within the confines of a Francoist aesthetic that imposed significant censorship limitations on the film-maker and thus is characterized by gaps in narrative and recurrent sustained silences, like a series of whispers and cries that can barely speak of repressed memories and hidden traumas. This is expressed particularly in the representation of the family and the *unheimlich* domestic space which they inhabit. As Paul Julian Smith (2006) notes, we never see all the members of the family in the same frame: they seem to lead parallel existences and only occasionally connect emotionally. In a piece of telling editing that is characteristic of the film, the viewer's first image of the father, Fernando, follows immediately the start of the showing of *Frankenstein*; we are led to expect to see the monster, but in fact see a strange figure in a bee-keeper's suit, his humanity seemingly disguised behind the protective clothing. The other key images associated with the father are the written word (he is writing some sort of philosophical memoir) and time in the form of a musical fob watch. Ana gives this to an anonymous 'fugitive' – probably a member of the maquis/anti-Franco resistance – whom she befriends in a belief that he is the manifestation of the film spirit/Frankenstein's monster. We next see the watch in the possession of a local Civil Guard officer as he shaves in a makeshift bathroom, a scene that re-emerges in *Pan's Labyrinth*; the fugitive has been killed in a fleeting, almost perfunctory night scene lit only by gunfire. Time here is equated with the kind of fixed and inflexible system also embodied in the beehive itself, which is associated with a relentless and ceaseless activity predicated on the subordination of its constituents, a metaphor that expresses both the nature of human existence and the essence of fascism. As Xon de Ros observes, a montage sequence of the village children entering the narrow door of the school creates 'a flickering effect that recalls the flight path of bees returning to their hive' (de Ros 2005: 142). The places and spaces of childhood – the family home, the school, the isolated village – contain and confine the imagination, but the film traces the way in which Ana becomes 'other' to this containment and through her identification with both real and imaginary outcasts – the fugitive and the monster – creates an imaginative space for herself that allows for the assertion of her independence and selfhood. In the mid-1970s Hollywood was imagining the child as a conduit for evil (*The Exorcist* (1973), *The Omen* (1975)), the product of a kind of moral panic around the state of contemporary childhood. For directors such as Erice (and later del Toro), the child can see beyond external layers of reality in ways that suggest freedom and liberation, even within an oppressive adult world. It is not for nothing that Ana, in one scene, places the eyes on the strange schoolroom mannequin, a scene that surely prefigures the early moment in *Pan's Labyrinth* when Ofelia replaces the eye in the stone stele, thus facilitating the release of the supernatural world into the real.

De Ros also draws attention to an aspect of the film that is sometimes overlooked by critics and that resonates in del Toro's own work: the casting of key roles. Momentarily leaving aside the two young girls played by unknowns, the actors playing the parents, Fernando Fernan Gomez and Teresa Gimpera, were both familiar to audiences, bringing as de Ros says 'a set of extra-textual connotations to the film' (de Ros 2005: 145). The former was very well known for his roles in a range of mainly realist Spanish films that were made within political circumstances requiring a significant degree of compromise in order to ensure their production. By contrast the Catalan Teresa Gimpera was associated with the 1960s Barcelona School, whose films were noted for their experimentalism in response to the theories and ideas of the French *nouvelle vague*. De Ros suggests that Ana's gradual breaking free from the sterile world of the family 'invites us to consider the film's position within Spanish cinema through the iconic associations on which the actors and their performances draw' (de Ros 2005: 145). Examining this tactical use of key central actors in del

Toro's films, particularly those early in his career that established his reputation, can open up helpful ways of reading them in relation, amongst other things, to their transnational and postcolonial credentials. Veteran Argentinian actor Federico Luppi appeared in all three of del Toro's Spanish films and Ann Davies has noted that the involvement of Luppi with the Mexican del Toro:

> suggests a dislocated desire for association, a call to care that both acknowledges the association of Spain with South America and the distance and dislocation of it (to say nothing of its difficulties: the association of Latin America with its former colonial master has not always, or ever, been an equal one). (2012: 27)

Similarly, the use in *Cronos* of Mexican Claudio Brook (ironically playing American capitalist De La Guardia) located del Toro's first film in a tradition linking back to Buñuel's time in Mexico, as Brook starred in two of the most important of these, *Simon of the Desert* (1965) and *The Exterminating Angel* (1962).

The Spirit of the Beehive has a sparing mise-en-scène that testifies to a society and nation haunted by loss and absence. This emptying out of the frame may seem in stark contrast to del Toro's richly populated visuals. But there is a common denominator of the painterly in both directors that also emerges in their referencing of Spanish art and culture. These are admittedly understated in Erice's film – the passing reference to Spain's most important work of literature, Cervantes's *Don Quixote*, with its tragic-comic representation of the collision between fantasy and reality, has already been noted. Erice also includes within his mise-en-scène some explicit references to classic Spanish art, notably the painting of St Jerome with the Lion that overlooks Fernando's desk and the little portrait of an angel leading children that graces the girls' bedroom. Above all, throughout the film, we are conscious of the piercing gaze of Ana, to which the camera often returns and which forms, perhaps, the film's most memorable image. It recalls Goya's portraits of children who fix the viewer with an unflinching and questioning stare; Goya's paintings repeatedly negotiated the line between socially and politically imposed conventions and subversive experimentation, rather like Erice's film. The aforementioned religious art carries with it a complex and ambiguous symbolism characteristic of *The Spirit of the Beehive* – the picture of St Jerome speaks of human mortality (the memento mori skull in the corner), the isolation of the self in his hermit state, even perhaps the co-existence with the dangerous, the ever-present lion hinting at a potential threat apparently tamed. All these intersect with the film's coded response to

Francoist Spain. Perhaps more significant is the way in which the iconography of Catholicism is both present but also absent – the spirit angel who leads the children is replaced in the narrative by Ana's imagined spirit, prompted by that most modern phenomenon, the cinema. The Catholic Church's complicity in Franco's dictatorship renders it spiritually empty and absent from the world of the film – we hear the bells tolling for mass on the soundtrack but see the villagers congregating for the showing of *Frankenstein*, which parodies the rituals of the Church. Del Toro's own response to religion in *Pan's Labyrinth* and elsewhere acknowledges its enduring presence not only in Hispanic and Latin American culture but also in his own psyche. *Pan's Labyrinth* perhaps offers the most extreme image of this in the Pale Man who presides in isolation over his own grotesque version of the last supper, ready to gorge himself on the minds and bodies of the young. This self-conscious referencing of Hispanic culture and religion, sparingly enacted in Erice's film, becomes a multi-layered mode of signification in all del Toro's films.

Film-maker as bibliophile

This section charts some of the key literary influences on del Toro, beginning with an investigation into some of the canonical figures which resonate in his work and then exploring the less familiar figure of H.P. Lovecraft, a writer who informs the bizarre and grotesque sensibility of his cinematic project.

In her recent biography of Dickens, Claire Tomalin describes the proliferating projects that the great nineteenth-century novelist was undertaking towards the beginning of his literary career in 1836:

> Dickens was now committed to the following projects: he had to continue *Pickwick* in monthly instalments for another year; he had to provide a few more pieces for the *Sketches*; both his farce and his opera were being published... he had promised a children's book... by Christmas: he had to start preparing for his editorship of *Bentley's Miscellany*... Chapman and Hall were hoping for a sequel to *Pickwick*... and Bentley was expecting two novels. Clearly this was not a possible programme for one man. (2011: 70)

It is hard to resist making comparisons between Dickens's obsessive multitasking and del Toro's own propensity to undertake multiple simultaneous projects, whether as director, writer, producer or executive producer. In 2012, the year of *Pacific Rim's* completion, the so-called busiest man in Hollywood, an oft-repeated phrase in relation to him, had at least 14 projects in various stages of development (Walkuski 2012). These included a number of animation movies resulting from his association with Disney and DreamWorks Animation, a TV version of Marvel's *The Incredible Hulk* for ABC, as well as literary adaptations of classic nineteenth-century English fiction, notably *Frankenstein* (1818) and *The Strange Case of Dr Jekyll and Mr Hyde* (1886). Although many of these were still at an embryonic stage, some were more advanced, including a film version of *Drood* (2009), Dan Simmons's epic novel about the last years of Dickens's life and the writing of his unfinished final work, *The Mystery of Edwin Drood* (1870). Whether or not this project finally materializes, there's an obvious clue here to the high status of Dickens in del Toro's pantheon of authors. Perhaps another is the naming of his domestic museum of curiosities, his 'Man Cave', after one of Dickens's greatest novels, *Bleak House* (1853). Although any linkage between a contemporary Mexican film director and arguably the greatest nineteenth-century British novelist may initially seem surprising, more detailed scrutiny reveals multiple connections that enable a more complex understanding of del Toro's art. Dickens's repeated focus on the experience of childhood, his Gothic sensibility, his near-cinematic visual imagination and his blurring of the borderlines between high and popular art are central commonalities here. Dickens was one of the first great novelists to reach a mass audience whilst at the same time achieving general critical recognition as a major writer. Above all, Dickens provides a powerful narrative template for del Toro, not only in the extraordinary inclusivity of his fiction, which critics such as Juliet John (2003) have seen as a kind of admirable democratic cultural populism, but also in the way he blends contrasting and often apparently conflicting narrative traditions: fairy tales, the macabre, sentimental fiction, historical fiction, the picaresque as well as social observation and critique. Hence it is more than possible to call Dickens a magic realist *avant le lettre* as a number of commentators have observed. As Katherine Kearns has suggested, 'Anyone who reads Dickens or the Brontes rides effortlessly on this continuum of real-surreal' (Kearns 1996: 76). In her seminal study of the fantastic in literature Rosemary Jackson identified within the apparently realist Victorian novel a 'camouflaged and concealed' non-realist inner text acting as a version of the Freudian unconscious. Her suggestion that '[a] dialogue between fantastic and realistic narrative modes often operates within individual texts as the second attempts to repress and defuse the subversive thrust of the first' (Jackson 1981: 73) could well be applied not only to Dickens's fiction but also to del Toro's approach to film narrative and his exploration of the dialogue or conflict between the real and fantastic, self and memory. In describing Dickens as a fantastic realist, Jackson talks of his prose as ' "fantastic" in its elisions, its grotesque images, its sliding from metaphor to metonymy. Nothing is stable, forms merge together, tending towards unification' (Jackson 1981: 78). For Jackson, Dickens's novels evidence a 'polyphonic mixing of realistic, grotesque, comic, fantastic, and horrific styles. Through their Gothic sequences, Dickens's texts move towards a dialogical structure, questioning from within the normative assumption of their "realistic" frames' (Jackson 1981: 77). Considering the recurrent stylistic features focused on in this book, a polyphonic mixing of narrative and genre might be a useful way of describing del Toro's hybrid approach to film-making.

In terms of pure chronology the connection between Dickens and the cinema is a totally anachronistic one – Dickens died in 1870, well before the invention of the medium. He has, of course, provided the basis for some of the cinema's classic films, above all David Lean's *Great Expectations* (1946), which del Toro nominated as one of his top films in the Criterion Collection poll (del Toro's fellow 'amigo' and compatriot Alfonso Cuarón filmed an adaptation of the book in 1998). There is also a well-established body of critical and theoretical writing that has linked Dickens and the cinema, beginning with Eisenstein's famous 1944 essay 'Dickens, Griffith and the Film Today' published in the collection *Film Form: Essays in Film Theory* (1949). In this essay Eisenstein argued for the essentially cinematic nature of Dickens's writing, citing the novelist as a key influence on one of the great directors of early cinema, D.W. Griffith. At the opening of his book *Dickens and the Dream of Cinema* (2003: 1), Grahame Smith cites Walter Benjamin's aphorism that 'every epoch sees in images the epoch which is to succeed it' as a starting point for his exploration of the proto-filmic qualities of Dickens's writing. Similarly, Garret Stewart begins an essay 'Dickens, Eisenstein, Film' by suggesting that 'Dickens was born for film. That's the truism. The further truth that film was born from Dickens is the burden of the most famous genealogical essay in the literature of cinema [Eisenstein's essay]' (Stewart 2003: 122). In 2012, as part of the celebrations marking 200 years since Dickens's birth, the BBC in conjunction with Film London produced a documentary *Arena: Dickens on Film* which again argued for his pre-visioning of cinema. Much of this kind of discussion focuses on the formal qualities of Dickens's writing – the use of rapid cutting, montage and other proto-filmic elements. Del Toro himself has parallel careers as a novelist and illustrator and published a theoretical study of Hitchcock before his filmic work. Grahame Smith also connects Dickens's fascination with the city, both as an aspect of modernity and also as a labyrinthine place of social and psychic trauma, with cinema:

> These themes – the city as dream and nightmare, its sounds and movement, its oscillations between light and dark, its prefiguring of cinema – are present everywhere in Dickens's work…. (2003: 70)

For del Toro, the city is also a site of strangeness and alienation. His first major film, *Cronos*, opens with shots of a deserted and desolate post-Christmas and post-NAFTA Mexico City and elsewhere the urban environment, whether it be New York, Prague or London, becomes a place of not always hidden horrors in *Mimic, Blade II* and the *Hellboy* films and positively apocalyptic in *Pacific Rim* and *The Strain* trilogy. These films and novels denote a repeated fascination with the subterranean and underground, with submerged layers and strata of the unknown or hidden that threaten to engulf the above ground. For Dickens, it was the abjected underclasses of the monstrous Victorian city that were implicated in a network of association and connection that also revealed the unstable nature of the social contract.

Dickens's relevance to del Toro's films is manifested in thematic as well as formal ways. For del Toro, Dickens's work is the pre-eminent representation of childhood trauma in English-language fiction. It is justifiable to say that in radically different ways the problematic experience of childhood for both writer and director was a central influence on their creativity. Dickens's own neglected childhood, particularly his being sent out to work in a blacking factory aged 12, sowed the seeds of this 'strange fascination exerted over him by child-suffering and sorrow' in the words of his first biographer and close friend John Forster. Del Toro has described his childhood as 'the most brutal and frightening period of my life' (Wood 2006b: 36). For both writer and director children are at once victims and agents, despite Dickens's Victorian tendency to mythologize and sentimentalize childhood innocence in some of his less successful portrayals. Peter Ackroyd suggested that *Oliver Twist* was 'the first novel in the English language which takes a child as its central character or hero' (Ackroyd 1990: 229), and this set a thematic pattern that was repeated many times, most notably in *David Copperfield* and *Great Expectations*. Likewise, del Toro is rare amongst contemporary film-makers, particularly in Hollywood, who put children and childhood centre screen without the soft focus or reassurance of nostalgia or sentimentality that mars their representation in more conventional mainstream movies. In this respect del Toro is closer to Michael Haneke's vision of the child as both victim and perpetrator of violence in a film such as *Das Weisse Band* (*The White Ribbon* 2009) than more mainstream Hollywood directors for whom childhood is seen as less traumatized, such as Steven Spielberg. Like del Toro, Haneke explores the ways in which children respond to and resist dominant ideologies that deny their right to ask questions of the adult world, interrogating received notions of childhood and innocence, albeit in Haneke's case from a very different narrative perspective. It is perhaps an exaggeration to claim that del Toro's films represent a kind of *homage* to Dickens, but the detailed level of reference and quotation is remarkable and intimate. Moments such as the scene in *Pan's Labyrinth* where Ofelia is reprimanded by her stepfather Vidal for shaking hands with the wrong (left) hand – her right hand is carrying books – echo Chapter 2 of *David Copperfield* where David refuses to give his future stepfather Murdstone his right hand – his left is linked with his mother's. Such apparently fleeting yet significant flickers of intertextual conversation suggest that Dickens's novels are a deeply embedded source of meaning and inspiration. The *Copperfield* connection is a useful one to pursue since surrogacy in parenthood and the orphan state is a core motif for both novelist and film-maker. Murdstone, David's stepfather, lives up to the implications of his name, with its explicit reference to murder, death and excreta – Vidal is a little more subtle in its ironic reference to the Spanish for life. For both director and novelist, the family is often if not always characterized by a sense of lack and absence as fathers in particular are often missing in del Toro's worlds; Whistler and Broom play the role of surrogate father in the *Blade* and *Hellboy* films, respectively, as does Jesús in *Cronos*, Casares in *The Devil's Backbone* and, in a very contrasting manner, Vidal in *Pan's Labyrinth*. Children are orphans in *The Devil's Backbone* and *Pan's Labyrinth* and are dying in *Mimic*, whose central character has her own problems with conceiving. Dickens counterbalances this view of the family by constructing alternative family groups or by mythologizing the comfort of hearth and home. Del Toro brings a harsher sensibility that refuses to ring fence children or childhood from the dangers of adult life, but also re-configures the nuclear family, particularly at the end of *Hellboy II*.

For a director who is soaked in a tradition of Hispanic history and film-making, del Toro does offer the viewer what is virtually a homage to the great European and American creators of fantasy and fairy tale: Lewis Carroll, Hans Christian Andersen, Frank Baum and C.S. Lewis amongst writers as well as artists and illustrators such as Arthur Rackham. In drawing together this range of cross-cultural references, del Toro effectively synthesizes some of the most influential fictional representations of childhood whilst at the same time offering a commentary on the brutality and monstrosity of contemporary history. References to mythological and fairy-tale figures also abound in his films, particularly in *Pan's Labyrinth*. From Pan to Pandora to Persephone, del Toro mines these archetypal narratives and tropes as a vital part of the film's palette, moving the viewer between the actuality of Franco's Spain and the extra-temporal world of the imagination and storytelling. The film's English title, with its reference to the Greek god Pan missing from the original Spanish *El Laberinto del Fauno*, offers a portal into a large body of literature, much of it written for children and adults in the later nineteenth and early twentieth centuries, that resonates throughout del Toro's work as a writer and director. The *Hellboy* films and *Don't Be Afraid of the Dark* (2010), where del Toro was co-writer of the screenplay and producer, also exploit the notion of real and fantasy worlds existing in parallel or in conflict, requiring the intervention of a child or childlike figure as intercessor or bridge. Indeed, for the latter del Toro co-wrote (with Christopher Golden) an elaborately illustrated text *Blackwood's Guide to Dangerous Fairies* (2011) which provides a kind of historical backstory to the film as well as a compendium of myths and legends from around the world. The fictional author/diarist Emerson Blackwood, who narrates the book (and who features in the opening scenes of the film), clearly references another of del Toro's favourite writers of ghost stories, Algernon Blackwood. The content also echoes Lord Dunsany's Edwardian fantasy classic *The Book of Wonder* (1912) and is embroidered with sometimes grotesque Rackham-esque illustrations.

Del Toro has suggested that for him the origin of the faun figure in *Pan's Labyrinth* can be found in a recurrent nightmare of his own childhood when, sleeping in his grandmother's house, he imagined he saw the image of a goat-man emerging from a wardrobe in the dark. He has spoken elsewhere about his association of childhood and trauma (Wood 2006a: 27–28). The faun, then, is a figure of profound ambivalence – a product of dreams and nightmares as well as a link back to the first golden age of children's literature at the end of the nineteenth and beginning of the twentieth century. The reference to Pan/the faun raises some further significant issues about the fictional origins of del Toro's ideas. Working backwards historically, the faun figure from children's literature that seems to have some kinship with del Toro's imaginary goat-man might be C.S. Lewis's Mr Tumnus in *The Lion, the Witch and the Wardrobe* (1950). Del

Toro rejects the version of the faun embodied in Lewis's sweetly domesticated figure, just as he rejected the redemptive Christ-figure of Aslan when he was invited to direct the film *The Lion, the Witch and the Wardrobe* (2005). He turned down the opportunity to direct because he couldn't see himself bringing Aslan back to life. Instead he returns, via his reading of writers like Arthur Machen (*The Great God Pan* 1894) and Algernon Blackwood (*Pan's Garden* 1912), to the often ambivalent and possibly dangerous late Victorian and Edwardian evocations of the great god that emerge in some key children's books of the period. As Seth Lerer has suggested of the mythological figure in an overview of this period, 'Pan is everywhere, not just in the Yellow Book but in the children's book' (Lerer 2009: 258), embodying the link between natural and human worlds as well as the lure of pagan and phallic eroticism. For writers such as Frances Hodgson Burnett (*The Secret Garden* 1911) and Kenneth Grahame (*The Wind in the Willows* 1908), the spirit of Pan inhabits their characters, breathing into them a sublime and restorative force of nature. For others, notably J.M. Barrie, Pan is a much more problematic, transgressive and potentially dangerous character, forever on the edge of sexual maturity. Like *Pan's Labyrinth*, Barrie's *Peter Pan* (1904, 1911) is essentially a fairy tale for adults, not for children at all. The Barrie connection re-emerges in a later project with which del Toro was closely involved, Juan Antonio Bayona's *The Orphanage* (*El Orfanato*) (2007), where the image of the lost child is central to the film's narrative and is, in turn, a metaphorical representation of Spain's 'lost innocence' under Franco. Bayona has described the film as a combination of 'the mother's story from *Peter Pan* with *The Turn of the Screw*, a ghost story by Henry James' (Moore 2007). *The Orphanage* focuses on a central female character, Laura played by Belén Rueda, who becomes a 'mater dolorosa' searching for her own albeit adopted 'lost boy' Simón, and by implication her own and her country Spain's lost past. Clearly influenced by del Toro, Bayona takes a very English classic text and reconfigures it to provide a meditation on the psychological legacy of Francoism. The film was released in 2007, the year that the Socialist government of José Juis Rodríguez Zapatero passed the *Ley de Memoria Histórica* (Law of Historical Memory), which acknowledged the rights of those persecuted under the regime and opened the way for the exhumation of mass graves.

Del Toro's own use of these intertextual flickers, mixed in with the visual references to Rackham and Tenniel, serves to shift these later Victorian and Edwardian texts out of a cultural and historical space that is often infused with a nostalgic and conservative construction of Englishness, re-contextualizing them in a Latin American director's account of one of twentieth-century Europe's bloodiest wars. Hence del Toro recycles established and familiar tropes from a golden age of children's literature in a new, transnational and transcultural context, at once defamiliarizing them and endowing them with new power and relevance. Interestingly, these tropes are mutated for the films, which are themselves about mutation and transformation, about the interface between humanity and monstrosity. So a clear link can be established between the stylistic elements of the films and their thematic preoccupations. A film such as *Pan's Labyrinth* is extensively reliant on a familiar and established literary heritage, but it is also able to play with and 'queer' its canonical referents in a way that more overtly commercial and studio-led screen adaptations (of the J.K. Rowling Harry Potter books and Philip Pullman's *His Dark Materials* (1995–2000) novels for example) aren't, enabling an intertextual creativity that is enhanced by its freedom from the corporate tyranny of franchise-building.

Del Toro is interested not just in pastiche versions of children's literary classics but in synthesizing a range of references to the modern literature of childhood in order to underline the power and relevance to contemporary reality of fairy tale and the story of childhood. Lindsay Steenberg underlines the 'Grimmian sensibility of his cinematic folktales' (Steenberg 2010: 156), which provide another source for the unsentimental and sometimes harsh fate that his children suffer. He also wants to remind us of the importance of the child's questioning gaze in a world where adult behaviour is characterized by a kind of mad unpredictability and brutality. In this respect Michael Rabiger's dubbing of Ofelia in *Pan's Labyrinth* as 'Alice in Francoland' seems entirely appropriate (Rabiger and Hurbis-Cherrier 2013: 206) as one of the most foregrounded intertextual figures within the film is Lewis Carroll's child heroine. At face value the feisty Ofelia, who encounters giant frogs, mysterious fauns and voracious, eyeless monsters, may seem a very distant cousin of Alice, the well brought-up, class-conscious girl who is apparently so concerned with decorum and propriety. There's a visual reference to Alice early in the film where Ofelia is dressed by her mother in a formal Victorian and green-and-white pinafore dress in preparation for the dinner given by her stepfather, only for it to drift away in the mud as she disrobes to encounter the repulsive frog, whose parasitical monstrosity arguably represents the dead hand of Francoist Fascism on Spain. Del Toro wants to foreground the Victorian classic for a number of reasons – it's another epic journey undertaken by the lone pre-pubescent girl-child, defying gender assumptions and facing a deeply disturbing, unreadable world. Most notably, though, is the link that emerges out of the motif common to both texts of the questioning self, the child interrogating an adult orthodoxy, whether it is Vidal's fascist paternalism or the anarchy of Wonderland that disallows her agency and individual autonomy.

Del Toro has described his use of the camera as attempting to replicate the child's interrogative gaze in visual terms, 'I try to use the camera as if it were a curious child, always tiptoeing and trying to get a better view but it keeps being pulled away' (Wood 2006b: 43). The potential for the child's gaze to be not only interrogative but also a corrective and transformative influence on the adult world is a central tenet of del Toro's films as well as the children's literature from which he draws images and ideas. As Rachel Falconer suggests:

> Her [Ofelia's] curious gaze becomes the viewer's conduit to another level of reality, accessed via a different mode of perception … As the film goes on to demonstrate, believing in this other magical reality may be one of the ways in which we can transform our own material and political reality, just when it seems to be beyond the point of repair. (2008: 104)

Other critics such as Lindsay Steenberg have felt that the use of the fairy-tale mode blunts the political edge of his films: 'Frequently the paternalist lessons of the fairytale push the political charge of the narratives to the background' (2010: 154); she quotes Michael Atkinson's (2007) sense of what he calls 'folklore materialism' where 'people's rebellions and socialist movements are subordinated to the patterns and ordeals of the hero's quest and the archetypal agonies of a traumatised childhood'. Perhaps closer to del Toro's methodology here and elsewhere, which often enacts a 'queering' of accepted norms and assumptions, is Rosemary Jackson's account of the way in which the focus of fantasy and horror on gaps, absences and silences rather than presence proves subversive and countercultural: 'By attempting to make visible that which is culturally invisible and which is written out as negation and death, the fantastic introduces absences … Undoing those unifying structures and significations upon which social order depends, fantasy functions to subvert and undermine cultural stability. It proposes what Cixous calls "a subtle invitation to transgression" by exposing the relative and arbitrary nature of those "responses [which men make] to death: ideological institutions, religion, politics" ' (Jackson 1981: 40).

In addition to the widely celebrated influences which can be found in del Toro's output, key cult writers play a significant role, no more so than H.P. Lovecraft. Del Toro is keen to attest the qualities of H.P Lovecraft's fiction and its influence on his own creative imagination. For over a decade he has attempted to launch his own adaptation of Lovecraft's *At the Mountains of Madness* (1936), in which a geologist provides a cautionary tale about an Arctic mountain range which contains a city inhabited by horrific alien ancients. Victoria Nelson contends that del Toro's principal aesthetic of blending bizarre yet beautiful creatures with scientifically plausible logic is influenced by a Lovecraftian sensibility (Nelson 2012). Del Toro claims that Lovecraft is one of the 'great unacknowledged writers' (Lambie 2011).

This influence can be located in key science-fiction horror hybrids and del Toro illuminates the influence of Lovecraft on two canonical films: Ridley Scott's *Alien* and John Carpenter's *The Thing* (1982). Indeed, del Toro claims that the similarities between *At the Mountains of Madness* and Scott's *Prometheus* (2012) have hindered his own adaptation. The influence of Lovecraft can be seen in more than just the tentacled creatures of the *Hellboy* films which so resemble Cthulhu. The narrative and thematic importance of parenting and primogenitor anxiety can be seen in both artists' work, and in del Toro's is often a source of great melancholy for both his protagonists and antagonists (Callaghan 2013).

Other overarching themes connect the work of Lovecraft and del Toro. Donald Burleson identifies the importance of 'forbidden knowledge', or 'merciful ignorance' in Lovecraft's fiction where 'there are species of knowledge only by ignorance of which humankind can maintain even the semblance of wellbeing' (Burleson 1990: 156). Although both are fascinated with the potency and potential dangers of hidden knowledges, del Toro tends much more towards the fundamental redemptive potential of knowledge rather than the apocalyptic tastes of Lovecraft, where revealed knowledge results in eventual insanity and a dystopian entropy. Although invariably powerful, the secrets of the Cronos device, the mysteries of the Faun's underworld and the arcane netherworlds uncovered by Hellboy are ultimately routes to self-awareness and are worth the high price with which they come. Those who seek to control and censor knowledge, such as Vidal in *Pan's Labyrinth* and the pedantic Tom Manning in *Hellboy*, are presented as anti-enlightenment figures. Del Toro has said in interview:

> I think that knowledge, as long as it comes with a spiritual dimension, is always great. What I don't like is knowledge that is purely, purely intellectual because that distances us from nature. I love the idea that knowledge can make us closer to the world, as opposed to making us feel superior to the world. (Elder 2013: 18)

This articulates an almost binarily opposite philosophy to Lovecraft's nihilistic worldview and in many ways embodies the moral message which dominates his cineverse.

Film-maker as connoisseur: The visual arts

> A horrific image can be as potent an image as what we normally qualify as art, because it depicts beauty. Some images of horror are very resonant, as fragile and beautiful as things that don't deal with the ugly side of human nature. (del Toro in Bovberg 2003)

This section explores del Toro's engagement with visual art, ranging from fine art, photography to comic books and multimedia. It is widely acknowledged that del Toro is one of the most aesthetically sophisticated film-makers of the twenty-first century and his dense visual style draws on a richly diverse gallery of images.

In his poem 'Les Phares', from *Les Fleurs du Mal* (1857), the Symbolist poet Charles Baudelaire begins with a series of eight stanzas celebrating a series of visual artists whose work has helped to define his own aesthetics. These include Rubens, Da Vinci, Rembrandt, Watteau, Goya and Delacroix and represent the 'phares', guiding lights or beacons throughout the history of Western art that have illuminated human experience for the poet, whose own writing is referenced on a number of occasions by del Toro and whose critique of Goya will be explored later in this section. To catalogue the painters whose art has contributed to the development of del Toro's visual imagination would be to write the history of art in the last two centuries and beyond. As with the equivalent filmic and literary sources, del Toro's eclecticism makes for a dizzying mix of genres and styles, from the fevered fifteenth-century imaginings of Hieronymous Bosch, through Goya to late nineteenth- and early twentieth-century symbolism to surrealism and comic book/graphic art and video games. Particularly important artistic beacons include Symbolist artists such as Odilon Redon (1840–1916), Felicien Rops (1833–1898), Carlos Schwabe (1866–1926) (who illustrated an edition of Baudelaire's *Les Fleurs du Mal*), Arnold Böcklin (1827–1901) as well as the Mexican Surrealist Julio Ruelas (1870–1907). Del Toro has blogged on his official website about all of these painters and illustrators whose sensuous and often perverse imagery is a continued source of inspiration for him. In interviews, del Toro has intimated his expansive and apparently insatiable appetite for painterly stimuli from whatever source:

> More and more as I grow older, I find myself looking for inspiration in painting, illustration, videogames and old movies. I love what many of my contemporaries are doing, especially people like Terry Gilliam, David Cronenberg, P.T. Anderson and Alfonso Cuarón. However, I get more charged up browsing through one of my art books or looking at some paintings or illustrations. I also feel there are very beautiful atmospheric moments in videogames. Language-wise, there's a lot to learn from them. Anime also. I love anime. (Jenkins 2008)

Perhaps surprisingly, the absorption of such richly diverse sources results in major and recurrent patterns, themes and tropes that emerge as a result of del Toro's capacity to filter and then alchemize what seem at first to be almost random influences. These might include (not an exhaustive list by any means) the subversive collapsing of borderlines between real and imagined, the indirect representation of politics and sexuality via fantasy and surreality, and what might be called a dominant discourse of perversity that correlates the human with the monstrous and that evinces on ongoing fascination, almost obsession, with the latter. These are conveyed and communicated via a visual palette that draws on historically diverse influences such as the later Goya's embracing a world of blackness and shadows, which emerges in del Toro's repeated use of subterranean settings and chiaroscuro lighting effects that operate as a coded visual narrative within the films. Goya famously claimed that '[i]n nature, colour does not exist any more than lines. There's only light and shadow' (Harris 1994: 24). Similarly, the Surrealist Paul Delvaux's (1897–1994) repeated use of an eerie blue light, which shrouds a landscape of unease and the uncanny, provides an inspiration for del Toro's use of similar blue tones, often a visual coding for emotional or psychological sterility or rigid ideology. Occasionally, particular paintings emerge as key specific references in the films. Perhaps the most obvious is one of the most famous of Goya's late *Black Paintings* (1819–1823), the image of Saturn devouring one of his children, a clear inspiration for the rapacious Pale Man of *Pan's Labyrinth*. However, there are also visual references to another of Goya's greatest political paintings, *The Third of May* (1814), in the execution scenes in del Toro's Spanish Civil War films, particularly *The Devil's Backbone* of which del Toro has said: 'Everything in the movie was meant to look like a Goya painting because he is one of the great painters of war' (Archibald 2001). Here the director is surely referring to the series of over 80 prints now entitled *Los Desastres de la Guerra* (*The Disasters of War* – Goya's own inscription for the etchings was 'Fatal consequences of Spain's bloody war with Bonaparte, and other emphatic caprices') which Goya created between 1810 and 1820. These extraordinary works, prompted by the Peninsular War and not shown during his lifetime, relentlessly depict the seemingly random barbarity of the conflict – the torture, rape and mutilation of bodies – in disturbingly graphic detail that seems to look forward to contemporary photojournalism. Del Toro has also spoken of the influence of another painting, *The Colossus* (now thought to be by one of Goya's assistants), on the design of his most recent film, *Pacific Rim* (Calautti 2012). The painting shows a gargantuan and mythic naked male torso, which fills the sky, turning its back on a fleeing and terrified populace. More generally, the most reproduced and reworked of Goya's Caprichos, the etching *El Sueño de la razón produce monstruos* (*The Sleep of Reason Produces Monsters*), expresses what is a fundamental premise for del Toro, the inextricable link between the human and the grotesque. In *Mimic* the misguided 'reason' of science does in fact produce monsters, albeit ones that evolve inexorably into the human. Goya wrote on some editions of the etching, 'Fantasy abandoned by reason produces impossible monsters: united with her she is the mother of the arts and the origin of their marvels', which could also be read as an essential dictum for del Toro. To foreground Goya as a key influence is not necessarily to deny the primacy of other artists, particularly the Symbolists, but to acknowledge the centrality of the Spanish master to Hispanic aesthetics as well as his position as the inaugurator of much of what is now taken as modernity in art as a whole, including film-making. For Robert Hughes, the art historian and writer, modern art begins with Goya's work in the 1790s. Hughes has also suggested that Goya's modernity has been a vital influence on a number of artistic careers: 'much of Manet, for instance, depends on Goya, just as much of the film imagery of Luis Buñuel does; and you can't easily imagine Picasso or Beckmann without him' (Hughes 2003a).

A further illustration of the importance of Goya to Hispanic film-making can be found in the work of Carlos Saura. In the most recently made feature film about Goya, Saura's *Goya in Bordeaux* (1999), the Spanish director traces the historical lineaments of the painter's life whilst also exploring questions concerning the ambivalence of representation and narrative. Antonio Lázaro-Reboll indicates in a review of the film: 'Saura draws on Spanish culture to frame his concerns about Spanish history and cultural representation, linking Goya's paintings back to the cultural preoccupations of the artist – war, violence, religion, art, and politics. Goya insinuates the inherent ambivalence of painted representation, as both artistic creation and historically situated narrative, and he warns us against seeing painting merely as narrative – that is, in terms of the event represented, where what really happened has already left the scene' (Lázaro-Reboll 2001).

This central ambivalence in Goya's work, expressing the tension between narrative and representation, politics and art, reflects some essential aspects of his career as an artist working within the realities of royal patronage and turbulent European history. Goya's career has often been seen as a divided one: on the one hand he became the highly successful court artist painting numerous portraits of Spanish aristocracy and monarchy; on the other he is the experimentalist explorer of the world of the supernatural and nightmare. The *Caprichos* and *Black Paintings* are haunted by images of violence, both human and other – witches and demons populate the landscapes of some of his most disturbing paintings such as *La Romería de San Isidro* (1821–1823) (*The Pilgrimage of San Isidro*) and *El Aquelarre* (*Witches' Sabbath* (1820–1824)). These two late works faced each other as part of the series of murals with which Goya decorated his house outside Madrid, Quinta del Sourdo (they were moved to the Museo del Prado after his death). In both paintings the human face becomes a monstrous landscape, scarred by superstition, religion, poverty and suffering. In an earlier painting, also entitled *El Aquelarre* (1797–1998), a similar scene is intruded upon by a horned figure, presumably Satan, who seems to be a possible precursor of the Faun in *Pan's Labyrinth*. It is illuminating to make a direct correlation between Goya's divided nature and del Toro, who has been described by the writer and critic Mark Kermode thus: 'In essence, he is a divided soul, a realist attuned to the strange vibrations of the supernatural, a lapsed Catholic ("not quite the same thing as an atheist") with an interest in sacrifice and redemption' (Kermode 2006a: 20). Kermode's final phrase helpfully indicates the essential point of contrast between del Toro and Goya. For the latter there appears to be little possibility of redemption for a humanity that becomes monstrous through violence, war, ignorance and superstition. In contrast, for del Toro redemption is possible through storytelling and fantasy – human choice, and if necessary sacrifice, can enact change and some form of liberation. Like the aesthetic imperative behind his *Caprichos* and the *Black Paintings*, Goya's vision of humanity is essentially a pessimistic one where the human all too readily metamorphoses into the grotesque and monstrous. For del Toro, human monstrosity is often concealed behind a handsome facade that has to be penetrated in order to be overcome – the bodies of both Vidal and Jacinto undergo this kind of process. Further to this, in what are arguably his most personal films, the *Hellboy* franchise, we are invited to love the figure of the exiled and outcast monster for his ironic embodiment of flawed but ultimately admirable humanity. One of the director's most elaborately conceived scenes, the Troll Market in *Hellboy II: The Golden Army*, constructs a universe running parallel to the human that celebrates a kind of monstrously imagined diversity. This is an animated Bosch canvas, full of Goya-esque monsters that seem to have emerged out of a Symbolist dream/nightmare landscape. Yet the Troll Market scene, despite its determined strangeness, contains little or none of Bosch's tortured Catholic imagery and apocalyptic hallucinations, nor is it haunted by the tortured interiority of much Symbolist and Surrealist art. In the end, it is simply there – a playful celebration of imagined otherness.

Baudelaire's description of Goya in the paper *Le Present* (1857) is uncannily applicable to del Toro:

> His monsters are viable, harmoniously proportioned. No one has dared to go further than he in the direction of grotesque reality. All these contortions, bestial faces, and diabolical grimaces, are profoundly human. Even from the technical point of view of natural history, it would be hard to fault them, every inch of them is so well-knit and so carefully integrated into the whole. In a word it is difficult to say precisely at what point reality and fantasy are knitted together and joined. The border-line between the two is so skillfully crossed that the subtlest analysis cannot trace it; the art behind it is so natural, yet so transcendental also. (in Glendinning 1977: 136)

Goya's last paintings, completed in the first quarter of the nineteenth century, provide a direct link to the Symbolist movement of the last quarter of the century and the beginning of the twentieth. Jodi Hauptman has described the relationship between Goya and Odilon Redon thus: 'For both Goya and Redon, then, the imagination is not at work alone; for what gives each of their oeuvres its mysterious power is this tension, this combination, this suturing of the real and the fantastic' (Hauptman 2005: 17). This suturing of the real and fantastic is central to the narrative in *Pan's Labyrinth* as Ofelia negotiates a path between reality and fantasy. It is also a given in such scenes as the Troll Market in *Hellboy II: The Golden Army*. For del Toro, the importance of Symbolist art is its capacity to represent the unknowable and communicate a sense of mystery. As del Toro has suggested on his weblog:

> [I]n this day and age we confuse hip smartness with intelligence and callousness with a point of view of the world. Knowing it all seems to be the way to gauge

an artist's worth. But Schwabe, Redon, Rops et al celebrate not knowing. They, in fact, celebrate the twilight of our knowledge, to them, the supernatural is absolutely real and mistery [sic] is the supreme goal of art. (http://deltorofilms. com/wp/)

This 'absolute reality' of the supernatural found in Goya and the Symbolists, and the lack of any mediating narrative, be it via dream sequences or hallucination, is key to del Toro's film-making and distinguishes him from his peers. As Hauptman says of Odilon Redon: 'Instead of choosing between imagination and mimesis, fantasy and nature, Redon employed one to get to the other: he closely examined nature in inventing his fantasies: he carefully observed reality as a way to take flights of the imagination' (2005: 24).

Elsewhere in this book we speak of a 'queer' sensibility that informs some at least of del Toro's work and it is possible to root some of that rejection of the culturally normative in the example set by the Symbolist and Decadent artists of the late nineteenth and early twentieth centuries. Decadence and Symbolism were both initially literary movements that became imbricated with avant-garde art of the time: early articulations of the movements by writers such as Jean Moréas in his 1886 manifesto and Albert Aurier in a groundbreaking 1891 article on Gaugin spoke of the 'polymorphous hallucinations' 'subjective deformations' and play of associations in Symbolist writing and painting. This creative confluence of word and image, of contrasting areas of imaginative activity, not only provides an aesthetic template for del Toro's own alchemic melding of diverse literary and artistic origins but also constructs a portrait of the artist as a kind of cultural explorer, questing after the creation of as yet unseen worlds. Elsewhere on his weblog he has spoken of the importance of Schwabe and Arthur Rackham to the crafting of *Pan's Labyrinth* and *Hellboy II* in comments that reveal some essential aspects of his own artistic enterprise: 'Their interpretation of the Fairy world is not similar at all but both men seem to approach it as explorers, trying to document a reality – a world – only revealed to their eyes' (http://deltorofilms. com/wp/). Before identifying him too strongly with the hypersensitive or effete Symbolist or Decadent artist, it has also to be remembered that del Toro is also the hard-headed pragmatist (as was Goya himself) who is necessarily able to manage huge film budgets and massive production projects and who also draws on popular cultural forms such as the comic book as extensively as he does the great painters of the past.

In addition to drawing upon 'high' art forms, del Toro is equally able to mine the wealth of pop-cultural artefacts and so fits in with the current

Hollywood zeitgeist of comic book and video game-influenced output, albeit with an emphasis on the darker and more Gothic-themed elements which bind together his work as a whole. It is worth noting that *The Devil's Backbone* is loosely based upon the comic series *Paracuellos* by Carlos Giménez and the narrative itself includes comic books as a means of fraternal bonding amongst the boys in the orphanage. As a famed collector of comics amongst many other pop-cultural forms and an active participant in the comic book fan community, as Antonio Lázaro-Reboll notices, del Toro is 'equally comfortable talking about films at Cannes as he is in discussing them at comic conventions' (Lázaro-Reboll 2012: 255). There is also a rich tradition of comic book production in Mexico. Tim Pilcher and Brad Brooks highlight the magnitude of comics in Mexican culture:

> It has often been said that the biggest market for comics in the world is Japan. While this is undoubtedly true, it isn't quite the full answer. Another country has, at times been just as voracious a consumer and producer as the Japanese, and that country is Mexico. (2005: 228)

This also involves a cross-pollination between film-makers and comic book artists. For instance, the film-maker Alejandro Jodorowsky (*El Topo* (1970)) collaborated with comic book artists to create *Anibal 5* (*Hannibal 5*) which involved a cyborgian agent who worked for the Latin-American Agency of Defense (ALAD), a situation echoed in the *Hellboy* franchise. Jodorowsky would later collaborate with Jean Gerard (Moebius) on a doomed adaptation of Frank Herbert's *Dune*, another influence on del Toro. Jean Gerard worked in the *bandes dessinées* tradition of Franco/Belgian comic books. Gerard's aesthetic blends fantasy and science fiction in an organic-looking style which is heavily surreal and psychedelic. The other seminal fantasy artist to influence del Toro is Frank Frazetta. Frazetta was an American artist who worked in, amongst other media, paratexts such as album covers, book covers and posters which are valued amongst the fan and geek community, as discussed in Chapter 2 of this book. Frazetta worked on the animated adaptation of *The Hobbit*, and no doubt his influence would have been seen in de Toro's production of it should it have progressed any further. Del Toro describes Frazetta as an 'Olympian artist' who 'gave the world a new pantheon of heroes…who somehow created a second narrative layer for every book he ever illustrated' (Boucher 2010). But ultimately the most directly influential artist on de Toro's oeuvre is Mike Mignola, who has collaborated with the director on the *Hellboy* franchise. Mignola's style has been described as 'dark and expressive', and in all of his work (including *Hellboy*) he brings a distinctly Gothic sensibility to the fore in the artwork on titles such as *Cosmic Odyssey* (1988) and *Gotham by Gaslight* (1989).

Mignola came to popular attention and launched Hellboy with Dark Horse Comics, which have been a major force in comic book culture over the last 30 years. This influence is twofold. First, Dark Horse reflects the rise in adult and mature audience comics which tend towards more complex, challenging and even avant-garde content. This stems from the shift in the late 1980s, where writers and artists such as Frank Miller, Alan Moore and Neil Gaiman were involved in claiming a stake for comic books as artworks and which saw the rise of the 'graphic novel' and the establishment of 'auteur'-like figures. Second, Dark Horse became an outlet for the distribution of Manga to the West, which has helped to create a keen fan base for Manga (such as *Akira* (1982–1990) and *Ghost in the Shell* (1989)) which has had a significant effect on the comic book fan community and which has provided a fascinating alternative to the dominant superhero genre of publishers, Marvel and DC Comics. It is no surprise that del Toro has collaborated with and drawn from Dark Horse, given its status as a home for alternative, bleaker visions and comics from non-US producers. *Hellboy* and *Hellboy II: The Golden Army* themselves represent a darker, symbolic and surreal version of the hyper-commodified shine of *Iron Man* and *Spiderman* franchises and *Pacific Rim* adds a brutal Manga, Gothic-influenced air to the ideologically simplistic, tech-fetishes of the *Transformers* franchise.

Perhaps the most pertinent visual reference points for a director so fascinated by the capacity of the image to capture or construct strangeness and reality in a simultaneous moment are the great photographers of the twentieth century, particularly those who used the photographic image in ways that radically subvert expectations of the medium or those who combine reportage with particular visual creativity. Examples of the former, cited by del Toro, include two controversial photographers of the generation born in the 1930s: the American Joel Peter Witkin (b. 1939), and the Czech Jan Saudek (b. 1935), and the more familiar and highly influential Surrealist Man Ray (1890–1976). Witkin explores sometimes extreme images of death and otherness in ways that are comparable to the work of Diane Arbus. As Gerry Badger has suggested in an important essay on Witkin 'Like Arbus, Witkin has elected to deal with the torment of his existence, what Bruno Bettelheim called the 'nightside of the Janus figure that we call identity'. But whereas the torment of Arbus derived from her sense of dislocation within society, her sense of being 'other', alone, a freak, Witkin confronts an altogether metaphysical issue, the eschatological nightmare, the pain of bodily existence and the anguish of death' (Badger 1999: 139). Badger's description of Witkin's work could well be applied to del Toro, '[h]e mediates, supplementing his raw subject material with metaphor, myth and allusion, constructing a dense contextual narrative for each image without entirely obfuscating its initial impact' (1999: 139). Witkin and Saudek, who is also a painter, challenge the boundaries of taste and acceptability, continuing the agenda of the earlier Symbolists and Decadents. In contrast, the photographers del Toro admires, who deal with elements of reportage or photojournalism, are at first glance less obviously disturbing. Amongst others he cites figures who established photography as a major art form, such as Henri Cartier-Bresson, the Mexican Álvarez Bravo (1902–2002), Arthur Fellig (Weegee) (1899–1968) and the Hungarian Robert Capa (1913–1954), whose reporting during the Spanish Civil War and the Second World War provided some of the most powerful images to emerge from those conflicts. Capa's extraordinary visual record, informed by his own anti-Fascist politics, provided some of the definitive images of the Spanish War and his juxtaposition of bloody conflict and 'ordinary' life offers a template for such scenes as the village execution of International Brigade fighters in *The Devil's Backbone*. Two other important photographers, both from Latin America, offer perhaps the closest parallels to del Toro's imaginative world. Juan Rulfo's fiction will be discussed elsewhere, but in addition he assembled an important body of photographic work, often of landscapes in which old and new worlds are contrasted, sometimes creating a surreal or dreamlike effect. As in his great 1955 novel *Pedro Páramo*, he juxtaposes the mythic and the real to the point at which distinctions are blurred. This desire to set the ancient and the new alongside one another in order to explore the relationship of the past to the present or to represent the dislocation between them is also evident in the work of Manuel Álvarez Bravo. Álvarez Bravo was one of the most important Mexican artists of the twentieth century and his photography records the shifting nature of Mexican society over a long period, decoding and recoding some of the stock images of Mexican culture in order to redefine and/or subvert received or clichéd notions of *Mexicanidad* (Mexicanness). John Mraz describes Bravo thus: 'Conscious both of Mexico's otherness and the way in which that has led almost naturally to stereotypical imagery, he swam counter to the stream of established clichés, using visual irony to embody contradiction' (Mraz 2010: 86). Also relevant to del Toro is Álvarez Bravo's focus on the ways in which the uncanny continually inflects the ordinary – he does this by focusing on apparently insignificant details which are imbued and invested with almost mythic meaning and power. The rootedness of del Toro's world in the here-and-now of reality, whatever the narrative context, has its most recent manifestation in *Pacific Rim* where he very specifically evokes some of the twentieth century's most famous photographs, those taken by the great American photographer Lewis Hine during the construction of the Empire State Building. These record the vertiginous working conditions of the construction teams as they laboured and rested on the sky-high skeletal beams of the building, with little or no safety equipment to protect them. In del Toro's most recent film, Hine's pioneering work in recording labour conditions and the heroism of the workers is referenced in the scenes that depict the construction of the ironically named Wall of Life. The disillusioned Jaeger pilot Raleigh Becket is seen working on a high beam above the city before he is brought back into active service by Pentecost. This section of *Pacific Rim* self-consciously evokes the 1930s and 1940s, not only in the referencing of Hine, but also in the almost sepia colour palette of the filming and the crowds of men gathering to find work dressed in what closely resemble period work clothes. The iconography here also evokes the wartime spirit of 'Rosie the Riveter' (we later see women working in construction at the Shatterdome) – the image that represented American women's labour contribution to the war effort and which famously appeared in wartime propaganda posters. These images reflect the director's acknowledged fascination with the period, but also convey a powerful sense of collective heroism that the film's ideology strongly endorses. They move us away from the often darkly pessimistic world of Goya, Symbolism and Decadence into a perhaps less complex and nuanced aesthetic, but one which celebrates human potentiality as opposed to human perversity.

2

Accented Fantasy and the Gothic Perverse

This chapter further interrogates Guillermo del Toro's relationship with two key areas of screen studies: transnationalism and Queer cinema. We situate del Toro in the context of contemporary transnational cinema, both as an exilic film-maker who has worked in a number of transcultural bases and as a prominent figure in both Hispanic film and Hollywood production. We also locate a number of transnational themes and motifs in del Toro's work and explore his own characteristic approach to transnationalism which blends the fantastical with the diasporic. This surrealistic 'accented' approach to film-making also has relevance to the process of 'queering' and we expand upon del Toro's creation of films which raid the vaults of the Queer uncanny.

Magical transnationalism

As early as 1995, when Guillermo del Toro's debut feature film *Cronos* was garnering critical acclaim and the film-maker was working on his first Hollywood production *Mimic*, he was critically identified within the shifting discourse from national cinema-bordered traditions to nascent transnational border-crossing culture. Anne Marie Stock identifies *Cronos* as an example of multicultural collaboration and dialogue which not only drives the mode of production of the endeavour but is also woven into the fabric of the narrative itself. She highlights the fact that del Toro 'and his film defy binary classification within "either/or" categories' and that on many levels it typifies Latin America's exploration of 'cross-fertilisation' as a potent source of film-making (2006: 159). Seen in this light, *Cronos* is striking in that cross-fertilization, blending and hybridity are impossible to ignore. Indeed, the blending together of elements to create new entities are so prevalent, the mix so overwhelming, as to obscure the component parts as distinct. Jesús's symbiosis with the Cronos device, the co-dependent relationship with Aurora, his granddaughter, the intermingling of the old and new, the multinational characters, the heteroglossic dialogue and the genre-bending narrative combine in a film which is paradoxically held together by the sheer commitment to a bricolage structure.

Stock, though, notices a tension in the critical reception of *Cronos* and other films working as a part of a transnational dialogue in the tendency to seek out an authentic national drive, hidden within the seemingly diverse filmic creation. She points out that critics repeatedly fall back upon del Toro's Mexican heritage, aesthetic temperament and perspective in a tendency which seeks ultimately to privilege the 'genealogical rhetoric of blood', a phrase which incidentally resonates thematically throughout del Toro's oeuvre (159). This section explores further del Toro's position in the development of transnational cinema; he has flourished in this area, benefitted from it and made a unique and increasingly influential contribution to it. In addition to extending the investigation into del Toro's Spanish-language films as prime examples of transnational, cosmopolitan and 'accented' works of art, we also incorporate his Hollywood productions into this discussion and contend that it is in the most iconic of contemporary American genres, the comic book adaptation, where del Toro's trans-thematics are most successfully and subtly played out.

Will Higbee and Song Hwee Lim chart three main methods that have been deployed in the theorization of transnational cinema as an area of film scholarship (2010). These are, firstly, a focus on alternative modes of production, distribution and exhibition of films outside national cinema boundaries and practices, secondly, an approach which takes into account regional phenomena in terms of a shared geopolitical cultural set of interests (such as Latin-American or Chinese cinemas) and, thirdly, an exploration of the cinema of diaspora that can be split into two interconnected areas. These are an analysis of the work of exiled, diasporic or postcolonial film-makers working in the West and informed by an outsider's perspective, and the thematic inclusion of figurative and literal issues relating to 'migration, loss and displacement that lead to identities in flux, which, again, challenge the stable and fixed (hegemonic) concept of the national' (9–10). This section will locate del Toro in relation to these methods.

In terms of production, del Toro's *Cronos* sets a precedent for his mode of operation which has been remarkably resilient (or perhaps, vital) considering his success across film industries. As well as including an international principal cast from Mexico, Argentina and the US, *Cronos* is also a co-production between Mexican and US production companies (the dual language of the film mines a transnational Hispanic audience base). The collaborative team of del Toro, Bertha Navarro (producer), Guillermo Navarro (regular cinematographer) and Ron Perlman (a recurrent acting presence) defines a mode of production across film cultures from the 'art house' *Cronos* to *Pan's Labyrinth*, through Hollywood action adventure films in *Hellboy* and *Hellboy II: The Golden Army* and to the blockbuster spectacle in *Pacific Rim*. In addition, as a Hispanic film-maker, del Toro can be seen as part of a generation of directors who have raised the industry profile of their geopolitical region and gained an international audience. Others, such as Alfonso Cuarón and Alejandro González Iñárritu, have mobilized as Mexican artists, developing a platform for the work of others (not least in the formation of their production company Cha Cha Cha).

'The Three Amigos' as they have been referred to, as well as other directors such as Fernando Solanas and Walter Salles, have participated in what has led to a widening appreciation of Latin American cinema as a fervent field of artistically credible and politically engaging cinema which itself reflects the effects of shifting cultures in the twenty-first century. Del Toro's role as a producer of emergent talent from Latin America should not be underestimated. Just as Pedro Almodóvar used the platform that he found himself on after the success of La Movida Madrileña movement to help launch other talents (del Toro included), del Toro has introduced a number of Hispanic film-makers to a wider audience keen to access non-Hollywood fare, often using the widespread appetite for genre fiction as a vehicle for such an exchange. The directors Juan Antonio Bayona and Andrés Muschietti amongst others have been promoted by del Toro as a part of a continued effort to establish a global audience for contemporary Latin American and Hispanic film. This also involves developing English-language films produced from within the Hollywood system, a factor that feeds into the third criterion outlined by Higbee and Lim, and it is here where the work of Guillermo del Toro begins to become more influential and interesting (Shaw 2003).

When del Toro was interviewed about the growing critical buzz surrounding *Cronos* and the attempts to garner a US audience for the film, he depicts a journey which in itself illustrates both the opportunities and the tensions brought about by the existence of a transnational network of film-making activity (DePalma 1994). We see the Mexican-born artist gaining plaudits on the international festival circuit and receiving attention from the US film industry, all the while resisting the opportunity to accept inferior Hollywood fare, maintaining a connection to Mexican heritage and staying true to the 'auteur's vision'. If we look fleetingly at what followed, a familiar narrative seems to unfold: the struggles with the limited Hollywood take on genre (*Mimic*); the see-saw between larger-budget Hollywood product and more personal 'foreign' work presented to the US (*Pan's Labyrinth*); and the potential for sublimation into the mega-budget blockbuster market (*Pacific Rim*). Del Toro evades, appropriates and subverts these narratives, and his alchemic filmic mode is central to this. The DePalma article sketches a journey from Mexico to the US and in it del Toro provides a sound bite which illuminates the very 'transnational' nature of film-making informed by multiculturalism and cosmopolitanism as recognized by Stock. Del Toro's comment that he is a 'round-trip ticket' film-maker galvanizes an element of transnationalism which widens the participatory scope of the cinematic workshop and leads to multicultural, heterogeneous film art. However, *Cronos* is the first and up until now the only film of del Toro's made or set in Mexico, and Spain is the source of his two further non-English-language productions. This is the result of his father's kidnapping whilst in Guadalajara and his subsequent release, prompting del Toro and his family to emigrate to America. On a surface level, del Toro's films appear to be split between Hispanic heritage and US émigré productions. In fact, *all* his subsequent films (with the exception of *Mimic*, the production which he was working on during his father's ordeal) have been made in exile and this has had a profound effect (Cruz 2009).

On the surface level it can appear that del Toro maintains a binary split between personal, politically relevant and revealing projects such as *The Devil's Backbone* and *Pan's Labyrinth* (the former set during and the latter in the after-effects of the Spanish Civil War), which garner critical and credible acclaim as a part of a transnational cinematic boom, and commercial franchise products such as *Blade II* and the *Hellboy* films, which are a part of an American-led boom in comic book adaptations. However, this binary is a façade, and del Toro's alchemic mode, whilst stemming from the material and commercial realities of transnational cinema and chiming with the thematic concerns of many transnational films, is more profound, more genetically encoded into his practice and cinematic philosophy. It is woven into all of his oeuvre and most completely realized in his *Hellboy* series.

Higbee and Lim observe that 'transnational cinema' as a term and as a concept is potentially reductive in that, for example, it seems to negate 'national cinema' or at least appears to counter national cinema as a mode of cultural expression (2010). They note that there are a number of concepts and concerns (some of which work in tension with one another) that are potentially taken for granted or seen in a reductive manner. Back in 1994 del Toro characterizes his modus operandi when discussing *Cronos*, saying that it 'in many ways reverses the clichés of a regular horror film while following them religiously' (DePalma 1994). This equation can be broadened out to include the other genres in which he works (the ghost story, the fairy tale, the action adventure film) and also the narrative of the transnational film-maker working within Hollywood. Much of the scholarly analysis concerning transnational cinema begins with the complex modes of production which have resulted in metropolitan/collaborative/cross-cultural output and trends. Increasingly, the narrative, figurative and diegetic have been taken more into account as complex areas of interest. The work of del Toro clearly has a transnational attitude, aesthetic and philosophy which transcend the material reality of production. We discuss the use of language in the films, border-crossing and identity, exile and melancholia and finally kinship formations as a response to disenfranchisement.

It is fitting that Hamid Nacify deploys the term 'accented' to describe the cinema of exile and diaspora, and although this goes way beyond lexis itself, the diegetic importance of language in transnational film should not be underestimated (Nacify 2001). As an influential film, Ridley Scott's *Blade Runner* (1983) is important to transnational genre film in that it imagines a post-national world. The 'city-speak' hybrid language of the film acts as a plot device but also as a voice of the environment which is so powerful in the narrative. In Takashi Miike's *Sukiyaki Western Django* (2007) the phonetic English spoken by Japanese actors in a hybrid postmodern Western world adds to the confusing, playful nature of the film and instils a level of post-structuralism where incomprehension and incongruous juxtaposition and the lack of voice become a key subtext (Rawle 2011). Translation in a heteroglossic world can also act as a powerful figurative device to represent a scenario where connections can be difficult and dangerous things. In David Cronenberg's *Eastern Promises* (2007) for example, the translation of Tatiana's diary acts as a metaphoric portal to an underworld of crime where a terrible by-product of transnational exchange is human trafficking. Language and its potency plays a part in almost all of del Toro's films, and some of its particular uses provide a thematic thread that adds a level of cogency to his seemingly disparate body of work.

From the outset of his feature-film career, language and the move to multicultural exchange are prominent in del Toro's films and this is never more evident than in *Cronos*. The film depicts a near future where Mexico has signed a freetrade agreement with the US; we are intoduced to a rapidly changing world where Jesús and his antique store are archaic islands in a world of flux.

The street signs are written in multiple languages, a juxtaposition which is heightened by the opening scene, where an archaic-sounding voice narrates the tale of a sixteenth-century alchemist who creates the Cronos device. This use of language as a framing device sets the scene for the dramatic projection of language (or its lack) by the characters. Stock contends that *Cronos* is a film which flaunts 'migrancy and hybridity' and that this is due in part to language. Scenes are a blend of English and Spanish, rejecting a notion of authenticity in a narrative where transformation is central (159). The film's engagement with the voice as a figurative device is also evident in the lack of speech from Aurora. She spends the film largely in silence, a witness to the trauma of change, only connected to an ageing man who is concurrently revitalized and moribund throughout the film. If we see Jesús's journey as a metaphor for a Mexico caught between the old world and the new, then we can see Aurora's silence as symptomatic of the fact that she is caught between worlds, unable or unwilling to speak the language of either.

Silence from the child as witness to the turbulence of change and conflict can also be seen in *The Devil's Backbone*. Abandoned at the beginning of the film, Carlos is silenced and marginalized, bullied by fellow boys expelled from their homes and terrified by the ghost of another silenced child. Carlos's voice grows throughout the narrative though and he is able to defend and speak up for himself against the aggressive Jaime and, in a final revelatory moment, communicate with the ghost Santi. Carlos, Jaime and Santi are initially alienated from one another, uncommunicative and alone, inhabiting the same border space but literally and figuratively from different worlds. It is only from joining together that they can defeat Jacinto, their violent oppressor, and although Carlos ends the film in exile, he is nonetheless emancipated from his role as victim. The fact that children feature so heavily in del Toro's work and that these children find voice may reflect his own status as an artist in exile, who over the course of his career has become bi-lingual out of necessity. Yana Meerzon argues that '[t]he move to a new land forces one to relive an earlier stage of his/her cognitive development. The need to learn a new language, to find some new means to communicate with the world takes a grown up person to their childhood' (Meerzon 2012: 24). In this respect, the character of Hellboy is pertinent: on one level an adult immersed in all American, beer-swilling popular culture but on another in stasis as a perpetual child as his name reminds us, and struggling to deal with his alienation and lack of voice.

The written word and the power of storytelling as potent alternative to dangerous reality is also a trope in del Toro's work. Similar to Carlos in *The Devil's Backbone*, Ofelia finds herself re-homed because of conflict in *Pan's Labyrinth*. The film seems to attest to the need for fiction when such monstrosity as fascism is encountered. For Ofelia, the fantasy world of fairy tale and the labyrinth offers an opportunity not just for escape but for a dynamic role in the processes of her own identity creation. This self-creation is often solidified through the construction of narrative and there are multiple examples of Ofelia (who is an obsessive reader) writing and realizing her own narrative agency through texts. The film offers a meta-textual dimension which attests to the transformative potency of fiction itself. Considering this, the whole of the narrative can be seen as an ode to storytelling as liberation. Del Toro is not just interested in pastiche versions of children's literary classics but in synthesizing a range of references to the modern literature of childhood in order to underline the power and relevance to contemporary reality of fairy tale and the story of childhood.

Naficy explores the ways in which accented cinema often employs a fractured multivocal display as a stylistic feature (2001: 121). This use of a cinematic 'free indirect discourse' destabilizes dominant narratives and presents a world where the milieu and its confusing and intoxicating elements collide to colourful effect. This is typified in del Toro's work in the 'Troll Market' sequence in *Hellboy II: The Golden Army*. When Hellboy and his group infiltrate the Troll Market they enter a cacophony of sight and sound, which consists of an overlap of languages, accents and dialects. Some of this is incomprehensible, some subtitled and some heavily accented English, including Hellboy's gang, which includes American, Germanic and Received Pronunciation English. In addition, Hellboy speaks via radio to Liz but is admonished by fellow agent Johann Krauss for fear of blowing their cover. Later Hellboy and Krauss interrogate two creatures who have information concerning the mysterious Prince Nuada. This meta-language combined with the market which is a mish-mash of bazaars, fashions from around the world and intertextual referents (such as the cantina from *Star Wars: A New Hope* (1977)) draws attention to the familiarity and alien nature of the netherworld and in turn the alienated nature of Hellboy and his troop in the cityscape above; as Hellboy states to Liz, 'nobody's looking at us, we blend right in'. Del Toro's films also conjure up archaic languages that are deeply powerful and mysterious. *Cronos* opens with narration about the Veracruz alchemist Fulcanelli who forges the device in the sixteenth century. In *Pan's Labyrinth*, when Ofelia meets the faun and asks his name, he responds that he has had many ancient names that 'only the wind and the trees can pronounce'. *Hellboy II: The Golden Army* is filled with Elvish and other strange languages and symbols as a part of the film's mythology. Chris Wahl uses the phrase 'polyglot cinema' to describe films which employ sub titles and international linguistic meshes in order to both acknowledge and intensify the 'diversity of human life' (in Berger and Komori 2010: 117). Verena Berger and Miya Komori notice how in the context of transnationalism migration and alienation polyglot cinema illustrates the 'breadth of languages with which migrants are confronted' (1995: 9). The use of fantastical non-human languages in his films (which is a recurrent motif) has a threefold effect. First, it accentuates the complex and confusing environments and situations which the characters must navigate. Second, it pits the urban, multicultural 'human world' against a backdrop of far more complex and ancient mythology which makes some of the concerns of the overworld to be petty and fleeting. Third, it makes all viewers of the films migrants in that we are all experiencing these languages as non-natives drawn into the mythical netherworld.

Key in all these examples is the motif of potent ancient languages which may have been overshadowed by new lexical formations and urban, modern linguistic transactions, but nevertheless hold within them substance which can bridge the void between worlds and peoples. Lindsay Steenberg contends that '[t]he transnational success of these films is due in some part to del Toro's combination of mythic themes and imagery with narratives about political strife and an honesty in the representation of the brutal violence so much a part of both worlds' (Steenberg 2010: 157). Of the many traversals between worlds, more often than not the intercultural language exchange is both disorientating and potentially dangerous, yet also holds the power to break down barriers and forge new alliances and friendships. This reflects more broadly the transnational tension and relief points in the wider worlds and their cinematic representations.

These exchanges often take place on borders, and the borderland is a consistent motif in all of del Toro's directorial output. Sometimes, these border-crossings involve voluntary or involuntary symbiosis, be they symbolic or literal transnational exchanges. In discussing *Cronos*, del Toro has stated that the vampiric relationship between North America and Mexico in a post-NAFTA world is a subtextual influence (Wood 2006a: 34). This use of the vampire as border-crossing 'consumer' is a transnational updating of one of the many tensions in Bram Stoker's incarnation of the vampire, where trade and travel reveal anxieties and desires emerging from a changing world. Writing on *Dracula*, Laura Anne Diehl concludes:

> No other fictional text distills the mutually enriched relationship of the 'life' sciences and the monstrous quite like *Dracula*. The Count is a palimpsest for contemporary discourses that inscribe pathology onto a racialized, sexualized and politicized body. The medical detection novel *par excellence*, *Dracula* is cyclopean in its drive to detect racial parasitism and the foreign invasion/ colonization of the white body. The world of the novel is organized not around good and evil or the scared and the profane, but around a symbolics of bodies and anti-bodies, good blood and bad blood. (2008: 117)

This tradition is given a pop-noir Gothic spin in *Blade II*. Set on the border between the human overworld and the vampiric underworld, the narrative involves a 'reaper virus' strain of vampirism that paradoxically threatens the vampire community and their ancient customs. Similar contamination threats can be seen in *Mimic*, where genetically modified 'slave' cockroaches are used to wipe out a virus and later turn on their human progenitors. The mutated race have grown in an underground realm, forgotten now that their use has run out in what seems to be metaphor for labour exchanges and the 'developed' world's manipulation and consumption of the capacities and resources of those deemed inferior. Here is the horror movie equivalent of a capitalist/Darwinian parable where the battle for survival is fought on the borders where the blood of children is spilled along the way.

Perhaps this borderland existence is most successfully explored in *Pan's Labyrinth*. Ofelia finds herself on a crossroads, caught between the worlds of the Falangist order, the resistance militia and the mystical underworld. Stranded in a world which makes little sense to her and where her continued safety is at risk, Ofelia gains access to a transformative world in which fantasy acts both as an escape and also as a means of making sense of her situation. The ability to traverse worlds does not solely offer an escape, though; it also begins to unify the two realms in a more consistent way. She has the ability to flee from reality to fantasy, but perhaps more importantly, she is able to shift successfully (but not painlessly) between the estate and the forest, between childhood and adulthood and between dictatorship and democracy, and in doing so gains a fuller perspective on the whole. This traversal, however, ultimately requires her death, and it is her spilled blood which opens fully the otherworld dimension. In this respect, the spectacle of children experiencing trauma is itself scrutinized and the perverse nature of such spectacle is revealed. The constant in all of the potential paths offered to Ofelia is the inevitability of change and the pain that comes with this. Rosemary Jackson explores the ways in which metamorphosis reveals an unconscious desire/fear dichotomy and the impossibility and implausibility of escape:

> Metamorphosis in the modern fantastic suggests that the slipping of object into subject is no longer redemptive and that 'perverse' images of mutilation/horror/monstrosity have taken precedence over superhuman or magical transformations of the subject. (1981: 81)

This disavowal of the redemptive narrative is fundamental to *Pan's Labyrinth*. It is on the one hand a war narrative in which the child bears witness to the traumatic historic event and on the other a fantasy which draws on existing children's literature as a vehicle for symbolic discourse. However, neither world takes precedence and as a result Ofelia dies between the two, torn apart by the apparent failure of each realm to work symbiotically without destruction. Whereas (as the Faun explains) the fantasy dimension is ancient and slow-moving, the swift and violent revolutions of the twentieth century make it impossible for the worlds to coexist without violent consequences. Ofelia is a victim of these ultimately incompatible spheres, exiting at the end of the film by returning 'home' to her parents, who are rulers of the fantasy realm.

Ofelia begins her journey into *Pan's Labyrinth* in transit (a staple motif of the Gothic genre), expelled from her own home and taken to the oppressive house of Captain Vidal. This echoes *The Devil's Backbone*, in which Carlos begins the film homeless and ends it as a part of a nomadic child group, and *Hellboy*, who is exiled on Earth from another dimension. Although the superhero franchise and the political horror film may seem radically different in terms of their delivery, a deep sadness can be found in each and all three protagonists are profoundly melancholic. Naficy equates such melancholy to the mourning of the loss of a stable homeland, '[t]hose in exile did not choose to lose their homes and homelands; mourning is not their fault but a fate. Moreover, nomadic identification often preys on the other without giving anything back. Metaphoric projection and political persecution go together' (Naficy 1998: 34). It is in the blending of direct references to political violence (in *Hellboy*, a Nazi plot to summon the power of the occult results in the protagonist's displacement) with symbolic and fantastical formations that del Toro engages with transnational diaspora. His position as an exiled film-maker plays a part in these representations, and he has said in an interview:

> I'm not a filmmaker who can speak directly about politics without addressing it through fable or parable. It's just not in my makeup, and the horror film is a very

political genre … Every day, every week, something happens that reminds me that I am in involuntary exile [from my country]. But to talk about life in a direct way is the work of other types of storytellers. As a man, the kidnapping defined my life. As a storyteller, I try to define myself. (Cruz 2011)

In this respect, the autobiographical finds a curious place in the fantastical narrative. Part of del Toro's 'makeup' involves complete ease with the fantastical and a complete unwillingness to consider 'realist' representational practice as the authentic vehicle for diaspora. Yana Meerzon contends that:

[T]he search for the 'essentials' often makes an exilic artist 'a modernist by default'; someone who in today's age of postmodern reproduction and simulacra resists cultural entropy. In one's artistic utterances, an exile is bound to simultaneously become autobiographical and to search for wider audiences. An exilic artist, therefore, seeks out a multilayered discourse that remains deeply personal to the artist but also allows others to see experiences that may be analogical or different to their own lives. (2012: 24)

This highlights a tension in Guillermo del Toro's work. On one level, his oeuvre is the epitome of the cinema of postmodern reproduction and simulacra, as all of his films are re-constitutions of existing narratives and symbols, steeped in the codes and conventions of well-worn popular genres. On another though, the films are also highly personal, drawing from a troubled past.

By its nature, exile is a result of trauma and change, and all the films in del Toro's output exhibit this feature as in the rifts in time and space which we see in *Pan's Labyrinth*, *Hellboy* and *Pacific Rim*. In *Pacific Rim*, monstrous creatures emerge to wreak transnational carnage and it is only through the power of combination that humanity can survive. Combination is redemption in all of the films and it is through making new bonds out of suffering that a way forward is found. Steenberg contends that del Toro's cinema explores 'humanity's place within a crumbling universe and the responsibilities we have in preserving its balance and preventing its disintegration' (2010: 153).

The group of misfits joining together in the face of adversity is a staple of popular culture and cinema and is a remarkably resilient trope. Dorothy and her friends on the Yellow-brick Road, Luke Skywalker and his rebellious gang, Gandalf and his fellowship and the X-Men united are all groups of seemingly incongruous individuals who benefit from their bonds. This convention suits del Toro's stories well. As well as the generic elements which pay homage to the 'rag-tag' group of outsiders defined by the genius of L. Frank Baum in the *The*

Wonderful Wizard of Oz (1900), there is a transnational element to del Toro's use of kinship. This can be seen not only in the fact that friendships borne out of trauma, political strife and displacement develop in *Pan's Labyrinth* and *The Devil's Backbone* but also in the fact that the groups themselves are at times made up of an international crew thrown together and alienated from the homogenous whole of their new environment. This is most notable in the team of *Hellboy II: The Golden Army*, which comprises international and inter-special individuals. The Bureau of Paranormal Research and Defence is, on one level, made up of comically stereotypical parodies as seen in the effeminate English postures of Abe Sapien and the hysterical Germanic barkings of Johann Krauss. However, on another level these work within a narrative structure centred on the revival of dormant empires based upon military rule which are startlingly Aryan in appearance. In addition to this, Hellboy, Sapien and Krauss are all non-human and are in fact performing nationality (a camp, heavily accented performance at that) which italicizes their alienated circumstances. Compared to the more directly relevant exploration of friendship, race and alienation in films such as *La Haine* (1995), del Toro's transnational action adventure movies may seem frustratingly apolitical. However, this ignores the long tradition of political discourse in genre work and del Toro's allegiance to Horror and science fiction, as well as the fact that transnationalism resounds throughout cinema and even into the popcorn multiplex.

Queer Gothic

His films are gleefully impure. Thanks to the breadth of their allusions, literary, graphic, and cinematic, they are not easily boxed into any one mode, 'high' or 'low'. Among other sources they draw on alchemy, martial arts, comic books, antiquarian ghost stories, symbolist painting, Christian and Pagan iconography, Mexican popular culture and an encyclopaedic array of international cinema. The mix varies from film to film but typical ingredients include horror, science-fiction, fantasy and the Gothic. (Davies 2011: 88)

Gothic literature originated in the eighteenth century as a reflection on and criticism of cultural tensions between rationality and irrationality in Enlightenment society … Gothic, in eighteenth century ghost stories as well as nineteenth and twentieth century cinema and music signifies the transgression of such limits, a crossing of borders in order to engage in the ongoing dialectic between seemingly opposed cultural forces. Gothic disentangles the societal conventions that establish such conventions and explores the ir/rational and super/natural borderlands where opposites converge: it places its audience in the twilight zones where the past lives in the present, phantasm is part of reality, where death and life concur and where evil resides in good. (Van Elferen 2011: 98)

It is far from difficult to locate del Toro's work within a Gothic-inflected context. Apart from the director's own frequent assertion of his Gothic credentials, the intertextual presence of such diversely 'Gothic' film-makers such as F.W. Murnau, Terence Fisher, Alfred Hitchcock and Mario Bava in his films is a central feature of their visual and narrative richness. Similarly, canonical Gothic writing from the eighteenth and late nineteenth centuries, including occasionally neo-Gothic writers such as Dickens and Henry James, provides him with a kind of encyclopaedia of the uncanny, enabling him to re-interpret and reconfigure familiar tropes and stories. The conventional 'terrible places', spectral beings and monstrosities of the Gothic narrative re-emerge in empty factories, isolated orphanages, New York subway systems, remote mills turned military garrisons, museums, Piranesian vaults and remote landscapes reminiscent of Shelley's *Frankenstein*. Indeed, it would be easy to nominate the latter as a kind of ur-text for del Toro, with its seminal portrayal of the outcast 'monstrous' figure, exiled from human contact (*Hellboy, Blade II*), ambiguous and anxious portrayal of humanity's relationship to science, knowledge and Nature (*Mimic, Cronos*) and cautionary awareness of the destructive potential of obsession, rigidity and intolerance on both the nuclear family and wider society (*Pan's Labyrinth, The Devil's Backbone*). To fix del Toro's work in such literary heritage would be convenient but also somewhat limiting, ignoring as it does the key elements of his oeuvre that derive from a Hispanic and Mexican literary context. Perhaps the most significant of the latter is the classic and highly influential novel by Juan Rulfo, *Pedro Páramo* (1955), which was a profound influence on a generation of great Latin American writers such as Carlos Fuentes, Mario Vargas Llosa and Gabriel Garcia Marquez. Del Toro has spoken of his early conception of *The Devil's Backbone*, which was originally to be set during the Mexican Revolution in the second decade of the twentieth century, as 'un homenaje al relato *Luvina* de Juan Rulfo' (in Khan Omar 2001). 'Luvina' is one of a collection of short stories that Rulfo published in 1953, two years before his only novel which depicts an isolated village seen through the eyes of a narrator, Juan Preciado, in search of his father Pedro Páramo. The narrator gradually realizes that the place is inhabited by the ghosts of a past that can't be fully known as time shifts and recedes beyond the grasp of memory or consciousness. As Susan Sontag remarks in her foreword to a 1993 translation, 'The novel's premise – a dead mother sending her son out into the world, a son's quest for his father – mutated into a multivoiced sojourn in hell' (Rulfo 1994). The spectral nature of Rulfo's narrative re-emerges in the persistent question that begins del Toro's *The Devil's Backbone* and which seems to echo throughout his work 'What is a ghost?', doubled surely by the unspoken question 'What makes a human?' – that essential interrogative that underpins science fiction and fantasy. Like Erice's *Spirit of the Beehive*, which itself depicts an isolated village inhabited by almost ghost-like figures, Rulfo's novel seems to be part of the director's cultural DNA in the way it blurs the borderlines between past and present, life and death, landscape and dreamscape, memory and the unconscious. Indeed, the opening of the novel, with its depiction of an individual traveller arriving in an unfamiliar yet uncannily familiar place, prefigures the opening of *The Devil's Backbone* and *Pan's Labyrinth*, '[t]he road rose and fell. *It rises or falls depending on whether you're coming or going* ... I had expected to see the town of my mother's memories, of her nostalgia – nostalgia laced with sighs' (Rulfo 1994: 4).

A rather too easy summing up of Rulfo's fiction (and del Toro's Spanish-language films in particular) would be to generically categorize them as magic realism. Lucy Armitt has explored the borderlines between magic realism and the contemporary Gothic, focusing on fiction by other key Latin American writers such as Isabel Allende, whose *The House of the Spirits* (1982) inhabits a similar narrative territory, albeit with a more consciously politicized agenda. Armitt has written that 'what we find in magic realism (particularly in the dark end of its spectrum where it meets the Gothic) is a double-edged *frisson* which oscillates around the disturbing aspects of the everyday' (2000: 306). Elsewhere she suggests a synergy between magic realism and the Gothic that could well describe del Toro's aesthetic: 'When magic realism meets the contemporary Gothic we start to carve out a cartography for the unconscious' (308). Films such as *Pan's Labyrinth* clearly illustrate this process whereby magic, realism and fantasy are interwoven and interchanged in order to explore not only the unconscious dreams and desires of the young girl as she attempts to deal with the experience of trauma but also the unconscious of a nation and culture itself traumatized by war, politics and history.

To return to Davies's remarks, it has often been argued that the Gothic is itself an impure, even perverse mode (Haggerty 2006; Smith and Hughes 2009). The gleeful impurity that he rightly recognizes in del Toro's films, their characteristic postmodern bricolage of allusions, a Frankenstein's monster-like stitching together of diverse elements, closely aligns them with a Gothic modality consistently associated with the heterodox, the transgressive, indeed the Queer/ uncanny. In her recent study of new Gothic perspectives (entitled *The Queer Uncanny*), Paulina Palmer remarks on the close interrelationship between the uncanny, spectrality and queerness:

> The spectre and phantom, key signifiers of the uncanny, carry connotations of 'excess' since their appearance exceeds the material, and this is another concept that connects the uncanny with 'queer'. The role of the uncanny as a signifier of excess is reflected in its ability, as Rosemary Jackson describes, to uncover the unfamiliar beneath the familiar and, by challenging the conventional view of reality as unitary, to prompt the subject to question mainstream, 'common-sense' versions of it. (2012: 7)

A cinema audience's experience of film is, of course, inflected with notions of the uncanny, even the Gothic, as we sit in the dark and enclosed environment, vicarious, voyeuristic observers on scenes sometimes familiar, often unfamiliar, sometimes excessive. Tom Ruffles locates cinema as an intrinsically spiritually inflected, supernaturally informed medium. We enter into séance with fellow audience members looking at after-images of moments captured but over, often seeing actors who have long since passed; he even goes so far as to suggest that '[p]erhaps the decline of Spiritualism in the twentieth century can be in part attributed to the growth of a rival means of moving back in time and across space more reliably, at the flick of a switch' (Ruffles 2004: 7). Del Toro's early films exploit this positioning of the audience in ways that sometimes echo his masters, Erice and Hitchcock. The use of voice-over and single-character identification implicates the viewer from the outset; like Jesús, Carlos and Ofelia, all of whom are questing figures that resemble the heroes and heroines of traditional Gothic narratives, when we watch a del Toro film we embark on journeys into a cinematic heart of darkness, often subterranean and inhabited by monsters. Del Toro's ongoing love affair with monsters, both 'other' and human, situates his films firmly within a Gothic tradition populated with vampires and freakish, sometimes mythic beings. However, del Toro's monstrous anti-heroes, particularly those originating in comic book narratives such as *Hellboy*, serve to 'queer' the conventional and ideologically conservative underpinnings of such familiar types as the twenty-first-century superhero figure. Critics such as Elizabeth Grosz have highlighted the ways in which the monster embodies an ambiguity that disturbs and challenges dominant categorizations and binaries (quoted in Palmer 2012: 152). Given the often hybrid, border-crossing nature of the monster, a recurrent feature in del Toro's work (viz. the insects in *Mimic* and the central characters of *Blade II* and the *Hellboy* films), established notions of male/female, human/animal, man/demon become unstable and unfixed, challenging the defined boundaries that demarcate what is socially and culturally acceptable from that which is abject, excluded and taboo. The finale of *Hellboy II: The Golden Army*, after suitable epic confrontations with that most Gothic gargoyle-like of creatures, the Angel of Death, uncanny cyborgian clockwork monsters of the Golden Army and similarly uncanny doubled figures of Prince Nuada/Nuala, constructs a queerly heterodox version of the family consisting of the three abject outsider figures of 'Beauty' (Liz, human but a monstrous pyrokinetic and pregnant with twins), 'Beast' (Hellboy, demon and monstrous) and 'Abe' (camp/monstrous). In the traditional Gothic narrative and film, the family is the originating site of conflict and destruction and is often 'monstered' by the narrative, as in Shelley's *Frankenstein*. (There are other salient examples of this ambiguous vision of the family in del Toro's work, if not quite as extreme as in *Hellboy* – for example, Mercedes and Ofelia's mother–daughter relationship replaces her 'real-world' parentage. More problematically the Faun operates as a kind of substitute father figure, as embodied in the neo-Mayan stele in the labyrinth with its sculpted image of the faun, girl and baby.) At the end of *Hellboy II: The Golden Army*, del Toro queers not only the superhero but also the all-American nuclear family as the transgressively ironic happy ending is matched by a very heterodox vision of 'family'. This is not necessarily offered as overt political or social critique, but as a perfectly natural outcome. As Smith and Hughes suggest, '[q]ueer is, in this respect, a matter of both setting oneself aside (personally or artistically) as different, and of reflecting upon that process by a textuality that may lie at any point between camp parody and confrontational acerbity' (3). Del Toro's films may mostly shy away from either extremes of camp parody or confrontational acerbity, but their Queer Gothic politics is well embedded in both narrative and image. As Smith and Hughes suggest, '[q]ueerness, in this sense, is a quality which may be said to inflect a sense of difference not confined simply to sexual behaviour but which may equally inform a systematic stylistic deviance from perceived norms in personal style or artistic preference' (3).

In his emphasis on the diverse nature of del Toro's allusive art, Lawrence Davies echoes our repeated acknowledgement of its richly intertextual nature (2011). Davies lists the varied sources that del Toro mines, which have the effect of blurring the borderlines between high and popular cultural forms, creating an accented hybridity of form and subject matter that is wholly his. In this respect, he builds on the work of earlier Gothic as a genre that 'prioritises both spectrality and intertextuality' (Palmer 2012: 78). As Palmer notes, 'strategies of repetition and return, with their uncanny significance' are a key element of the Gothic, and Julian Wolfreys points to the ways in which ghosts of other texts haunt and inhabit Gothic writing, creating what he describes as 'the sense of the unfamiliar within the familiar' (2002: 117). To note that this kind of haunting pervades del Toro's cinema would be to state the obvious – every one of his films is populated by ghostly and not-so-ghostly textual presences from literature, film, art and transnational popular culture, which enhance and extend the meaning and significance of what are often ghostly narratives themselves in terms of their subject matter. Furthermore, the films' narratives and imagery seem to generate ghostly images of themselves within the arc of the story. *Pan's Labyrinth* is constructed on the basis of an internal narrative haunting: the dominant frame narrative of the Civil War aftermath is 'haunted' by the story of Princess Moanna and her relationship to the Faun, collapsing any differential between real and fantastic as the two narratives interact and interweave. This process works alongside the more overt textual references to parallel worlds and the literature of fantasy as exemplified in the use made of Carroll's *Alice* amongst others. A comparable kind of internal dynamic, albeit in a more literal ghostly mode, exists in *The Devil's Backbone*. In a scene that is central to the film's meaning (as underlined by its use in the title), Dr Casares tells Carlos the story of the preserved foetuses from which he extracts the amber liquid sold as a cure for impotence in the village. Here del Toro takes a common trope in post-*Frankenstein* Gothic film in particular – the mix of scientific knowledge, superstition and the grotesque – in order to construct an internal narrative that tells the story of adults literally feeding upon children (yet another classic fairy-tale trope) in their search for power. This in turn echoes the film's main narrative depicting the victimization and traumatization of children in war. Textuality as spectrality is perhaps the nearest we can get to summarizing the kind of nuanced multiplicity of del Toro's breadth of reference. What makes his films so distinctive is that their often ghostly or monstrous subject matter is itself rendered through this kind of spectral storytelling.

One of the marginally less visited areas of del Toro's oeuvre is the significance of religion, in particular Catholicism, in its intricate network of influences, but the presence of religion in his work can fruitfully be read through the lens of the Gothic. Representations of Catholicism have always played a significant role in the Gothic. From its earliest manifestations in the eighteenth century, Gothic writing displayed a highly ambivalent approach to Catholic faith and rituals, often treating it with a heady mix of deep-rooted, Protestant-inspired suspicion and feverish fascination. Settings associated with the Catholic Church provided many of the locales for early Gothic, as convents and monasteries became the favoured loci for often radically sexually transgressive behaviour (one of del Toro's favourite novels, Matthew Lewis's *The Monk* (1796) can hardly be matched for its taboo scenes in tombs and cemeteries). As George Haggerty suggests, 'When in *The Monk* Matthew G. Lewis uses the details of conventual life to suggest lurid forms of sexual excess such as necromancy, incest, matricide, and same-sex love, he does not need to explain his choice of a Catholic setting... or religious life' (2006: 64). Anglo-Saxon assumptions about the insidious dangers of the faith are sufficient to justify the context. Del Toro's own highly ambivalent relationship to the dominant religion of his home nation has been well documented in interviews and elsewhere (Kermode 2006b). His difficult relationship with his devoutly religious half-deaf grandmother, the dedicatee of his first film, his own avowed rejection of faith as well as his acknowledgement of its inescapable influence on him are all key determinants of its significant place in his psyche (DePalma 1994). Anthony DePalma's interview, which appeared around the time of the release of *Cronos* in the US, opens with an account of the director's recollection of an early Gothic encounter he had in a Belin cemetery where:

> in 1982, he dug a grave for a scene in a corny Mexican thriller. He was only 17 then and had to get permission from his high school to work with the film crew. After that, he kept visiting the eerie cemetery in the center of Mexico's second largest city just to look at the crumbling granite skulls on the monuments and to read the woeful expressions of mortality and faith engraved on the 19th-century tombstones. (1994)

Later in the interview del Toro talks of the moment when he was 13 and happened to be in a Belin hospital, where 'wandering down to the Morgue he saw a pile of discarded foetuses. "I understood right then that there was no God," he said. Afterward, he became "a raging atheist," which turned his grandmother against him. "She exorcised me," he said. "She threw holy water on me"' (1994). Out of these suitably Gothic experiences emerges a submerged religious discourse that is part of a sustained quest for the spiritual in his work, whereby art, storytelling and the sublimity of horror take on would-be religious connotations.

Cronos begins with an appropriately Gothic scene – the flight of the transgressive alchemist/scholar Fulcanelli from the Inquisition, but perhaps the single most Gothic moment in *Cronos* occurs a little later in the film when cockroaches crawl out of the decayed wooden saint's statue within which Jesús finds the device. As a shocking visual fusion of decay, corruption, salvation and faith this is hard to beat, although it does come straight from a grammar of horror in a direct line from influential films such as Jack Clayton's *The Innocents* (1961). It ushers in a line of religious iconography that pervades all del Toro's work: the paraphernalia of worship, rosaries, crosses, statuary appear with regularity, but virtually always in incongruous situations that radically decontextualize them from their apparent significance or stress the heavy weight of guilt imposed by Catholicism (viz. the cross the boys have to carry in *The Devil's Backbone*). Disused churches appear in *Mimic* and *Blade II* as settings for moments of violence or horror, and in the first *Hellboy* film our hero opens up a grave in order to strike up a useful conversation with a talking corpse, which he then carries on his back, a weirdly parodic pietà that seems laden with strangely reverse or perverse religious iconography as the demon carries the resurrected. It would be a bit heavy-handed to over-interpret this scene as it is largely played for comedy (another underestimated element of del Toro's art), but another pietà moment at the end of *Blade II*, where Blade cradles the dying vampire who has chosen death by sunlight in order to escape the deviant poison injected by her 'brother's' bite, is played as a moment of salvation. The comic undertow of the *Hellboy* scene indicates that del Toro rarely strays into religious territory that is self-consciously mawkish, but the argument with his former faith is an ongoing dialectic that is fundamental to his art. DePalma locates this firmly within a Mexican cultural context – what DePalma describes as 'that very Mexicanness of connecting decay and salvation-crossing horror with hope' (1994). This could be read as a colonialist approach to the subaltern culture of America's 'difficult' neighbour, and del Toro, like his other two 'amigos' Cuarón and Iñárritu, has been particularly adept at managing the issues that have arisen from their crossing that ever-problematic border. Rather than read this Catholic/Horror strand as a 'Mexican thing', better to see it as part of del Toro's engagement with his wider cultural genes, in which the Gothic provides some crucial elements.

A defining element of Queer is both its commitment to exploring issues relating to non-heteronormative identities and practices and sexualities and its inclusion of wider non-conformist relationships and anti-hegemonic practices and communities. Harry Benshoff sums this up by stating that Queer is 'insistent that issues of race, gender, disability, and class be addressed within its politics, making interracial sex and sex between physically challenged people dimensions of queer sex also, and further linking the queer corpus with the figure of the Other' (1997: 5). In this context, a great deal of cinema from a vast array of cultures can be considered in the light of the Queer, and this perspective opens up fascinating readings of everything from Shakespeare to Pixar. Surely though, no other filmic genre is better suited to Queer reading than the Gothic. Consider, for instance, James Whale's incarnation of *Frankenstein* (1931), where a melancholic Other figure, banished from the mainstream because of its difference and desire, wanders on the outskirts of society. This queerness is also to be found in *Bride of Frankenstein* (1935), where the relationship between the creature and its muse provides a template for antisocial desire (this film also features in diegesis in *Hellboy II: The Golden Army*). These core Queer Gothic films are later intertextually linked to New Queer Cinema in *Gods and Monsters* (1998), where Frankenstein's creation becomes a cipher for Whale's subconscious manifestation of his lover, killed in the trenches of the First World War (Keller 2002: 62). Benshoff contends that in horror film, a web of 'subtextual and connotative avenues' inscribe queerness into the narrative and one of the most fundamental of these is in the presence of the monster and 'his/her relation to normality' (15).

Del Toro's work is full of Queer figures and relationships which go against the grain of heteronormativity, questioning the binary opposition between the monstrous and the normal. Hellboy and Liz's romance follows the *verboten* trajectory, deemed inappropriate as interspecial and as a danger in exposing their covert group. Covert relationships are also seen in one form or another in almost all of del Toro's films; in fact, it is hard to locate a 'traditional' heterosexual romance in any of del Toro's cinema. Marc DiPaolo contends that the comic-book incarnation of Hellboy is a celebration of 'old-world, blue-collar machismo' and certainly the beer-swilling, hyper-muscular protagonist struggling with the complexity of his emotions echoes this to some extent (DiPaolo 2011: 255). However, this machismo is undercut in del Toro's translation. Consider for example a male-bonding scene in *Hellboy II: The Golden Army* in which a drunken Hellboy and Abe Sapien drown their sorrows. In a comic/camp nod they listen and then sing along to Barry Manilow's *I Can't Smile Without You*, in what becomes a tender scene rather than a display of machismo. This queering of the 'bromance' which permeates the *Hellboy* films is all the more effective considering the strong heteronormative narratives associated with the superhero movie. This can be seen in the hyper-confident, hyper-sexual and hyper-commodified excesses of characters such as Iron Man and Thor and in the trope of the weak alter-ego hiding immense masculine power in characters such as Spiderman and the Hulk. Christina Adamou notices that characters such as Spiderman and Superman '[B]ecome leaders as superheroes and peaceful citizens as their alter egos. Their superhero identity is more masculine: it is stronger and more active in the public domain and thus embodies a masculinity that they cannot represent in their everyday lives' (2011: 100). Hellboy does not have the benefit of an alter-ego, his crimson skin, tail and stumped horns are all manifestations of his difference and he remains closeted. He is of course eventually outed to a public who reject him despite his heroic deeds, and it is only in the company of his equally Queer peers that he finds solace. Adamou contends that the twenty-first century has seen an evolution of some superhero movies that provide a counter-narrative to the received heterosexual script (as can be seen in the *X-Men* franchise and films such as *Hancock* (2008)) and the *Hellboy* films should be situated as a Gothic addition to this evolution. Steenberg notes that del Toro's work:

> shies away from a Manichean imagining of a world divided into good and evil; or a straightforward struggle between man and monster. His villains are rarely without (quasi-) justifiable motives and are typically treated with sympathy for their doomed situation. (2005: 153)

Such sympathy for the monster figure dominates del Toro's film-making and where there is true malice and viciousness it is to be found in human characters such as Vidal in *Pan's Labyrinth* and Jacinto in *The Devil's Backbone* who are obsessed with their own sense of importance which is coupled with a macho sense of entitlement and a disrespect for women.

Travis Sutton and Harry M. Benshoff contend that one of the perversions of Gothic fiction involves the appropriation of Christian symbolism and the representation of it in a discourse of sexuality. This appropriation highlights:

> the cultural links between Christianity and gothic horror, blood and other bodily fluids, penetration and sexuality. The conflation of those various tropes arguably constitutes the appeal of all gothic literature, which tends to displace aspects of sex and sexuality onto monstrous signifiers, inviting readers to experience the thrill of the sexually deviant within the safe or 'innocent' zone of a fictional make-believe generic construct. (2011: 204)

In many ways displacement of desire, the erotic and the perverse can be seen in del Toro's films where overt sexual content is rare. For example, in *The Devil's Backbone* Carmen and Jacinto are seen having sex whilst the impotent Casares listens on in the room next door. There is a palpable aggression between Carmen and Jacinto; they dislike one another but both are driven by desire, she by libido and he by monetary greed. Then, in a post-coital moment he steals a key to a safe where he believes gold is stored and Carmen begins to put on her prosthetic leg. Then there is a rare moment of tenderness as Jacinto assists Carmen and they begin again to have passionate sex. If we take into account the quasi-incestuous nature of the scene, given that Jacinto was once an orphaned resident under Carmen's care and the fact that the gold is hidden in a secret compartment in Carmen's leg, then the odd, Gothic, Queer nature of the moment is illuminated. One romantic and sexual relationship that del Toro has developed is between Elizabeth Sherman and Hellboy, a relationship that remains platonic in the original comic book series. One can see where the attraction to the character comes from; Liz is a lapsed Catholic whose pyrotechnic powers manifest themselves when she is emotionally aroused in what is a familiar motif for followers of Gothic and Horror fiction (in, for instance, Brian De Palma's *Carrie* (1976)). In the films, sexuality manifests itself in Liz's dangerous pyro-passion and Hellboy's ability to withstand her passionate episodes; typically, a colourful symbolic spectacle acts as a substitute for the sexual act. In *Cronos*, for example, Jesús's revived libido is manifest in his thirst for blood and the iconic scene where he licks blood from a bathroom floor arguably acts as a substitute for an erotic cruising encounter to satiate his desire. This desire for blood and use of haemal imagery is of course a part of the Gothic tradition and typified in the figure of the vampire. Patrick O'Malley notices the symbiotic symbolism between sexual deviance and religious deviance in Gothic depictions of blood consumption which is 'deeply entwined'. In discussing the famed scene where Dracula forces Mina to drink his blood, O'Malley illustrates this conflation: 'while the image of the cutting of the chest and the feeding of the blood from the wound may evoke a displaced fellatio or cunnilingus it more directly points to the traditional iconography of Christ as pelican, slicing open its breast to feed its young' (2006: 159).

In this light, Jesús's licking of the blood on the floor of a public toilet is as much Eucharist as it is psycho-sexual and the image of the public toilet as church and place of Holy Communion takes on a religiously deviant dimension. Another recurrent trope involving haemal exchange and the sacred involves the spilling of blood on a talismanic surface revealing a gateway into the otherworld. In both *Pan's Labyrinth* and *Hellboy* blood unlocks the gate to another dimension in scenes which evoke occult sacrificial practices. The stakes that del Toro sets in his scenes are immense: characters not only fear their corporeal mortality but it is often the future of their races, the future of humanity or their spiritual existence which are at risk as these inter-dimensions collide. In an interview del Toro has said:

> Well the deepest horror is the one that deals with the worst kind of things. When you're dealing with somebody that may die or be maimed, you can always have the possibility of survival. There's always that part of you that says, 'Well, if I lose an arm, I would always have the other one … well if the monster tears up my leg, I can always have a prosthetic one made or something. But when you're dealing with the soul, there is no solution. There is no prosthetic for the soul'. (in Elder 2013: 22)

The occult elements of some of del Toro's work place it alongside a side-canon of Gothic film, which often evokes perverse sexual-deviance blended with religious deviance. Films such as Ken Russell's *The Devils* (1971), Pupi Avati's *Arcane Sorcerer* (1996) and Robin Hardy's *The Wicker Man* (1975) inhabit a dangerous place where the grimoire meets the Queer and where religious iconography is put to use as a perverse figurative device.

3

Fan as Film-maker

It is the intention of this chapter to argue that del Toro has a unique place in contemporary 'geek' film-making as a director who is lauded as an artist with an accomplished ability and authorial mission and a fellow fan with vested interest in maintaining the integrity of the material he both creates and shepherds into existence. This is not to maintain that del Toro is the only much-respected film-maker to flourish since the upsurge in geek screen output. Directors and writers such as J.J. Abrams, Joss Whedon and Robert Rodriguez have managed to create, develop and release 'geek' couture which is critically successful and lauded as original and in tune with the loved source material from which they draw, with at times much more commercial success than del Toro. However, the ambition of this chapter is to argue that a collision (a term that implies some form of accidental entropy, which is open to debate) of factors results in del Toro resonating with the fan community in a number of interconnected ways and in a specific cultural context. This includes the ways in which he has embraced DVD culture and accompanying special features as a means of providing a paratextual discourse alongside textual (across film and other media) output. It also involves an analysis of the ways in which he has incorporated his own biographical detail into this paratextual input in order to create and maintain an auteurial mythology (although he himself has dismissed the relevance of auteur theory). We will explore the ways in which his own encyclopaedic and wide-ranging knowledge of cult and geek culture have informed his work with the result that he has been identified as an insider (a fan as film-maker) and curator as well as director (or direcurator). In addition, del Toro has benefitted from and has benefitted the rise of the Internet as fanternet and the evolution of the fan convention from niche spectacle/network environment to the media extravaganza it has become.

Alongside the mythology which revolves around del Toro as 'auteur' and collaborative film author, there is the increasing fascination with the mythology surrounding his experiences and relationships with the film industry. These further enhance his position as insider, protector and defender of the canon of material which is so used and abused in popular culture, especially since the turn of the twenty-first century.

The recent investment and resulting proliferation in comic book franchises, fantasy, science-fiction and horror-based material are clear to see and have received considerable media attention. However, in order to understand the rise in all things geek it is important to understand the intermingling of modes and genres which it entails. Using the phrase 'comics culture' Rob Salkowitz explains the hybrid nature of fandom:

> Comics culture is the blend of superheroes, animation, movies, videogames, television shows, art, fashion, toys, accessories and personalities that has emerged as the result of a postmillennial convergence of media and the concurrent explosion of online channels for connecting fans with the objects of their fandom. (2012: 15)

Critical here is the fact that del Toro's alchemic modus operandi chimes with this culture, a culture of which he is both architect and product.

Much has been made of the ways in which fandom operates not as separate and insular communities working independently from a broader 'mainstream' culture, but as a means of responding to, circumventing and resisting mainstream culture. Lewis writes, '[b]y participating in fandom, fans construct coherent identities for themselves. In the process, they enter a domain of cultural activity of their own making which is, potentially, a source of empowerment in struggles against oppressive ideologies and the unsatisfactory circumstances of everyday life' (2002: 3). Lewis and others such as Henry Jenkins attest to the counter-cultural political potency of fan culture as a means of galvanizing energies opposed to homogenized ideological tides and dynamics. Other commentators such as Nathan Hunt have questioned the assumption that fan organization and activities are acts of symbolic resistance and that paradoxically such communities themselves replicate hierarchical ideological structures (Hunt: 186). What scholars of fandom do agree on though is the fact that fan audiences are active, ardent and invested in not just consuming the products but also in perpetuating an active discourse which is a part of a live enterprise. The fact that del Toro is not just a fan of the particular sub-sects of genre film-making, literature and art which influence his own work but also a collector of paraphernalia, uber-cinephile and champion of others in the field positions him as speaking the same language and understanding fandom as a fellow zealot. Matt Sienkiewicz and Nick Marx point out the fact that intertextual layering often involves active audiences engaging critically with a web of referents which form a discursive whole and that this awareness of the knowledge base of the audience separates 'discursively integrated media' from the merely intertextual and that such 'media also asks its audience to critically engage with the modes of discussion in which these secondary texts are participating' (2009: 5).

No other document more fully perpetuates the notion of del Toro as master archivist, preserving and replenishing geek lore in the face of ephemeral franchise trash than *The New Yorker* profile of him published in 2009. A good deal of the profile describes 'Bleak House', del Toro's house-cum-archive-cum-workshop filled with, amongst other things, a host of movie memorabilia, a library of occult reference books and effects kit from his own and others' films. Del Toro is portrayed as having a deep intellectual and instinctive connection to this place, which acts as a temple of fan worship, inspiration and means of maintaining a treasury of archaic lore, totemic collectables and paraphernalia so valuable to the geek community. In a telling section of the article, which illustrates *The New Yorker*'s complicity in developing such an alluring persona, Daniel Zalewski writes:

> I knocked, and an assistant hollered for me to come in. When I opened the door, a rectangle of California sunshine invaded the dark entryway, landing on the hideous face of a large, lunging demon. It was a life-size cast-resin model of Sammael, from 'Hellboy', standing where a decorator would have placed a welcoming spray of flowers. Behind it, French doors offered a shimmery view of the back-yard pool. Sammael was far from the only model on display. Del Toro had filled the house with dozens of monster maquettes from his films – scale models created by special-effects shops during the early design phase, allowing the imaginary to become palpable. Del Toro had given Sammael, who has a lion's mane of writhing tentacles, a subtle motif of asymmetry; one front limb is slightly longer than the other, setting his gait off balance, and he has an extra eye on the right side of his snout. Doug Jones, a mime turned actor who has played creatures in dozens of films, including 'Hellboy' and 'Pan's Labyrinth', says that, in the subculture of monster design, del Toro's creatures are couture. 'It's because he's a fanboy', he said. 'He knows *exactly* how fanboys critique movies. He anticipates the "That wouldn't really work!" response'. (2011: 2)

The disembodied voice of the assistant and the grotesque coterie that greets the visitor itself draws upon a whole host of horror movie clichés (which are nonetheless sources of joy for fans of such movies) and establishes the foundations of a portrait of film-maker steeped in a living geek fantasy and, more crucially, making films that are entirely in tune with the nuanced tastes of the geek community.

Other than the commitment to a geek sensibility and 'curation' that is so evident in the paratextual accoutrement highlighted in the article, there is a sense of scholarly devotion to the origins of the mythologies so popular in contemporary culture. The precise attention to the obscure origins of vampires, the varied design of dragons beyond the stock Hollywood flying lizard depiction and the devotion to the corporeal detail of how exactly Frankenstein's creature should appear all feature in the article and present trivia not as an insignificant 'fanboy' obsession but as a vital part of expertise which is woven into the fabric of much fandom. This elevates del Toro beyond industry moviemaker to master storyteller replenishing myths by a process of reimagining. Hunt explores the ways in which trivia in the science-fiction fan community (and by extension its interrelated sects) are part of an internal ecology of status which self-generates a hierarchical system. He writes of how:

> [t]rivia are used to establish who is an insider and to declare others to be outsiders who do not have the right to participate within fandom and how once recognized, a secure knowledge of the trivial acts as a beacon to others who share a similar understanding, who recognize trivia as a community held discourse. (186)

In doing so, fans are able to claim ownership over the texts and wider mythologies surrounding them and also a privileged position based upon perceived cultural capital (198). Hunt highlights the ways in which these notional insular economies of information may take on the very hierarchical functions which some have claimed they work against. For example, he points to the homosocial competitive environment in which the capital of trivia thrives. Del Toro acknowledges this in *The New Yorker* profile, playfully referring to Bleak House as his 'man cave' and recognizing the masculine-heavy environment of creature design (although he champions Milicent Patrick, the under-appreciated designer of the *Creature from the Black Lagoon* (1954)). In addition, Hunt argues that within fan communities, hierarchies of knowledge are perpetuated to value those with existent dominance within such systems rather than opening up a more egalitarian mode of participation. If we accept the value of trivia en masse as a powerful form of currency within fan communities, then del Toro's significance as a master of such knowledge and as a professional and celebrity trivia archivist is a key part of his position within the community itself.

As discussed, del Toro's dedication to both the canonical works of geek culture and more obscure works from the annals is central to *The New Yorker* profile. That is not to suggest, though, that del Toro operates as a slavish film-maker with a mission to present detailed and authentic depictions or remakes of classics in the field on screen. In fact, del Toro's compulsion to transform the origins and influences so evident into his own imaginative territory is acute and a key part of his modus operandi. Del Toro is a film-maker who is extremely open when it comes to explaining the vast array of influences which can be found in his work. This openness is a part of the wider appeal of the film-maker who has an evangelical enthusiasm for others, from the legendary writers, artists and film-makers who have shaped the pantheon of genre fiction, mythology and popular culture to the unsung craftspeople and storytellers who have striven to create powerful imagery in seemingly throwaway formats. However, del Toro's work rarely, if ever, functions as a part of a simple adaptation; instead, it emerges in a far more radical and dynamic manner. The reworking of the *Frankenstein* and *Dracula* stories told from transforming individuals in *Cronos*, the *Alice's Adventures in Wonderland* imagery and thematic rhythms woven in *Pan's Labyrinth* and the reframing of *Hellboy* from darkly melancholic brooding Gothic hero to awkward but lovable man child all illustrate del Toro's dual approach to storytelling, which is both acutely aware and indeed reliant upon the legacies of previous incarnations but entirely committed to extensive re-interpretation and reframing of such incarnations. In a segment of *The New Yorker* profile which charts del Toro's attempts to launch his interpretation of *Frankenstein*, his ambitions to re-tell the canonical tale whilst filtering it through his own sensibilities in line with his growing body of work are presented in the most artistic of terms, '[f]or someone like del Toro, giving birth to a new Frankenstein's Creature is even more exciting than designing an original monster. Just as a Renaissance painter relished the challenge of rendering the Crucifixion, a true monster-maker wants to take on the icons' (6).

This is absolutely key to del Toro's esteemed reputation in the film world and in the wider fan community. Just as his knowledge and influences are far reaching, ranging from canonical and obscure literature and folklore, the visual arts, cinema, television, comic books and pop-culture detritus, seemingly free from the boundaries of class-informed taste formation, so too are his skills as a storyteller and artist. Emerging from a guerilla approach to film-making, where invention develops out of an ability to participate in many levels of the creative process, arguably heightened by genre film requirements of effects work such as creature design or special effects (other notable genre film-makers who began on miniscule productions punching far above their weight include Sam Raimi and Peter Jackson), the perception of del Toro as a director who is also a designer, monster-maker, writer and innovator is a key part of his particular, and particularly popular, image amongst the fan community. In this context, he is both artist and artisan, and this singles him out to an extent in a world dominated by blue-screen landscapes, digital effects and motion-capture performances. For instance, del Toro's dedication to elaborate, time-consuming original creature effects work is not only a refreshing alternative which would appeal to many casual filmgoers but also a veritable model of commitment to the historic lineage of genre film-making and the roll call of pioneers and artists (Harryhausen, Giger, Karloff, etc.) who precede him.

Del Toro's influences are extremely varied and draw from a wealth of knowledge of 'high' and 'low' transnational cultural output. This is interesting in itself in relation to the fan networks which he appeals to. John Fiske, amongst others, draws attention to the key role that the writing of Pierre Bourdieu has in providing a framework by which to explore taste formation and its maintenance in a cultural system fuelled by economically endowed power relations. In Pierre Bourdieu's model, 'high' and 'low' culture feature in a hierarchical system (mirroring class taxonomies and their surrounding cultures), which perpetuate rarefied elitist artworks as 'tasteful' in opposition to pop culture that is denigrated as a subordinate and ephemeral gutter culture (2010).

Fiske has pointed out some of the absences in Bourdieu's research when it comes to exploring the nuances of popular culture, its consumption and its uses. Fiske also contends that fandom distils popular culture and in doing so paradoxically disengages from the mainstream whilst simultaneously replicating the taste formations which it seeks to shun. He writes, '[f]andom then, is a peculiar mix of cultural determinations. On the one hand it is an intensification of popular culture which is formed outside and often against official culture, on the other it expropriates and reworks certain values and characteristics of that official culture to which it is opposed' (Fiske: 448). Certainly, there is a value system within geek culture which like other fan cultures may seem impenetrable to the casual consumer. Such systems which provide levels of prestige to knowledge that may otherwise be derided in the 'mainstream' have been satirized in television shows such as *The Big Bang Theory* (2007–) and comic books such as *Kick Ass* (2010). Del Toro can be seen as the geek's aficionado when it comes to such capital. What is accentuated with del Toro, and enveloped in his mode of working, are the ways in which the spectrum of low and high culture is exploded and re-established in a bricolage construction held together by the film-maker's stylistic strategies. For instance, del Toro's approach to drawing from a whole range of cultural output both within and without the film industry is distinct. He maintains that '[t]he worst thing that you can do is be inspired solely by movie monsters. You need to be inspired by National Geographic, by biological treatises, by literature, by fine painters, by bad painters' (Zalewski 2011). This results in a textual strategy which will see straight to video movies combined with Goya-esque figures brought to life (this perhaps separates del Toro from another intertextualists, Quentin Tarantino, whose many references most often come from other films). In the work of del Toro, the essential quality of the heterosis is its range and disregard for received spectrums of taste. *Mimic* provides an example of this composite approach to film design. Although a relatively minor item in del Toro's oeuvre, the film nonetheless illustrates creative alchemy at play. Obscure B-movie and comic book references work in conglomeration with painterly references to Goya and biblical allusions. These references to 'high' culture are not included in order to elevate the films out of their genre positions; rather they are included to add texture to the genre work which deepens their grotesque clout, dragging the prestigious out of the galleries and into the monster movies. Del Toro has spoken of his apparent disregard for intellectually-driven plaudits, saying that '[i]n emotional genres, you cannot advocate good taste as an argument … I don't see myself ever doing a "normal" movie … I love the creation of these *things* – I love the sculpting, I love the coloring. Half the joy is fabricating the world, the creatures' (Zalewski). This is not to say that in utilizing pop-cultural material and B-culture sources the films themselves are intended to mimic or satirize 'trash' as a niche (in the ways Tarantino and Rodriguez's *Grindhouse* (2007) double bill does), rather that the B-cultural content is symbiotically presented alongside high art content in order to engender new mythologies spliced together from all the influences freed from the world of class-driven cultural currency.

One of the many narratives which influence the perception of Guillermo del Toro as a storyteller dedicated to preserving the standards which have gone before him, alongside his own interpretive licence which allows him to replenish the old as new, is the story of the projects he has struggled to make, turned down and haggled with studios over, which are presented as trials of the artist's odyssey. The list is extensive and includes classics such as *Frankenstein*, franchises such as the *Harry Potter* series and the *Narnia* book adaptations, and famously the development of *The Hobbit*. The reasons for such rejections and disappointments are complex; however, a recurring issue is the fact that del Toro requires artistic licence in order to proceed with a project (and the lessons learnt by del Toro's experiences in making *Mimic* cannot be underestimated in this context). This failure to adapt much-loved texts, or at least the unwillingness to proceed without creative freedom, paradoxically generates a further mythos around del Toro as an authentic fan-cum-film-maker, committed to invention over bland commercial reproduction.

This highlights a balancing act evident in the geek community's reception of new cinematic interpretations and additions to canonical texts. For example, a good deal of critical attention has been paid to the reception to *Star Wars Episode I: The Phantom Menace* (1999), particularly in regard to fandom. Hunt explores the ways in which the release of the film, with all its narrative sojourns and inconsistencies, identified by some as betraying the mythology from which it came, resulted in contestation and struggle over which audiences 'owned' the discourse surrounding the film. On this level it appears that altering aspects of a much-loved mythology is disparaged within fan networks and that the source material represents hallowed ground. However, too literal interpretations of canonical works also receive significant criticism. For instance, one of the elements of Zack Snyder's much-anticipated adaptation of the venerated graphic novel *Watchmen* (2009) which came under debate on its release was the evident faithfulness to the source material, which was seen by some as properly faithful and by others as overly reverent to the detriment of the film itself. Similarly, Bryan Singer's take on Superman in *Superman Returns* (2006) received criticism for slavishly following Richard Donner's much-loved take on the character which resulted in a film lacking in imaginative flare. Thus far, del Toro has avoided significant criticism of his use of canonical genre work, which is not surprising considering the films in which these works find a new home (*Cronos*, *The Devil's Backbone* and *Pan's Labyrinth*, respectively). In addition, his more straightforward adaptations (in *Hellboy*, *Hellboy II: The Golden Army* and *Blade II*) come from source material with significant fanbases, but both are relatively new creations in comparison to the likes of Superman. Considering this, a freer reign over the material is perhaps deemed acceptable. It may then be a simple case of misplaced industry expectations that when faced with widely known adaptations of 'tent-pole' properties (and the assumptions that accompany these) del Toro's insistence on artistic licence renders him the wrong person for the job. Nonetheless, the two oeuvres, the completed films themselves and the incomplete shadow companion films, complement one another and add to the reputation of del Toro as a film-maker with creative integrity, unwilling to bend to the industry demands involved in franchise building.

In addition to the media coverage of del Toro which paints an alluring and affectionate picture of the fan-made film-maker and creative pioneer, del Toro's own biography and willingness to inject this into his work and the surrounding paratexts which accompany it add to the mythos of the storyteller. These biographical details, particularly in relation to his childhood, are often remarkable and their influences on his creative output are explored in other parts of this book. What is striking in the context of this particular discussion, though, are the ways in which the geek cultural products, which are so relevant to the work he produces and the wider artefacts that hold significance, instilled in del Toro an avocation which would later develop into a career. Like many in fandom, the passion for the area which becomes the site of celebration is seeded in the formative years and del Toro's recollections of scouring stores for comic books and devouring movies and cartoons will strike a familiar chord. However, an important factor which is discussed in *The New Yorker* profile and which underpins del Toro's entire relationship with fandom involves a reference to Forrest Ackerman. In the late 1930s, Ackerman founded The Boys' Scientifiction Club, ostensibly the first geek culture group, and later went on to found *Famous Monsters of Filmland*, the inaugural geek fanzine. In addition, he filled his house (the 'Acker-mansion') with movie memorabilia and other paraphernalia in what was to become a legendary collection for fans. In the interview, del Toro is open about the fact that 'Bleak House' is inspired by the troves of Ackerman, whom he refers to as his 'hero of heroes'. *Time Magazine*'s obituary to Ackerman in 2008 acknowledges his prolific career as an editor, writer and agent but understands these roles as an:

> exponent of his educated ardour for science fiction, fantasy and horror, and his need to share that consuming appetite … [as] the genre's foremost advocate, missionary and ballyhooer. His love for the form, stretching back more than 80 years, godfathered and legitimized the obsessions of a million fanboys. His passion was their validation. He was the original Fanman. (Corliss 2008)

As well as being intellectually and stylistically drawn towards genre film-making, it is important to note that del Toro is an avid defender of an often-maligned mode of storytelling which is only rarely seen as an art form. He said: 'I see horror as part of legitimate film. I don't see it as an independent genre that has nothing to do with the rest of cinema' (http://www.criterion.com/current/posts/1692), and these assurances, amongst others, position his intentions as similar to Ackerman. Del Toro is transparent in his devotion to Ackerman and his desire to retain the tradition of fan as proponent and patron:

> He was a huge influence in my life. When I was a kid, I actually wrote him a letter asking him to adopt me. Unfortunately, my father found the letter before I could mail it and he gave me quite a belting. But Forrey and I saw each other many times over the years. I was lucky enough to be a speaker at his tribute about a month ago. My library home is essentially my version of the Ackermansion. It's me trying to imitate my hero. (Cruz 2009)

What is key here is the fact that not only is del Toro an uber-fan of movies (and their related geek works) and the paraphernalia, artworks and legacies which they leave behind but that he is a fan of *fandom* itself. Considering this, it is no surprise that he is a much-admired figure who seems to have a particular line into the spirit and workings of fandom, as he sees himself and is seen by fellow devotees as a leader of fandom, given the energies and resources to act as both custodian and innovator of the geek strata.

Del Toro's fascination and utilization of paratexts is significant in maintaining the public persona of the film-maker as fan insider. But what of his films themselves and the ways they incorporate such a preoccupation with cultural artefacts, collection and identity formation? In this context, it is clear that many of del Toro's films employ the impulse to collect and represent the totemic power of artefacts. This is perhaps most prevalent in *Cronos*. The film's opening provides a recurrent motif which increasingly drives the narrative. Jesús Gris, the film's protagonist, owns a struggling antique shop, which sits anomalously in the busy Veracruz, whose inhabitants seem intent on leaving the past and rushing towards the future. The bazaar is of course filled with curios and relics, not least the rescued statues of archangels (so reminiscent of del Toro's maquettes) in one of which the Cronos device is hidden. The device itself is unique, a fabulous contraption which is presented as 'once in a lifetime' and which is filmed in the earlier parts of the narrative from the perspective of a collector's desiring eye. The device itself invigorates Jesús, and later, when its power envelops and then overruns him, he resembles a fading model, more suited to an antique collection of oddities than the world of the living.

The Devil's Backbone also includes references to antiquated and outré collections, powerful and enigmatic objects and pop-cultural ephemera able symbolically to bond disparate and lost individuals. The orphanage, not unlike

Jesús's antique store, is host to an array of disregarded statues, stored away from a violent and fast-changing outside world. On this level the boys themselves are lost property, discarded by a world whose struggles have overcome the adult capacity for parenting. These children are left in the hands of Carmen and Dr Casares, who is a collector himself. Casares's laboratory-cum-surgery is filled with now unused appurtenances and medical samples, the most bizarre of which is a collection of deformed foetuses, preserved in rum, which he sells to the villagers as a remedy for ailments and male impotency to make ends meet. The doctor is also a bibliophile and bonds with Carlos over a shared reading of *The Count of Monte Cristo* (1844). The boys, too, bond over a shared passion for comic books and seemingly insignificant cultural detritus, which is treasure itself to these children who seek a surrogate family in a world from which they are disenfranchised (touchingly, some of the boys fantasize about becoming comic-book creators in a world where art and entertainment are again allowed to function). Carlos's small collection provides a means for him to share with others and engage in a mutual passion in a small but exclusive fan club where the boys swap trinkets, read together and bond in spite of the collapsing world around them. Such bonds provide a narrative means to create a sense of fraternity and patronage in contrast to the political and national schisms of the civil war. They also instil in the young band of brothers a selfless honour which puts Jacinto (who is also obsessed with objects, but with monetary value rather than intrinsic beauty) and his ruthless, greedy individualism to shame. These bonds do though act as a testimony to textuality itself, as a means of forming individual and group identities based upon a shared passion for pop-cultural entertainment imbued with a symbolic depth and dimension. Perhaps the most iconic object in *The Devil's Backbone* is the undetonated bomb lodged into the ground of the courtyard. The bomb literally symbolizes the precarious position of the orphanage which is under the flight path of overhead warplanes and symbolically represents the impotence of Dr Casares and the boys themselves, who eventually gain power by working together as a force against the vile Jacinto.

Textuality and creation contrast sharply with morbid fascination with objects of control in *Pan's Labyrinth*. The fascist Captain Vidal is obsessed with keeping time and in particular with his dead father's watch which is petrified in time from the moment he was killed. There is no love, affection or wonder in the connection of the watch, a wonder that is clearly seen in the intricate mechanics of the Cronos device. This negative fixation on a dead object illustrates Vidal's damaged and static nature and his manic autocracy and is in opposition to

Ofelia's love of books and her revelatory findings that textual creation itself is a means of exploration, escape and growth. Clark and McDonald write:

> *Pan's Labyrinth* seems to attest to the need for fiction when human monstrosity, as represented by the Spanish fascists, is encountered. For Ofelia, the fantasy world of fairy tale and the labyrinth offers an opportunity not just for escape but for a dynamic role in the process of her identity creation. This identity formation strengthens the link to Anne Frank, whose diary represented an alternative existence over which she had some control. Ofelia's self-creation is often solidified through the construction of narrative and there are multiple examples of her (as an obsessive reader) writing and realising her own narrative agency through texts; moreover, the film offers a meta-textual dimension which attests to the transformative potency of fiction itself. In this way, the whole film can be seen as a celebration of storytelling as liberatory. (2010: 59)

As the boys in *The Devil's Backbone* fantasize about a world where they can write their own stories and share their passion for fantastic narratives, Ofelia devours stories and filters them through her own potent creative sensibilities as a means of escaping and subverting the oppressive system which stratifies her. This element of *Pan's Labyrinth* is almost an extraordinary realization of Henry Jenkin's conception of 'textual poaching', where marginalized individuals purloin elements of established media and reconstitute them into an arena where fan authorship means agency with emancipatory possibilities. Jenkins writes:

> Like the poachers of old, fans operate from a position of marginality and social weakness. Like other popular readers, fans lack direct access to the means of commercial cultural production and have only the most limited resources with which to influence entertainment industry's decisions… Within the cultural economy, fans are peasants not proprietors, a recognition which must contextualise our celebration of strategies of popular resistance. (2012: 26)

Jenkins originally wrote this in 1992, and it is arguable that a sea change has occurred where fandom's power has increased dramatically in certain key areas and that the creative industries themselves are far more heavily populated with fans-cum-producers.

In del Toro's other films, there are galleries of strange, beautiful and enigmatic devices, texts and talismanic relics which unleash their often-astonishing power (these reach something of a pinnacle in *Pacific Rim*, which fetishizes uber-toys in the form of the *Jaegers*). The *Hellboy* films depict a hidden shadow culture where mythical creatures war for control of a general population blind to the powerful sub-currents which are only apparent to a group of ostracized individuals deemed freaks by the mainstream (a narrative trope established in comic book lore in amongst other things the *X-Men* universe, a trope which is now commonplace in film and television texts). This shadow culture is littered with peculiar fascinations which reveal their supernatural potency once activated: the ancient occult seal which is activated when it comes into contact with blood (a motif seen again in the closing moments of *Pan's Labyrinth*) to become a portal to another dimension and enchanted eggs which re-spawn creatures who can evade death add to the mythology of *Hellboy*, where the ancient and mythical begin to invade and shape the modern urban environment.

This mythology is deepened in *Hellboy II: The Golden Army*. Due perhaps in part to the relative commercial success of *Hellboy* and the rising star of del Toro as a creative force, *Hellboy II* sees the director's realization of fantastic miscellany go up several gears. This is perhaps most evident in the Troll Market sequence, which is both a densely populated bazaar revealing the extent of the mythological netherworld below New York and a celebration of creature effects work (in contrast with the CGI-heavy creations of so many other films) highly valued within fan communities. More central to the narrative is the Golden Army itself, a vast collection of beetle-like mechanoids which once activated (again, by the utilization of supernatural forces) hold immense destructive power capable of engulfing the world. The scenes in which they become active are startlingly similar to the scenes in *Cronos* where the device is set in motion. The number of devices and their scale may have increased, but at their core is the fascination with the complex and beautiful inner-workings of automata, uncannily brought to life for dramatic effect.

Eric White charts the history of automata, intricate machines which imitate the movement and mannerisms of living things (often insectoid in appearance), in relation to ideas raised and debated in Cartesian discourse and its far-reaching philosophical disciplines. Not least of these are the ways in which automata have been used in the arts as a locus of meditations on the potency of imagination as abstract phenomenon versus the concrete displays of wonder by mechanically driven spectacles. White observes:

> From the Romantic era onward, representations of insects and automata have provided compelling metaphors for conflicting manifestations of imaginative process in the literature and, more recently, cinema of the fantastic ... [del Toro's] depiction of the simultaneously monstrous and marvellous prospect of insect life powerfully suggests a biological substrate underlying both the automatism

that transpires as a swarm of desiring impulses multifariously engaging the phenomenal flow and its disturbing other, a stance toward the world in effect determined to swallow up the totality of existence. (2008: 363)

The complexity of the argument put forward by White and its relation to del Toro's cinema reveals the ongoing interest in narratives which call into question the 'natural' state of humanity (or its equivalent sentient state) as inherent to humans only. The question of humanity is spliced with the totemic object in *Cronos* and its reframing of the vampire myth. Del Toro's drive to retell both the *Frankenstein* and *Pinocchio* stories is illuminated in this context. The central question of where humanity is located has fascinated many film-makers, not least Stanley Kubrick and Steven Spielberg whose *A.I. Artificial Intelligence* (2001) is a re-imagining of the *Pinocchio* fable. Tim Burton splices together both the *Frankenstein* and *Pinocchio* stories using Americana kitsch and Gothic fairy tale in *Edward Scissorhands* (1990). Such preoccupations are taken to darker places and find a perverse logic in the work of David Cronenberg. Whereas a significant amount of del Toro's imagery concerns the dormant artifice animated by some supernatural or elemental trigger, Cronenberg's early to mid-period output sees the corporeal take on mechanical functions in often deeply unsettling moments where flesh takes on mechanistic form. For instance, the typewriter insect in *Naked Lunch* (1991) locates the writing process as an abject form of creation (in line with White's exploration of the ambivalence of imaginative processes) and the 'meat gun' which fires teeth in *eXistenZ* (1999) draws attention to mechanized violence as an extension of primal and vicious impulses.

Such body-horror leitmotifs are certainly evident in del Toro's films from the outset and represent amongst other things his fascination with Lovecraftian mythology, where corporeal grotesquery leads to mental collapse. However, del Toro has also demonstrated the ability to convey such ideas into action adventure cinema, retaining the core ideas they hold but exhibiting them in pop-cultural releases targeted towards an audience who value popcorn entertainment with an intellectual foundation. This can be seen in the ways in which *Mimic* (essentially a blend of science-fiction, horror and action movies) presents the rise of a grotesque insect species that mirrors human behaviour leading to a Darwinian fight for survival which destabilizes any notion of humankind as divine or elevated out of corporeal vulnerability. Although *Blade II* essentially sees del Toro complete a film as a director for hire on an existing franchise, upon scrutiny the design of the film and its narrative drivers are distinguishable. One could disregard *Blade II* as simply an action movie, with choreographed fight scenes, a rock soundtrack and ingenious gadgets and weapons (and it has all of these things in abundance), but at its core lie tropes which relate to fan-community dynamics. Not least of these is the protagonist's search for a confederate group of which he feels a part. Although outwardly the loner figure, Blade is motivated by a need for companionship, be it with the paternal figure of Whistler (Kris Kristofferson), the vampire shadow council and its agents or the reapers, he is involved in one way or the other with all these factions yet separated due to his inter-species parentage and resultant hybrid identity (perhaps the key leitmotif in the director's oeuvre). One of the key dimensions of the superhero comic book archetypes is the orphaned or ostracized figure seeking redemption through acceptance into a welcoming community (Kaveney 2008). Mythological figures such as Superman, Batman and Spiderman embody heroic ideals of course, but also through hypostasis symbolize a fundamental melancholy fuelled by the forlorn knowledge of their own isolation and difference. These melancholic tones have become more accentuated since the 1980s, when a darker trend in comics as adult-themed entertainment emerged. The characters of Hellboy and the resurgent Blade can be seen as a part of this continuum (Wolk 2007). Genre films which have been celebrated within fan communities also employ this central character dimension. The *Star Wars*, *Matrix* and *Avatar* mythologies all begin with central characters who are aware of a fundamental isolation and strive to fill this void with an extended family of outwardly disparate individuals with a shared quest. The allure of such archetypes is key to del Toro's oeuvre and his mainlined understanding of fandom and its communal identity.

Del Toro's position as a figurehead of fandom and its associated customs derives primarily from the density of his films, their textured interactions with other works of art and their emergence as innovative compositions. There are, however, other influential factors which have provided a platform from which to showcase his talents and develop the dialogue around the work and its fruition. It has been acknowledged that fandom, a necessarily organized or semi-organized entity by nature, is now more than ever an influential force in part because of the banding together that has emerged from networked interaction and the resultant digital cultures (DiMare 2011: 310). Building upon the ideas of Jenkins *et al.*, Axel Bruns develops the idea of the 'produser' – the individual who is both a consumer of a media product and the user with agency through participation and endorsement in a networked culture (2008). Bruns argues that one of the key factors which facilitate individuals as produsers is the environment which is populated by fellow produsers willing to engage in shared exchange in a number of contexts. Digital innovations have enhanced this, in that:

> [t]he same technology which makes possible many-to-many communication and distribution of content also enables peer-to-peer modes of organizing the collaborative engagement of communities in shared projects: this means that users can now communicate and engage directly with one another on a global scale, entirely bypassing traditional producers and distributors of information. (14)

Technology and the distribution of information are key here: del Toro typifies a film-maker whose position has been enhanced by technological factors that have affected film culture, in terms of the mode of distribution of films themselves, the growth in the production and importance of the paratext and the heightened agency through connectivity of fandom. Three interconnected techno-cultural phenomena are clearly key: the commonplace use of DVD and Blu-ray formats, the emergence and mass endorsement of web-environments as a hive of fan exchange and the popularization of fan conventions from underground cultist events to hyper-commodified media spectacle.

Aaron Barlow notices that the successful marketing and influence of the DVD (and by extension, Blu-ray) has not occurred in a bubble but has been a part of a wider digital revolution since it originated in the 1980s and came to prominence in the 1990s (2005). The proliferation of digital media and its resultant cultures mark a sea change in our relationship with the industrial producers of information and entertainment. In line with this, film culture has been affected in no small way. The exponential rise in TV channels has led to niche outlets for genre-specific output, classic movies, national cinemas and independent and cult productions. File-sharing technologies have created a crisis in the eyes of the industry, in which the established modes of distribution, capital and ownership are evaded and disregarded. The technological manipulation of digitally created and transferred film itself has also impacted upon the medium and the creative reshaping of films in fan-edits, and fan-created texts lend a new lease of life to 'textual poaching'. Perhaps the most fundamental change in terms of the context of cinephilia is the establishment of the disc as a film medium and the important 'special features' which accompany it. The various moments which see an innovation or invention go from being a potential product to a ubiquitous part of mainstream culture are described by Chris Chester as 'acts of invocation'. Our reliance upon email and the Internet, on mobile and smart phones and GPS systems are just a few examples of media which have become established through acts of invocation. The most significant development in cinema from a technological perspective has been the arrival of DVD and its generic subsidiaries (in Fuery 2009). Of course, home cinema is no new phenomenon, dating back to the 1950s and finding relative popularity in home video in the 1970s and 1980s. However, perhaps because of the storage capacity of the technology itself and certainly because of its association with the wider media shift, disc formats have changed a good portion of film culture.

Del Toro's films, their accompanying paratexts and their audience have been undoubtedly affected by the advent of DVD. This is influential in a number of ways which themselves illustrate the different aspects of disc modes in relation to the consumer. A prominent element in the proliferation of DVD products, not just as a readily available home version of Cineplex releases, but as an outlet for a far more prolific selection of multifarious cinemas, is the release of 'foreign-language' films into a wider English-speaking market. Audiences' access to such material has been enhanced by web access, which facilitates, amongst other things, online vending and discussion forums for enthusiasts (Barlow 2005: 59–61). For example, along with positive Internet reactions, the tenth anniversary release of *Cronos* in 2003 broadened its audience in part on the back of the success of *Pan's Labyrinth* (similarly, the DVD release of *The Devil's Backbone* mined associations with *Hellboy* and *The Others* (2001)). This release contrasts to the cursory treatment often afforded to non-Hollywood (and mid-budget genre) titles released on VHS, where, for instance, one version of *Cronos* was dubbed into English on an extended play tape (which compromises both image and sound quality). Located as a part of the 'art-house and international' market, the release came with the disc special features which are increasingly commonplace for products intended for a cine-literate or cinephile audience. Fan culture is of course central to cinephilia and fandom's traditional propensity for collection, enthusiast promotion and preference for quality format and technical specifications make it a boon audience for distributors.

Barlow notices that '[b]ecause of all of its "behind the scenes" extras, the DVD, in addition to everything else, makes the fan feel closer to the actual making of the film than was even possible before with earlier technology' (64). Proximity to texts and their production translates to notions of ownership in the fan community, as discussed by John Fiske amongst others. The DVD offers the allure of access to the creative processes involved in film-making, providing the illusion of peer-engagement with the professional producer; it also often features a relatively specialist register which aficionados will recognize as a non-patronizing acknowledgement of expertise. In contrast to the press junket or other more promotional interviews, often acknowledged as a contractual engagement accompanying the opening of a film, the DVD interviews and accompanying documentaries, are presented in many cases as complicit with artistic aspirations understood by the audience, heightened by the format which sees the film-maker directly addressing the viewer. This treatment of the DVD or other disc format as fan-centric mode is heightened by the release of special editions. Del Toro's academically informed creative pursuits and unashamedly scholarly understanding of film techniques as well as cult genealogy make him a cinematic innovator perceived as 'multifarious' in terms of knowledge, skills and willingness to engage in erudite cinephile discourse (Chun 2002; Contreras 2009). This presentation of knowledge and the willingness to engage with others in an intellectual manner about shared passions are key to the establishment and maintenance of 'art-worlds' and subcultural intellectual and social environments which are bonded by discourse. David Carrier writes of the ways in which enthusiasts of contemporary art relate to one another in order to belong through exchange, a notion which fits smoothly into the conception of fan communities:

> The art-world community has no dues, formal membership requirements, or lists of members, but belonging to it is not an entirely subjective matter. Unless you know a certain amount about contemporary art, you cannot belong to this community. A community is defined, in part, by a willingness to engage in intellectual exchange. (2003: 188)

Barlow proposes that many of the now 'standard' features of the special edition DVD (including commentary tracks, making of documentaries and the inclusion of and historiographical sources) have a quasi-academic function and that they legitimize cineaste culture through detailed engagement with the film-maker and film-making process and by proxy the viewer as cinephile, invited behind the curtain as a privileged guest (75–108). Certain gold-standard distribution outlets, which strive to provide a film experience as close to the intended specifications of the film-makers as possible, accentuate disc media as key components of cineaste culture.

Notable amongst such distributors is the Criterion Collection, a rarefied archive of notable films presented as close to the original format as possible and with a specially made and collected surrounding array of audio visual, image and textual features with the intention of framing the film itself as an exemplar. It is no surprise to those interested in the growing critical celebration of del Toro from the fan and cinephile community and in the academy itself that Criterion have turned their attention to his work. In 2010 Criterion released 'director approved' DVD and Blu-ray editions of *Cronos*, complete with all the splendour associated with the collection, including a video tour of 'Bleak House' and all its treasures, a completed version of an early del Toro attempt at horror, *Geometria* (1987), and two commentary tracks, a platform on which del Toro excels.

The audio commentary, a feature developed for the laserdisc, developed and standardized on DVD and now a regular component of a Blu-ray release, caters for the audience's appetite to understand film in relation to the wider world. Barlow acknowledges that the audio commentary takes on many forms, involving uncomfortable participants wary of seeming pretentious, unprepared speakers filling dead air and technically substandard aural tracks (2005). In del Toro's case though, the enthusiast, fan and academic elements of his persona are undeniably showcased on the audio commentary. Not only are his commentaries available for all of his major films and clearly suited to someone who enjoys talking about his own work and the work of others, but they also are a testament to someone who believes in the *value* of an articulate engagement with the form. This can be located as a tradition of fandom and as an important component of identity formation in geek circles. Writing about fan communities and the ways in which they bond through discussion, debate and the expression of a shared enjoyment of the text (the term 'geeking out' means much the same in fan vernacular), Fiske uses the term 'enunciative productivity' to describe the ways in which fan discourse (and its related networks) are initiated and maintained. He writes:

> An enunciation is the use of a semiotic system (typically, but not exclusively verbal language) which is specific to its speaker and its social and temporal context. Fan talk is the generation and circulation of certain meanings of the object of fandom within a local community. (450)

Language here is key; the formation and exchange of an interpretive code function in the same manner as a speech act. Just as a speech act (an oath, a declaration of marriage, etc.) is performative and illocutionary in the moment of utterance, the ongoing discussion, analysis, celebration and criticism of texts through language keep them alive and central to the continuation of the interpretive community (Searle 1969). Carrier asserts that the art gallery, the museum and other shared exhibitive events are vital to the maintenance of the community and its ability to situate the production of new texts in relation to the continuum of past texts. He contextualizes this community ethos in the light of the emergence of Salon culture in mid-eighteenth-century Paris and the later Modernist art public culture where 'Aesthetic values are defined by discussion in the public art museum' (Carrier: 141). Whilst museums and galleries do exist to showcase the texts of fandom, more natural informal institutions can be found in the comic book shops, the cinema, the convention and on fan sites and forums. Gang mentality can also be found in the various sub-cultural strands (superhero comics, J-Horror, etc.), with their own codes and conventions and shared knowledge exchanges. The audio commentary is of course a more exclusive format than the peer-to-peer discussion, and del Toro holds a rare and privileged position as a professional producer of such texts. He speaks the same language and identifies with and is identified as a member of geek fandom, and the commentary provides us with a simulation at least of an exchange amongst peers, an exchange he clearly relishes (as can be seen in his candid commentary about his early short film *Doña Lupe* (1985)).

In addition to the paratextual features of home entertainment products, this fan discourse is increasingly displayed and exchanged on computer-mediated forums, where the concept of a networked community of active users with a shared base interest is more fully realized than in smaller peer groups, conventions and letters pages. Websites such as Aintitcoolnews, Dark Horizons and Chud provide a mixture of news, reviews and interviews and, crucially, provide 'talk-back' forums where fans can interact with one another. It's no surprise that del Toro features heavily on sites such as these, not least because he is particularly forthcoming and knowledgeable about the cultures themselves. Jenkins illuminates the ways in which fandom acts as a template for the now ubiquitous switched-on network culture, where fan communities are

> [e]xpansive self-organizing groups focused around the collective production, debate, and circulation of meanings, interpretations, and fantasies in response to various artefacts of contemporary popular culture. Fan communities have long defined their memberships through affinities rather than localities. Fandoms were virtual communities, 'imagined' and 'imagining' communities, long before the introduction of networked computers. (2006: 147)

Alongside the rise in popularity of such virtual sites, there has been a significant elevation of the convention circuit. Trade shows used to be places where fans could exchange and buy paraphernalia, comic book-back issues and occasionally vie (or pay) for an autograph or photo with a star of a TV show or comic book writer. The shows themselves also provided a prerogative stage where cultish behaviour deemed odd in the mainstream could be celebrated and exhibited and fans could dress up, geek out and generally flout their shared passions. Such conventions have famously been credited with reviving the *Star Trek* franchise and 'Trekkers' are a testament to fan collective power. In the past decade, such 'Comic-Cons' have become big business, and whereas once the focus of attention may have been an ageing star of a cult television show forgotten by the mainstream or an effects pioneer from 1970s gore cinema, large shows such as the Comic Con International San Diego are, as Salkowitz contends, 'the pop culture industry incarnate', where directors such as Steven Spielberg and stars such as Tom Cruise will attempt to create a buzz for their product via the passion of active fan audiences (19). Of course, del Toro features in such events. A full year before the release of *Pacific Rim*, the director featured on a panel which presented footage and engaged with his fans. This in turn resulted in fans distributing handheld video footage of the event online and the talkbacks which followed. *Pacific Rim* typifies genre cinema in the early twenty-first century – effects-heavy spectacle steeped in the lore of geek culture and blending together geek cultural forms and concocted by the fan as film-maker.

Part Two

Texts and Thematics

4

Twisted Genres: *Cronos* and *Mimic*

This chapter considers del Toro's first two feature films, *Cronos* and *Mimic*, as case studies of his approach to the horror genre and as early examples of his artistic sensibilities. The modes of production of these two films are radically different and illustrate transnational cinema in contrast to the Hollywood production model. However, we argue that each film draws upon del Toro's thematic and symbolic fascinations and his intertextualist discourse. *Cronos* is a highly lauded film and *Mimic* is seen by many as an artistic failure and at the very least a minor work in del Toro's oeuvre. However, we wish to re-appraise *Mimic* as a film with unexcavated qualities and as a work that applies del Toro's Surrealist Gothic sensibilities in a Hollywood creature feature genre. We begin with a discussion of *Cronos*, a film which takes that most perverse Gothic genre, the vampire tale, and re-interprets it as a Mexican fairy tale.

Alchemical beginnings

'[Francois] Truffaut used to say that in the first few thousands of feet of your work is your entire work, and I think that's true of *Cronos*,' del Toro told *Hero Complex* before the event. 'You have a view of childhood that is not common, not Hollywood childhood, and the girl of *Cronos* perfectly could have grown up to be the girl from *Pan's Labyrinth* in a way. You have the idea of the mundane being invaded by the extraordinary, but in a really kind of grungy way; it's not a spectacular invasion of the fantastic. And the idea for making a genre that is normally spectacle or gore and making it about a family and a small group of people and their relationships, and writing it in a way that is not the Hollywood way of writing. ... All of that is in [*Cronos*], and it's true of the rest of the movies.' (Clark and Boucher 2010)

I was actually more interested in opening the movie like a Hollywood movie, open it as if you are about to see a super-expensive production but then this production only lasts three minutes. Then you go in to meet the most boring guy on earth. This is what I was attracted to. It's like beginning with a Mexican version of *War of the Worlds* with all the spaceships arriving and then cutting to a Mexican family working in their fields on their cows and see the invasion from their perspective. It's really about the everyday-guy perspective on a Hollywood premise. (Wood 2006a: 36)

Mimic can be seen as del Toro's apparent defeat by the Hollywood production machine and its intrinsic conventionality and cultural conservatism, although the version of the film that has emerged over the years represents a far more interesting and original vision than was perhaps first thought. In contrast, his debut feature film, *Cronos*, and his subsequent movies speak much more directly of his delight in exploding generic boundaries and alchemizing given narratives, modes and tropes into new forms. As Laurence Davies has noted, del Toro's films are 'not easily boxed into any one genre or mode' (88). In his essay equating the film's medieval alchemist Fulcanelli with both vampire myth and *Frankenstein*, Brad O'Brien notes that '[a]lchemists thus combine science with the supernatural', an observation that could well be applied generally to del Toro's film-making, particularly early in his career where reality and fantasy merge and re-emerge in new combinations (172). Just as *Mimic* takes the 'bug invasion' B-movie and infuses it with body horror, slasher motifs, gender politics and millennial anxieties around science, technology and the city, so *Cronos* reworks vampire and Frankenstein narratives into an often intimate, tender and comedic meditation on time, love and human existence. The abovementioned 'family and small group of people' centring on the elderly and appropriately named Jesús Gris provide the film with its unorthodox narrative core. Del Toro has described the film as 'an exploded view of my brain' (Criterion DVD), and *Cronos* can certainly be read as a kind of primer for his ensuing work. As del Toro further suggests on the *Cronos* DVD commentary, 'all my movies are one big movie'.

The film's title sets in motion important mythological references that resonate throughout del Toro's oeuvre. Cronos is in Greek mythology the youngest and foremost of the Titans, known for acts such as the castration of his father, Uranus, and the devouring of his own children, visually memorialized by painters such as Rubens and Goya. As discussed elsewhere, the latter's art, particularly the *Black Paintings*, underpins much of the visual palette of del Toro's films; commentators have remarked on the recurrent presence of one of Goya's most famous works *Saturn Devouring His Children* (Saturn and Cronos were conflated within Roman mythology) (Derry 2009). The most obvious manifestation of this is the Pale Man in *Pan's Labyrinth*, but there is a key moment in *Cronos* where the vampiric grandfather Jesús comes close to 'devouring' his beloved granddaughter Aurora but finally resists, beginning a process of death and redemption that resonates within his forename. The unusual agency of the child in this process, another recurrent trope, exemplifies del Toro's resistance to Hollywoodization of the child figure, discussed later in this chapter in the section on *Mimic*. Aurora, who acts as the silent witness to the film's events, utters no word throughout the film until the moment where Jesús is vampirically drawn to the blood dripping from her hand, at which point she says 'abuelo' (grandfather), thus reminding him of his identity and humanity. This is a scene that reworks the famous moment in James Whale's *Frankenstein* (1931) between the Monster and Little Maria, but in del Toro's film the child survives, despite seeming to offer herself to her grandfather. It is at this point that Jesús destroys the device and repeats his own name as an act of self-identification and recognition of his mortality – the repeated *Gris* here finally distancing him from the link with Christ. The character of Aurora pays homage to another child-as-witness, Ana in Victor Erice's *Spirit of the Beehive*, a film which arguably provided del Toro with the narrative template upon which to elaborate his own individual vision. Like the also near-silent Ana:

> Aurora bears witness, and looks on as Jesús gives himself over to the *Cronos* device, to addiction, hunger, momentary youth and death. By turn visibly angry, jealous, dumbfounded, and afraid, she watches over him … Classically, she recognises and confirms the mythical foundations of a shaken symbolic order, whose sacrificial logic, from having been threatened, is now, once more, in place. (Kraniauskas 1998: 157)

In portraying Aurora (the name suggests the dawn Jesús will not see) as witness, del Toro draws on earlier filmic representations of childhood and trauma, such as Spielberg's *Empire of the Sun* (1987), as well as nineteenth-century narratives, such as Dickens's bildungsroman fiction, particularly *Great Expectations* (1861) and *David Copperfield* (1850), with the crucial difference that del Toro never sentimentalizes the child figure, nor is the child portrayed as lacking agency – Aurora plays an important part in Jesús's overcoming of la Guardia. The title also speaks of the film's engagement with questions of time and mortality, given that the Greek Cronos is often conflated with Chronos, the Graeco-Roman personification of time. The Cronos device (the film's initial Spanish title options were *Sangre Gris*, *El vampiro de Aurelia Gris* and *La Invención de Cronos*) is in essence a cyborgian time machine for the body, where time travel is replaced by time transcendence (its inventor Fulcanelli has had his life extended by 400 years – his dying words are 'suo tempore' (in his own time)). It is replete with recurrent and characteristic motifs of cogs, wheels and mechanisms as well as a vampiric living insect at its core. The scarab shape stems from a number of influences, both mythic and mundane: the ancient Egyptian symbol for creation and the sunrise god Khepri (this echoed in Aurora's name) and the fashionable jewellery featuring live insects that del Toro observed women wearing in Mexico at the time of the making of the film (DVD commentary). Del Toro's fascination with insects (he wanted to be an etymologist or marine biologist when young) emerges strongly in his first two films and melds in later projects with fantasy creatures such as the 'fairies' in *Pan's Labyrinth* and *Hellboy II: The Golden Army*. The Fabergé-like golden egg which stores the Cronos is decorated with potent alchemical and other symbols including the ourobos, the ancient symbol of the serpent eating its own tail and thus forming an unbroken circle of creation and re-creation, which may also stem from Egyptian myth. It is characteristic that the pagan takes a significant role in a film which, like much of del Toro's work, is also suffused with a powerful if damaged Catholicism: a religious sensibility that treats the iconography of the faith with an ironic yet troubled sense of its contradictions yet also its insidious and irresistible power.

If *Cronos* offers an early compendium of del Toro's symbolic and imagistic vocabulary, then it also reveals many of the films and film-makers that have shaped his film language and visual sensibility. The film is enhanced by a rich intertextuality that draws on and sometimes ironizes horror movies from the 1920s and 1930s (Expressionist classics such as *Nosferatu* (1922), Fernando de Fuentes's *El Fantasma del Convento* (1934), the Universal classics), Hammer horror (in particular the work of Terence Fisher), art-house Gothic masterpieces such as Jack Clayton's *The Innocents* as well as more recent horror classics such as Mario Bava's 'giallo' movies and David Cronenberg's *The Fly* (1986). What is particularly noticeable in *Cronos* is the layering of ideas around and within the pivotal vampire myth. The film is remarkable in the way it comprehensively reconfigures the myth without ever explicitly mentioning vampires, whilst at the same time drawing hungrily from a wide range of cultural sources. Whilst locating the film within a developing genre of postmodern cyborg fantasies, Geoffrey Kantaris acknowledges the breadth of del Toro's achievement in the film: '*Cronos* plays with the multiple valency of vampire mythology, which encodes fears about hybridisation, racial-cum-sexual pollution, the corruption of virginal "nature" and the transfusion of body into simulacrum, whilst freely vampirising the stock repertoire of horror movies both within Mexico and internationally' (2007: 58). In 1992, the year preceding the release of *Cronos*, Francis Ford Coppola had made *Bram Stoker's Dracula* in a way that positioned the text firmly in relation to the cultural climate of the 1990s, particularly concerning AIDS and related anxieties. Coppola's film also purported to offer a more faithful version of the original novel, as did Kenneth Branagh's *Mary Shelley's Frankenstein* released in 1994, but both were roundly criticized precisely for their failure to adhere to the origins of the tales. Both were produced by Columbia and American Zoetrope, Coppola's company, and had 40-million-dollar-plus budgets, as opposed to the two million dollars at del Toro's disposal, which came mainly from local Mexican sources but still represented a very substantial level of funding for a Mexican film at the time. As the film's producer Bertha Navarro (who also produced *The Devil's Backbone* and *Pan's Labyrinth*) remarked: 'In Mexico it is virtually impossible to make films that cost over $2 million. *Cronos* made it clear, even to del Toro, that he needed another structure to bring his visions to the screen' (Wood 2006a: 39). However, these major mainstream studio productions such as Coppola's did relatively little to develop the classic mythologies and fictions with which they were dealing, despite their high-end production values and often voluptuous period feel. Indeed, Branagh's film in particular seemed unable to interrogate successfully Shelley's original and descended into melodrama with disturbing frequency. In contrast, del Toro's first film de-familiarizes and then reconfigures these familiar myths by drawing on images of postmodern simulacra, contemporary cultural and political concerns as well as a comprehensive filmic resource. It is almost as if in abandoning the source material to be adapted (for example, Stoker) he is able to get closer to the edge and spirit of classics by the very nature of being unbound from them. The extraordinary inventiveness of *Cronos* was acknowledged by its local and international critical success. (It won in nine categories at the 1993 Ariel awards – Mexico's equivalent of the Academy Awards – including best picture, director and original screenplay – and in the same year won the International Critics' Prize at the Cannes International Film Festival. Budgetary returns were considerably less favourable, however.) Recent commentators have focused on the film's radical revisioning of the vampire figure which looked forward to the seeming explosion of vampire films and TV series in the later 1990s, 2000s and beyond, when the filmic undead seemed to be reproducing at an alarming rate in ways that contrasted radically with previous manifestations, often melding realistic milieux with vampiric fantasy (for example, *Buffy the Vampire Slayer* (1997–2003), *Twilight* (2008–2012), *True Blood* (2008–), amongst others).

Cronos's representation of border territories offers a revealing contextual framework in which to explore the creative morphing of the vampire. As Barbara Creed notes:

> [T]he concept of a border is central to the construction of the monstrous in the horror film; that which crosses or threatens to cross the 'border' is abject. Although the specific nature of the border changes from film to film, the function of the monstrous remains the same – to bring about an encounter between the symbolic order and that which threatens its stability. In some horror films the monstrous is produced at the border between human and inhuman, man and beast (*Dr Jekyll and Mr Hyde, Creature from the Black Lagoon, King Kong*) in others the border is between the normal and the supernatural (*Carrie, The Exorcist, The Omen, Rosemary's Baby*). (2000: 66)

Vampire texts in particular feature infiltration and border-crossing of an often literal kind, involving domestic thresholds and territorial borders (Dracula's journey to England, for example, in Stoker's novel) as recurrent tropes. In *Cronos* all kinds of borders are subject to slippage and porosity – the film is full of encounters between aspects of the symbolic order (language, time, cultural specificity, geo-politics and economics, the patriarchal family) that denote an essential instability in given hierarchies. The relativity of temporal divisions is implied from the film's opening soundscape as the mechanical ticking of antique clocks is juxtaposed with the ominous synthesized sound of a great tolling bell, with its inescapable connotations of Catholic rituals, the mass and funeral rites, foreshadowing the movie's final ritualized deathbed scene. The superimposed sounds of clockwork mechanisms and ancient sounds fed through modern electronic filters wordlessly narrate the eliding of historical and cultural borders defined through notions of temporal specificity. The first image we see clearly on screen is a cogwheel (a recurrent del Toro device) introducing the film's exploration of the unstable interface between the machine and organic life, cyborg and human. The opening voice-over narration simultaneously moves us across 400 years, two continents and introduces Catholic repression (Fulcanelli the alchemist has fled the Inquisition) and inverted or parodied religious symbolism. The upside-down hanging man, whose blood is being drained for the now-dead alchemist, evokes a parody of the crucified Christ and the hanging man of the occult Tarot; later in the film, Jesús Gris's wounded hand and foot parody the stigmata and, more generally, the film is set in a post-Christmas period characterized by the tawdry detritus of a devalued 'festive season'. Del Toro moves us away from clichéd notions of the alchemist as obsessive pursuer of the transmutation of base metal into gold towards the more comprehensive definition given by scholars such as Stanton J Linden, quoting H.J. Sheppard:

> If, in the final analysis, a comprehensive analysis of alchemy is deemed necessary, it is useful to bear in mind one recently proposed by H.J. Sheppard … He states 'Alchemy is the art of liberating parts of the Cosmos from temporal existence and achieving perfection which, for metals is gold, and for man, longevity, then immortality and, finally, redemption'. (1996: 11)

The alchemical nature of film, with its capacity to elide and transcend time or simultaneously represent and transform reality, is fundamental to del Toro's output in the medium. On the DVD director's commentary he has spoken of his desire in *Cronos*, to utilize colours associated with alchemy: red, gold, black and white in the visual palette of the film. Like Fulcanelli, the first character in his feature filmography, he is haunted by his Catholic past (the film is dedicated to his ferociously Catholic grandmother) and alchemizes disparate filmic and narrative traditions and genres, taken from across time and from the earliest examples of human storytelling such as fairy tale to contemporary narratives of science fiction and fantasy always with a strong influence from horror. It has been argued that the horror film is a destabilization of cinematic 'reality' and a coherent rational world where order rules. Thomas Elseasser notices the fundamentally disruptive nature of horror, stating:

> The horror film especially permitted deviations and transgressions of the representational norm. In contrast to maintaining a coherent diegetic world and the rule of narrative causality, horror films almost by definition disrupt the cause and effect patterns of such classical devices as shot/countershot, continuity and reverse field editing in order to create a sense of mystery, of the unexpected, of surprise, incongruity and horror, misleading the viewer by withholding information or keeping the causal agent, the monster, off screen for as long as possible. (1998: 195)

Considering this, horror can be seen as essentially alchemic, melting and thus liberating cinematic elements from their cogent whole.

Time and haunting are, of course, key reiterated elements of del Toro's oeuvre, as divisions between past and present, history and the contemporary are constantly undermined or elided. This emerges visually in the repeated use of clocks, watches, cogs, mechanisms and timepieces in general (most notably, perhaps, the fob-watch that the fascist Vidal obsessively consults in *Pan's Labyrinth*). Significantly, in *Cronos* all the clocks have stopped in Jesús's antique shop after it has been trashed by De La Guardia's minions; the clock has also stopped in his tomb-like factory. For Jesús this marks the beginning of the end of his relationship to 'normal' time, a process that climaxes with his absence from the midnight countdown at the New Year's celebration, where a melancholy partygoer dressed as a clock seems to haunt the proceedings. For del Toro, adherence to the notion of time as linear and progressive is a marker of, at best, a certain rigidity and mundanity (in the case of Jesús – already a somewhat anachronistic, aimless figure) and, at worst, destructive authoritarianism (for example, Vidal in *Pan's Labyrinth*). William Faulkner's now over-quoted dictum 'The past is never dead. It's not even past' (*Requiem for a Nun* (1950)) crystallizes something of the feel of a del Toro film. A more nuanced reading can be developed using Derrida's marginally less familiar concept of hauntology, developed in his *Spectres of Marx* (1993), which has gained considerable currency in the last few years as a theoretical tool in the reading of post-millennial culture. As Jane Kenway *et al.* suggest, 'Derrida's notion of hauntology is built on a presence/present double gesture. The ghost confuses our sense of existence as presence. The ghost *is* but it does not exist. As it is neither present nor absent, it places "being as presence" in doubt. The ghost also confuses our understanding of time … Thus time is no longer ordered according to a linear progression from the distant past, to the present moment, and into the unseen future. The ghost's state of being desynchronizes time' (2006: 4). For Niall Lucy, Derrida's reading of spectrality has the result that 'all that metaphysics allows or restrains us to regard as certain (concerning time, identity, presence, and so forth) is open to the risk of becoming uncertain, of coming undone or being disjointed' (2008: 112). This seems particularly useful when constructing a reading of *Cronos*, since the film is closely concerned with both physical and metaphysical uncertainty at a number of levels: personal, political, cultural, national and international. Hauntology's near-homophonic closeness to ontology in French playfully underlines the concept's questioning of being, whilst at the same time clearly implicating language itself in the absent/present nature of the spectral. Del Toro makes this point very explicitly in *Cronos*, with its bi-lingual dialogue and multilingual visual content and context (a no-parking sign in five different languages appears in the opening title shots of litter-strewn post-Christmas urban streets, newspapers appear to be in Russian Cyrillic script), and the arguably pivotal figure of Aurora speaks only one word throughout the entire film, a silent and ghostly observer of human fallibility.

In *Spectre of Marx*, which originally appeared in the same year as *Cronos*, Derrida poses the question 'what is the *being-there* of a ghost. What is the mode

uly immortal character. And the character played by Federico Luppi becomes
nmortal and the moment he decides to die, the moment he says, 'Fuck it, I don't
ant to kill my granddaughter'. (Kermode 2012: 24)

·e are predominantly political spectres and monsters in *Cronos* which are
of central significance. Del Toro has spoken of the film's relevance to post-
·TA (North American Free Trade Agreement) Mexico:

wanted to show the vampiric relationship between the nephew and uncle,
nd, of course, the vampiric relationship between Mexico and the United States.
his is why the date in the movie, which we see on a newspaper – is 1997, even
1ough the film was made in 1993. I wanted it to be set in a post-NAFTA Mexico.
Wood 2006a: 33–34)

film that deals with the porosity of borders and borderlands, the relevance
1e NAFTA, which opened up Mexico's economy to a flood of US-produced
ds, hardly needs stating. Preparations for NAFTA included the revoking of
1es that protected traditional Indian land from privatization, prompting
Ejército Zapatista de Liberación Nacional (aka Zapatistas) to declare war
nst a Mexican state they saw as capitulating to US economic imperialism.
1ificantly, *Cronos* opens with a prologue evoking the Spanish colonial
.od, thus situating Mexico in a historical continuum in which national and
ural identity is inherently unstable and unfixed across time. As Ann Davies
3ests, the figure of La Guardia represents not only a parody of the Hughes-
reclusive American magnate, emblematic of inaccessible capitalist power,
also a blurring of national and cultural identities (2008: 402). His Spanish
1e (which evokes a famous New York mayor and perhaps also Franco's brutal
1rdia Civil) and the fact that he has dialogue in both English and Spanish
1fy to a latter-day, post-NAFTA colonialism that the vampirized Jesús Gris
sts. But *Cronos* is no simplistic David and Goliath narrative of US hegemony
·r Mexico. De La Guardia's cyborgian body is suspended between life and
th, frantically consuming the past – he eats Fulcanelli's manuscript and
:kpiles statues of angels in his obsessive bid to find the device. (It is interesting
1ote that del Toro's casting of Claudio Brook as De La Guardia links his film
k to Buñuel's Mexican period when Brook appeared in a number of great
nish director's films. Del Toro has even suggested his walking with two
.es references Orson Welles's *Lady from Shanghai* (1947)). His thuggish and
1ically named nephew Angel, played by Ron Perlman who has become a del
.o regular, is obsessively concerned with changing the appearance of his nose,

of presence of a spectre?' (1994: 38 original emphasis), wł
echoes the voice-over at the opening of *The Devil's Backbone*:
A terrible moment condemned to repeat itself over and ov
suspended in time'. This question is one to which del Toro ı
obliquely, in almost all of the movies he has directed and ot
produced and/or scripted (for example, *The Orphanage* (2007)
Ojos de Julia) (2010), *Don't be Afraid of the Dark* (2010), *Mama*
his central figures exist in a transitory, disenfranchised and nor
are literal and metaphorical orphans inhabiting a kind of ph_?
and psychological liminality. In *Cronos* the nature of the spe
though the representation of a number of contrasting ghost-lil
include the alabaster-skinned Fulcanelli who appears briefly
narrative and whose device serves to haunt the rest of the film
the cyborgian device itself with its organic beating heart seen on
encased within a gold shell (perhaps made from Aztec gold
symbols from pre-Christian myth that also speaks of one of *the*
of consumer capitalism, the Fabergé egg, and that crosses histc
promise of eternal existence to its user. The central modern-d
also come to embody this liminal state, so that Jesús Gris epitom
present nature of the ghost/spectre as we experience his metam
and resurrection, a narrative underscored by his role as an ant
curator of the past, which situates him as a borderline figure inha
and present. His uncanny double and antagonist La Guardia exi
Hughes-like hermetic and antiseptic environment surrounde
images of his own past – the preserved organs extracted from I
a macabre image of technology put to the service not only of a
vampiric capitalism (his factory is 'open all night', although it
to produce anything) but also a state of suspended being, deal
Aurora, the characteristic (for del Toro) child figure as witness, m
a spectral silent figure representing unmediated love and hoveri
of events until the moment late in the film when she speaks fo
and reminds her grandfather of his humanity and identity when
to take her blood. This scene echoes the moment in Erice's *Spiri*
where the Frankenstein figure does not harm Ana. For del Tor
moment in what he describes as the 'thesis' of the film:

> I share the belief that there is a state of grace that can be reached
> moral purity but through almost ethical purity – by being yourse
> immune to the world... In the film the girl who does not mind

his face being a particular target for his uncle's violent tirades. Del Toro has indicated that the violent and unsympathetic American characters are a kind of revenge for the clichéd but familiar representation of Mexicans in Hollywood movies as moustachioed bad guys. But there is a more complex set of meanings here as well, as Ann Davies suggests: 'The American body is collapsing – and malleable, as Angel's desire for plastic surgery on his nose suggests. In bodily terms, then, America seems diseased, infectious and repulsive' (402). Jesús's own bodily borders (in particular his skin) are wholly destabilized after his piercing by the device. Initially time runs backwards as he regains a degree of youthfulness, but his 'death' at New Year marks the making and remaking of new layers of being, underlined by a scene where he reads his own death notice which has been comically prefigured by Mercedes's own obsession with cutting out obituaries from newspapers.

John Kraniauskas gives a thoroughgoing Marxist reading of the film that develops further some of these ideas. In his introduction he cites a range of relevant Mexican cultural and historical referents that evoke the place of phantoms of the past or revenants which 'occupy an important place in the cultural histories of Mexico' (1998: 142). These include the traditions associated with the Day of the Dead and Juan Rulfo's novel *Pedro Páramo* (1955) with its 'dispossessed peasantry who haunt the text as living dead and as its narrators', the revolutionary Zapatistas' use of vampiric imagery in a manifesto issued during the 1994 rebellion and a Catholicism predicated on the symbolic consumption of Christ's body (142). For Kraniauskas, *Cronos* is 'a fantasy of the contemporary body, technology and of time in the accelerated age of late – transnational – capitalism' (146). Del Toro's re-reading of the vampire myth is part therefore of a resurgence of vampiric representations in the 1980s and 1990s that tallies with a 'massive deregulation of capital that is associated with it transnationalisation and the recent neo-liberal assault on the welfare state' (146–147). Kraniauskas misses the salient point that it is during this period that the vampire figure in film and fiction tends to become more sympathetic, equated in some cases with a kind of existential malaise that tempers the traditionally predatory image (see the fiction of Anne Rice amongst others and TV series such as *Buffy the Vampire Slayer* as well as its spin-off *Angel* (1999–2004)). This rehabilitation of the vampire is most clearly expressed in Francis Ford Coppola's reversal of the Dracula figure as villain into hero in *Bram Stoker's Dracula*. The Count is thereby reconfigured into a dandified neo-Byronic hero, consumed by poetic angst rather than a more visceral hunger (Craig and Fry 2002).

Whilst acknowledging the viability of such a predominantly Marxist reading, Laurence Davies resists a purely allegorical approach to the film, stating 'to characterize this film, though, as any sort of allegory – political, cultural, sexual, or religious – goes against its grain. Its moods are mercurial, its modes elusive' (96). Davies quotes from del Toro's director's commentary to the film to point out the director's attraction to 'that connoisseur of weird events', Charles Fort. 'I always look for the Fortean in life', says del Toro; hence Davies reads the films as celebrating incongruity, inconsequentiality, shifting meanings, the grotesque as an act of resistance rather than gothic anxiety (96). Davis continues, '[t]his is not anxiety at work, but ridicule, not existential uncertainty, but rebuttal of a crass and inadequate system of beliefs' (96). It is important not to underestimate del Toro's use of parody as a source of meaning in *Cronos*, as the film regularly employs a comic sensibility as a key part of its narrative discourse. This emerges particularly in the reworking of earlier filmic vampire conventions – Gris's post-death resurrection sees him dressed still in the traditional evening wear donned by the likes of Bela Lugosi and Christopher Lee, the familiar undead as lounge lizard, but now reduced to a pathetic clown-like tawdriness, his mortuary dinner jacket back-to-front as he wanders barefoot in the graffiti-strewn urban backstreets. This moment in the film is preceded by a grotesquely comic morgue scene in which Jesús's 'corpse' is made up by a gum-chewing embalmer to the accompaniment of Mariachi music. In his director's commentary del Toro talks of his desire for a comedic scene redolent of the gravedigger in the final Act of *Hamlet*, the dark humour capturing a kind of irreverent Mexican 'Day of the Dead' sensibility, with its grimly sardonic sense of familiarity with death. The scene also continues the working through of del Toro's issues with Catholicism: the embalmer wears a large gold cross over his dirty white vest and there is an incongruous shrine with candles in what is otherwise a grubbily sordid setting in which the dead are despatched unceremoniously and with little or no dignity (this scene was apparently the result of comprehensive research on del Toro's part into mortuary practice). In a further parody of Christ, Jesús 'resurrects' after three days and finds a red cape in a trashcan. Del Toro also stresses his desire to represent in the undead Jesús a working-class vampire, a 'poor devil' who is at the opposite end of the spectrum from Stoker's archetype, the masterfully aristocratic Count Dracula.

In contrast to a broadly Marxist approach, Ann Davies employs a Foucauldian discourse in her detailed study of the film's engagement with vampiric myth and meanings. In particular, she focuses on Foucault's notion of the heterotopic as a place where incompatible or opposed realities can co-exist and identifies the vampire as containing 'two conflicting, indeed opposed realities, of life and death. […] The vampire is a heterotopic form of the body, in which human bodily restraints (above all that of permanent decay) are overcome' (2008: 397). The body of Gris becomes indicative of this kind of destabilizing of the binaries that underpin notions of the human – life/death, light/dark, interior/exterior, speech/silence, good/evil. Davies suggests that 'Gris's bodily border of skin is constantly unmade and remade, thus literally embodying the porousness of heterotopias' (2008: 400). The second of these binaries is particularly key to both the representation of the vampire/monster figure (given its traditional shunning of light) and also the making of movies, the play of light on screen. Ann Davies cites Ken Gelder's discussion of the relation between cinema and vampire:

> Cinema may be a suitably nomadic home for the vampire; it, too, eventually goes everywhere – it has become an internationalised medium. […] film is an animating medium, bringing images to life in an otherwise darkened room, in a simulation of the night – a feature to which horror films in particular often speak directly. (Gelder in Davies 2008: 398)

It is intriguing just how many of del Toro's films feature long sequences in spaces that also replicate the darkness of night: subways, sewers, basements, subterranean caverns, secret installations. (This is perhaps ironic given del Toro's repeated and scrupulous concern for the light palette used in his projects. Each film is characterized by a carefully nuanced juxtaposition and interaction of screen colours – as already mentioned, *Cronos* replicates colours associated with alchemy – even in such apparently insignificant details as the red hair of Mercedes, Jesús's wife.) These nocturnal locales are not just the stock-in-trade of the horror movie in del Toro's hands – the sewer or subway are particularly key here in terms of the Foucauldian notion of opposed or contrasted realities; they are both of the city and not – part of the urban infrastructure and technology yet also places of abjection where the urban dispossessed construct their own alternative existence. Given del Toro's ambivalence towards religion, it is not surprising that churches are also represented as heterotopic space – places of darkness as well as light, and often more the former than the latter. The alchemic red (evocative of both gold and the philosopher's stone) is the focal point in perhaps the most notorious scene in *Cronos*, the New Year's Eve party (an appropriate locale for a film about transformation and time) where Jesús's thirst for blood becomes so uncontrolled that he licks the leftovers of a nosebleed from the floor of the men's bathroom. Del Toro has acknowledged the centrality of this scene which Kenneth Morefield describes as 'a sly homage to Hitchcock's occasional torturing of his lead actors' (Morefield 2008: 148):

> The image that better represents *Cronos* for me is that of the guy licking the blood from the nosebleed on the toilet floor. There were so many walkouts during this scene. What a waste, it was an extremely beautiful bathroom. There is, however, something about this shot that gets to the root of revulsion. (Wood 2006b: 35)

The socio-political associations of this scene are apparent given the then current anxieties surrounding AIDS in public spaces and the linking of toilets with public health scares, drug abuse and homosexualized spaces in cruising culture. This is the moment when Jesús himself finally becomes abject – it is the literal and metaphorical abasement of the still-human Jesús prior to his 'death' – the scene ends with him being kicked unconscious by Angel in the toilet and in the next being disposed of over a cliff. The scene can also be read as a perverse moment of Eucharist in which the public toilet is reconfigured as sacred ground.

A final aspect of del Toro's reconstitution of the vampire narrative can be found in the perhaps surprising focus in the film on an apparently insignificant old man. Certainly traditional vampire narratives such as *Dracula* construct the vampire as age-old and metamorphic. In Mario Bava's *Black Sabbath* (1963), it is the father figure who is the vampire. *Cronos* presents us with a seemingly redundant figure who, despite his close relationship with childhood (we see him playing hopscotch with Aurora early in the film), is cocooned in a doubled antique shell – his shop and his body. The piercing of his body by the device initiates the arc of the narrative. According to Ann Davies, there is significance also in del Toro's focus on an old rather than young vampire, given the tendency in 1990s film and TV to focus on 'gilded youth'; for example, the beautiful mock-family of Brad Pitt, Tom Cruise and Kirsten Dunst in Neil Jordan's *Interview with a Vampire* (1994) (2008: 400). She rightly notices that this stress on old age is a motif that reappears throughout del Toro's work, a point that may be nuanced further by noting that virtually all his films involve a key relationship between youth and age in which a parental presence is often by-passed. In the final version of *Cronos*, it is left unexplained as to why Aurora's parents are absent – del Toro cut about 30 minutes of the film that explained the parents' death in an accident. This allowed him to envisage the film more explicitly as 'a kind of love story between the granddaughter and the grandfather' (Wood 2006a: 30), emphasizing the sense of a continuum across time and generations. Comparable age/youth relationships exist between the boys and Dr Casares (also played by Federico Luppi) in *The Devil's Backbone*, between Ofelia and the Faun in *Pan's Labyrinth*, between Hellboy and Professor Broom in the *Hellboy* films and arguably between Whistler and Blade in *Blade II*. The absence of the father (it is perhaps telling that del Toro's father was kidnapped in Mexico whilst he was filming *Mimic*) not only underpins del Toro's concern with time and chronology but also allows his child figures a freedom to become central to the narrative, omnipresent and empowered. Aurora is present throughout the film and becomes a parent/carer figure to her grandfather, virtually confiscating the dangerous Cronos device from him and hiding it in her teddy bear, handing him a towel when he appears back at the house in his almost comically undead state and hiding him from the light in her toy box. These moments from the film prefigure the function of Ofelia in *Pan's Labyrinth* as the pivotal hero/quest figure, confronting the law of the father in the Francoesque figure of her stepfather Vidal. The relationship between the aged and the young is thus a recurrent and symbolic trope. Del Toro's aesthetic is informed by a set of creative interactions between a series of what appear to be binaries which he duly collapses: old and new world culture (Europe/the Americas), established art forms – film, fiction, painting – and newer formations such as comic and graphic fiction and video games, auteur film-making and pop-culture blockbusters. More broadly this could be read as a melancholic acknowledgement of decay which is spliced with a resilient belief in rebirth, since effectively Jesús dies so Aurora may live.

Cronos is perhaps del Toro's most personal film. It is the only one set wholly in Mexico and draws implicitly on his experience of childhood as well as the culture and politics of his home country. Arguably, the film's darkly comic representation of a dance with death draws from powerfully embedded Mexican traditions, not just the Day of the Dead but also the sardonic work of comic/grotesque artists such as José Guadalupe Posada. Its cast of characters, seemingly dislocated in time or place, tangential or 'foreign' to their immediate surroundings, reflects something of his own outsider tendencies and establishes a psychological template that he will return to again and again in later work. Jesús Gris's antique shop is itself redolent of del Toro's own mania for collecting, storing and using references to the past. *Cronos* is a repository of multiple and diverse references to filmic and cultural remnants that come to haunt the film like so many celluloid ghosts. Del Toro has described the film as 'an exploded view of my brain' (Criterion DVD), and in this respect it (and Gris's bazaar) prefigures the 'man cave' that del Toro has constructed as an annexe to his current house in Los Angeles which del Toro appropriately calls 'a modern cabinet of curiosities', since for him curiosity is the lifeblood of imagination. The film is densely woven with references, however fleeting or random, to del Toro's personal experience of the medium, not exactly in the form of homage, but more as elements in an alchemical process that acknowledges origins and influences but transforms them into something new. He began scripting *Cronos* when he was 21, finally shooting it seven years later, and it inaugurates many of the questions he was to explore further in other films: the nature of the horror genre, the relationship between fantasy and the real, the interface between time, existence, trauma and death, and crucially the centrality of childhood to human essence and experience.

Do be afraid of the dark

On the level of film text the theatrical version of *Mimic* resembles a kind of Frankenstein's monster, assembled out of a diverse range of disparate elements and lacking a coherent rationale. Del Toro has described in detail, both in interview and on the director's commentary supplied with the Director's Cut DVD (2011), the ways in which he felt 'raped' by the highly invasive processes of Hollywood production. Clearly this is a far from unusual circumstance for a young and inexperienced director in which to find themselves, but it is significant that del Toro has felt the need to reclaim the film and produce a version that, in his terms, is much closer to his original concept. This assertion of the auteur's rights has resulted in the erasure of all evidence of those producer invasions which manifested themselves particularly in the work of the second unit, which del Toro saw as introducing cheap thrills into an otherwise carefully crafted genre piece. Even the Director's Cut bears only relative resemblance to the original concept as scripted by del Toro and Matt Greenberg. However, as an act of reclamation the Director's Cut of *Mimic* seems relatively light-touch, unlike that of a film such as *Blade Runner* (1982) with which it has common concerns regarding the problematic differentiation between human and replicant. Scott's later 1991 version of his film famously offers a radical reworking of the ending which del Toro avoids in his new version of *Mimic*, despite having a more ambiguous and anxious conclusion available to him, included as an extra on the Director's Cut DVD. It is ironically appropriate in a film such as *Mimic*, so centrally concerned with birth and reproduction, that the production processes should themselves involve such difficult gestation. *Mimic* exists in del Toro's oeuvre as a kind of Shelley-ian 'hideous progeny' (1831 edition of *Frankenstein*), although the troubled production and release history of Scott's *Blade Runner* eclipses the problems del Toro experienced. These are explored in depth in Paul Sammon's *Future Noir: The Making of Blade Runner* which was published in the same year as *Mimic*'s appearance (1997). One revised version of the screenplay (available on Daily Script, http://www.dailyscript.com/scripts/*Mimic*_production.html) offers a much darker vision, particularly in its dystopian ending which unequivocally suggests the emergence and infiltration of the insects into the mainstream of urban New York, and therefore human, life:

> Commuters move to and fro, moving up and down and in and out of the illuminated areas of the station.
>
> In the crush of onlookers is one deadpan face- a *MIMIC*, hugging the shadows, waiting for its moment!
>
> We PAN 180 degrees to the other side of the platform- there, briefly glimpsed is ANOTHER, and ANOTHER.
>
> We TILT down to the throng below.
>
> > SUSAN
> > (barely audible)
> > They've come up …
>
> The electrified VOICE of the train ANNOUNCER suddenly FADES UP, telling of departures and delays-
>
> We raise above Susan's head-
>
> > TRAIN ANNOUNCER
> > The 11:16 local to Poughkeepsie, boarding now, Track 32- the 7:20
> >
> > > Connecticut local, making connections to South Norwalk-
>
> DOWN ANGLE
>
> -culminating in an OVERHEAD VIEW of the main terminal.
>
> The movement continues. But from here, the people are dots, their importance no greater than that of a colony of ants.

This 'original' ending makes far more explicit del Toro's concept of the film as a meditation on human arrogance and the concomitant likelihood that humanity is no longer God's favoured species. In this respect, *Mimic* continues the long-held tradition of science-fiction films which incorporate environmental concerns into their narrative. Pat Brereton attests to the durability of ecological angst within the genre, stating that '[o]f all the conventional Hollywood genres, science-fiction appears to be the most amenable to ecological and social questions – both formally and within a historical context' not least because 'by its very nature, science-fiction film, in some way or other, calls into question the world we live in and accept as absolute' (2005: 141). This inclusion of ecological issues into science-fiction film is typified by the eco paranoia of 1970s films such as *Soylent Green* (1973) and *Logan's Run* (1976) and the out and out eco-awareness message of *Silent Running* (1972). Certainly, one can take a reading of *Mimic*, with its inclusion of the Prometheus trope, where entomologist Susan Tyler genetically engineers a breed of cockroaches with catastrophic consequences, as containing an eco-centric thematic. However, del Toro's alchemist drive to blend genres, influences and motifs results in a far more hybrid film (echoed by the inclusion of genetic splicing as a key narrative device). In addition to being an eco-aware science-fiction film with a strong horror component, the film is heavily influenced by B-monster-movie sensibilities and slasher-movie notes. Brereton argues that the received readings of North American B-movies or Creature Features that have routinely settled on the presence of Cold War paranoia as the figurative presence have historically underestimated what he sees as notable fears over ecological concerns over mass-urbanization and the proliferation of consumer culture. He states:

> Academic critics affirmed that these science fiction films [such as *It Came From Beneath the Waves* (1955), *Them* (1954) and *Invasion of the Body Snatchers* (1956)] covertly addressed these historic tensions, reflecting the hysterical fears of a communist take-over by the 'enemy within' which swept across America in the 1950s. What is less appreciated, however, is that for the first time these films also helped construct a universal, if nascent, eco-consciousness through the growing understanding and fear of (non) natural forces and their resulting threats to human nature. (142)

Del Toro is a self-confessed enthusiast of the Creature Feature and something of a curator of B-movie paraphernalia, and it is no surprise to see such influences on his first Hollywood production with the genetically engineered human-sized sewer insect serving as a potent motif for human vulnerability in packed and decaying urban environments (Landis 2011). Whereas the 1950s Creature Feature blended together Cold War paranoia with eco-crisis fears, del Toro's take on the monster movie incorporates pre-millennial tensions, and in this respect it can be situated as part of an upsurge of 1990s science fiction which infuses fin-de-siècle angst with ecological trauma. Powerful images, such as Neo waking from a simulated reality to find himself in a battery field fuelling an artificial life-force in *The Matrix* (1999), the arrival of a genetically re-spawned Tyrannosaurus Rex to terrify the grandchildren of an arrogant showman in *Jurassic Park* (1993) and the creeping presence of bizarre monkey symbols on the streets of Baltimore in *12 Monkeys* (1995), combine to illustrate a popular trend in 1990s science-fiction film which mined both pre-millennial anxieties and ecological catastrophes in a marked renaissance in intelligent prophetic science fiction (other notable examples can be seen in *Dark City* (1998), *Gattaca* (1997) and *Strange Days* (1995)). *Mimic* is dismissed by del Toro himself as a minor work in his own oeuvre and is clearly less fully realized than the films mentioned above. However, the sheer brutality of the narrative and the ways in which it borrows from another B-movie phenomenon, the slasher genre, is noteworthy.

In many ways *Mimic* defies the conventions of the slasher genre as outlined (if at times with certain contestations) by the likes of Vera Dika, Carol Clover and Robin Wood. For instance, its science-fictional premise separates it from genre-defining films such as *Halloween* (1978), *Friday the 13th* (1980) and genre deconstructions such as the *Scream* movies (1996–2011). In addition, the slasher film narrative often relies upon a lone human killer, in direct contrast to the swarm of mutant insects which provide the key threat to their progenitors in *Mimic*, although, arguably the most effective and unsettling scenes involve one key creature stalking its prey in what can easily be seen as, at the very least, a nod to the slasher motif. The film's urban mythical core structure works in the context of the slasher genre and provides some of its more gripping moments. Mikel J. Koven provides a convincing argument that the slasher movie is at its core a visualization of the oral urban legend and that the narratological studies of the genre have often underestimated the correlation between the two. He states '[t]he slasher film, like the oral urban legends which these films so closely resemble, may be seen to share one final similarity, that of *affect*' (2003). Just as the urban legend seeks to draw the listener into the complicit suspension of disbelief that somehow, somewhere the terror tale could have taken place, the slasher film's gore aesthetic asks for the viewer to become the grossed-out spectator, to play along with the notion that what splatters on the screen is viscerally authentic. Del Toro brings a strong gore aesthetic to *Mimic*, in contrast to the well-worn dictum that less is more when it comes to engendering fear within an audience. Morris Dickstein asserts that '[t]he best horror films avoid overwhelming us with gore and violence, which can easily turn comical when overdone, or be pointlessly punishing to the audience' (1984: 61). Del Toro provides an alternative aesthetic principle to this, which is evident in *Mimic's* most brutal moments; he has stated, 'I'm tired of hearing that the best horror movies are the ones that don't show the monster. I love these movies! Representing fear physically in the movie is a celebration of my kind of film' (Contreras 2010: 61).

One of the key interconnections that Koven identifies between urban legends and slasher movies is the narrative structure which unfolds; he cites Daniel Barnes's articulation of the 'four movement structure' which underpins urban legends, a movement of 'Interdiction, Violation, Consequence, and Attempted Escape'. As Koven explains, the interdiction phase is often sub-textual and this phase is 'then violated, and the consequences are outlined. These stories then conclude with the protagonists' escape, sometimes successful, sometimes not, from the consequences of violating the interdiction' (2003).

This directly relates to the structure of *Mimic*: Tyler and her husband Peter Mann ignore all of the Promethean warnings, and interfere with nature with colossal consequences; the rest of the narrative involves them trying to both escape and rectify their violation of nature. On another level, the central mythology of the film, that of a dangerous breed of creatures reproducing in the New York City sewer system, draws from urban legend itself. Not least is the resilient myth of giant albino alligators in the New York City sewers which is an oral Creature Feature in itself (Coleman 1996; Brunvand 1981). Indeed, this legend produced its own film version in Lewis Teague's B-movie *Alligator* (1980), and it is perhaps worth noting that sewers feature as breeding and stalking grounds in the influential creature feature *Them!* (1954). Of course, this writer is aware of *Mimic's* smörgåsbord of cinematic and cultural influences, intertextual references and thematic drawing from Greek myth to forgotten B-movies, but this is *entirely* the point in relation to del Toro's alchemic process. In this instance, *Mimic's* central motif of a hybrid breed of creature, a new species manipulated and reinvented, is almost comically appropriate for a film-maker whose commitment to genre cinema is at once reverential and historically informed and yet entirely modern. In this respect, del Toro's intertextual strategies and hybrid cinema place him firmly alongside his contemporaries (such as Quentin Tarantino) as a product of the baby boomer generation (led by Steven Spielberg and George Lucas) who so enthusiastically re-invigorated B-movie genre work in the 1970s and 1980s. However, his formations of the genre have some striking dissimilarities to the adventures portrayed by the likes of Spielberg.

Perhaps the most striking scene in *Mimic* which illustrates del Toro's tonal disparity to Spielberg depicts Ricky (James Costa) and Davis (Javon Barnwell), two street kids who earn money by trawling the subway system in search of insect and pupae samples for Tyler. In an extraordinary scene they come across one of the giant *Mimic* creatures and are brutally and mercilessly killed. In many ways, the scene is very much like the conventional horror/science-fiction death scene in the mould of the *Alien* franchise. What makes the scene so unusual is the slaying of the children in a way entirely different from Hollywood conventions. The scene is striking on a number of levels. The children themselves exhibit many of the character traits associated with the 'streetwise' children typified by Spielbergian cinema. For instance, they are children out of their depth, forced for a time to explore a dangerous world without reliable adult supervision (a recurrent trope in Spielberg's films, not least in his take on the monster movie in *Jurassic Park* and *The Lost World* (1997)). One of the pleasures of Spielberg's films, though, is the way in which the children survive the bildungsromanian adventure through a combination of bravery and ingenuity (as in *E.T: The Extra Terrestrial* (1983)), the collective power of friendship (as in *Hook* (1991)) or the release of parental instincts (as in *Indiana Jones and the Temple of Doom* (1984)). The vicious, nihilistic fate of Ricky and Davis and the unsentimental meaninglessness of their deaths is in direct contrast to the Spielbergian child journey. Of course, children perish in films such as *Schindler's List* (1993) to huge emotional effect, such as when the girl in the red coat is seen dead by Oscar Schindler; however, this is a key turning point in the narrative and the emotional impact of the moment changes Oscar forever, again in direct contrast to the child deaths in *Mimic* which simply act as a signifier of the newfound violent potency of the creature. In an interview, del Toro has referenced this alternative view of child danger, stating:

> It is something that I really take very seriously when I make the movies. I feel that there is so much more danger in showing kids in a movie about giant dinosaurs and claiming that the dinosaurs won't eat them. In reality they would…for me my childhood was the most the most brutal and frightening period of my

life ... Horror is an extension of the fairytale and in fairytales ogres and wolves ate children and I think that it goes to the roots of storytelling to have children as vulnerable. (Wood 2006b: 36)

This scene, alongside the dystopian premise where thousands of children have perished before the narrative begins, provides a dangerous and brutal world where children are very much in mortal danger. John O. Thompson provides an insight into the taboo nature of child death in film and the narratalogical functions of this, following on André Bazin's writing on film. He cites Bazin's assurance that adults invest in children a nostalgic revisitation of our own memories of childhood, filtered through an adult formation of the world and in doing so see children as loaded symbols rather than characters per se, '[w] e are thus seeking to contemplate ourselves within them: ourselves plus the innocence, awkwardness and the naiveté we lost. This kind of cinema moves us, but aren't we in fact just feeling sorry for ourselves?' (Thompson 2000: 209). Del Toro's recurrent references to his own childhood and the brutal scenes which he witnessed would suggest that innocence and naiveté is something he does not relate to or long to recapture and is mirrored in the sobering reality of the death of children in *Mimic*. Thompson draws attention to the function that child death can have to the narrative trajectory of a film. For instance, he recalls *Gone with the Wind* (1939), where Scarlett and Rhett's daughter is killed in a riding accident as providing a pivot in the narrative (Thompson: 212). We would also add that the *killing* of children in film can act as an agent of character formation, in that it can illustrate the nature of the *killer*. In David Cronenberg's *A History of Violence* (2005) an anonymous young girl killed in the opening moments of the film serves no narrative function as such, but does serve a character function in that the brutality of her killer (who will stalk the main protagonist) is coldly apparent. In this sense, the girl in the red coat in *Schindler's List* functions in both ways outlined above, illustrating the abhorrent nature of the fascist regiments commanded by Amon Goeth and the pivotal moment when Schindler decides to intervene. What is key to all these examples is that the children who perish serve a function, but remain either anonymous or uncharacterized to any significant degree, serving as, what Thompson calls 'people functions'. What then of poor Ricky and Davis in *Mimic*? Certainly, they illustrate the bloodthirsty and callous nature of the beast and arguably the non-maternal aspect of Tyler who encourages them to go out on their potentially dangerous (and at least unsavoury) quests. They clearly provide a limited narrative function in that they reveal further the extent to which the new breed of creature has infested the denizens of New York;

however, these children are characterized, differentiated from one another (both physically and verbally), resembling young heroes from children's adventure movies, yet their death is uncharacteristically unsentimental. Furthermore, the similarities between their death scene and scenes of horror in slasher movies makes a spectacle (a guilty pleasure) out of their deaths, deliberately sidestepping the treatment of child mortality in much mainstream cinema.

The splicing together of genre conventions (the streetwise kid, the vicious stalker) and the commitment to presenting these in unfamiliar ways (the streetwise kid *killed* by the vicious stalker) further illustrates the controlled and creative chaos of del Toro's methodology and this extends to the landscape he creates in *Mimic*. The familiar depiction of a future noir, an urban dystopia in which darkness and rain envelope the characters, is hinted at in *Mimic* by the representation of New York as a bleak metropolis threatened initially by a devastating plague that kills the city's children and later by rapidly evolving creatures that are on the verge of becoming monstrous replications of the human. This is no cleaned-up New York of the 1990s (in fact *Mimic* was filmed in Toronto), but one in which the main character, entomologist Tyler, can light-heartedly share a joke with an audience about the city's inhabitants' familiarity with cockroaches, the initial cause of Strickler's disease which in the film's prologue is the cause of child death. (Strickler's syndrome does in fact exist as a genetic disorder affecting bodily tissue.) New York here is more Gotham noir than *Sex and the City* (1998–2004), and del Toro has acknowledged that his version of the city is a figurative fantasy which 'does not bear any resemblance to the real New York' (Wood 2006b: 36).

Perhaps more than any other cinematic city, New York has provided a startlingly malleable backdrop ranging from the utopian pleasure-dome of *On the Town* (1949) to the corrupt nightmare of *Taxi Driver* (1976). Murray Pomerance captures the mythic and malleable nature of New York on screen which so many film-makers have been drawn to, stating, 'New York is an eidolon, surely – an image which is possessed of a phantasmatic, apparitional, haunting quality, and that rests out of history as a mark of aspiration, memory and direct experience' (2007: 4). The New York of *Mimic* draws from the long science-fictional tradition of utilizing the geographical tension of co-existent underground and overground worlds (established in H.G. Wells's *The Time Machine* (1895)) as well as the New York-based slasher movies of the early 1980s (such as William Friedkin's *Cruising* (1980) and Daniel Petrie's *Fort Apache: The Bronx* (1982)). Like many 1900s films which depict contamination, AIDS metaphors resonate and are perhaps italicized by the setting of the film in New York and having the main protagonist work for the Centre for Disease Control (CDC). The inclusion of a virus which seems to target specific sections of the population (not least children) attains heightened significance in a city which saw the rise of the HIV epidemic in the previous decade.

The result gives much of the film an apocalyptic and nihilistic feel (admittedly demolished by the Hollywoodized ending), where New York's rehabilitation is reversed and the darkened, rain-soaked environment is only briefly lit when we see a preacher fall to his death under a neon cross and 'Jesus Saves' sign. Wheeler Winston Dixon recognizes the potency of the New York night landscape:

> New York at night is more nocturnal than any other place onscreen. The deserted streets become invitations to danger and violence; the depopulated spaces of the night are the mirror image of the bustling metropolis in the day time. New York has a hold on our imagination because it is so compact, so violent ... Mutability is the key characteristic of New York at night, a realm transformed the absence of illumination'. (2007: 243)

In a film inherently concerned with mutability, New York itself becomes a character whose sharp contrasts, violence and sacrifices add to the overall bleakness of the film. Considering this, the denouement in which Tyler is confirmed to be pregnant has a perhaps unintentionally absurd quality to it; in a world with such a terrible past and such devastating potential, who on earth would want to bring a child into existence?

Indeed, this debate about procreation and responsibility runs throughout the film. In an earlier scene, the film's central couple discuss pregnancy and their difficulties with procreation surrounded by a museum exhibit of dinosaur bones as a perhaps none-too-subtle indication of potential human obsolescence and sterility, a theme developed further in Alfonso Cuarón's later dystopian noir, *Children of Men* (2006). This dislocation of human existence and divine favour is further emphasized through the prevalence of del Toro's trademark visual signature of broken and distorted religious iconography, beginning with the neon Jesus Saves sign which illuminates the exterior of what purports to be a church but is in fact a diseased sweatshop out of which the dark angel insects emerge like sinister priestly figures swathed in black. This revisits a key moment early in *Cronos* where a cockroach emerges from the saintly statue that also contains the alchemist's gold bug. Like the plastic-wrapped statues and icons in *Mimic*'s disused and misused church, the religious statues in *Cronos* have become disassociated from any original significance, but are now part of a ruthless capitalist's search for immortality that does not involve God or Heaven, a situation where man is indeed attempting to become God (Hansen 2011).

Ridley Scott's earlier film *Alien* (1979) emerges as a more developed intertextual presence in *Mimic*, as recognized by many of the film's reviewers and critics; indeed the film seems itself to be a *Mimic* of a film del Toro publicly adores (Landis 2011). Further exploration of these links opens up del Toro's film to a rich set of interpretative possibilities; in fact, the entire *Alien* franchise is relevant to the development of del Toro's oeuvre which is hardly surprising given its longevity and involvement of directors whom del Toro particularly admires: James Cameron, David Fincher (whose *Se7en* (1995) provided inspiration for *Mimic*'s titles) and Jean-Pierre Jeunet. Del Toro has spoken of the relationship between *Mimic* and the *Alien* films in sometimes negative terms, seeing it as a result of studio interference: '[a]t the end of the day, with a cold head and a cool heart, I see they wanted to do *Alien* and I wanted to do *Mimic*, and so we ended up with *Alien-three-and-a-half*' (Wood 2006a: 44). However, it is certainly possible to construct a far more productive set of interactions that enrich any reading of del Toro's difficult child.

The splicing in *Alien* of science fiction, gothic fantasy, body horror and gender anxiety make it a richly rewarding intertext for directors of del Toro's generation. Scott's deconstructing and reconstructing of genre prefigure del Toro's own ongoing project to synthesize and evolve given film and literary types into new forms. Visual echoes of *Alien* occur within the first few minutes of *Mimic*. An early scene where Susan Tyler (Sorvino), dressed in what resembles a space suit, releases the cockroach-destroying Judas Breed in a womb-like subterranean space clearly references scenes in Scott's film where the crew of the Nostromo are exploring the hostile planet prior to the alien's attack on Kane. The hole through which Tyler emerges also echoes the vaginal spaces that permeate the visual landscape of *Alien*. These provide a visual underpinning of the film's anxiety about the female body and the mother/monstrous feminine in particular and prefigure *Mimic*'s own concern with motherhood and reproduction. Furthermore, del Toro includes a clear visual pun as the layered hive-like container that houses the Judas breed replicates in miniature the 'pod' from which the Nostromo crew emerge nappy-clad from their frozen slumber. In both situations, the image of scientifically clean 'birthing' is an ironic prelude to death and the creation of the monstrous. In the case of *Mimic* this is the first step towards the evolution of the Judas Breed into semi-human clones where

Tyler is, albeit unwittingly, acting as 'monstrous mother', not only in genetically manipulating the Judas Breed, but also introducing it into the very core of the city and therefore humanity. We are always made aware of the altruism underpinning her actions, the necessity to save the child population of New York which is made evident in the opening scenes. But this is always ironized by her own apparent incapacity to reproduce and the transgressive nature of her science. A later scene sees her in conversation a kind of scientific Father/God figure (Gates, played by F. Murray Abraham) who both upbraids her for playing God/Frankenstein and yet thanks her for saving his grandchildren. In this respect, Tyler's actions echo the myth of Pandora as a transgressive and disobedient female and the film is generally underpinned by an anxiety around the politics of gender. At surface level, the film appears enlightened in its choice of a cool-headed female scientist as a central protagonist. The casting of Sorvino is interesting here as previously she had played very contrasting roles as a prostitute and porn star in Woody Allen's *Mighty Aphrodite* (1995) and Marilyn Monroe in a TV miniseries, both earning her major awards. Sorvino's character is forced to confront her doubled identity as symbolic mother-figure and saviour to the children of New York and monstrous mother to the Judas Breed – she is a female Frankenstein whose 'sleep of reason' over genetic tampering gives birth to Goya-esque-winged monsters.

Further parallels between *Mimic* and *Alien* proliferate as the movie develops, from the female scientist as central protagonist, the tell-tale monster excretions, the P.O.V. shots as an alien tail swings menacingly behind a doomed character, the uterine and labyrinthine dark tunnels in which much of *Mimic* takes place, which echo the cargo ship Nostromo's ducts and passageways. Prevalent also are comparable thematic links – the interface of humanity, capitalism and the monstrous, the problematic construction of the family as well as gender issues and anxieties, particularly the use of the 'final girl' which Carol Clover sees as a key characteristic of slasher films of the 1970s and 1980s (1992). Most significant are the relative ways in which the two films explore issues of reproduction, gender and the interface between humanity and alterity. One of the most influential readings of *Alien* has been Barbara Creed's account of the film through the lens of Kristevan ideas on abjection. Creed describes Scott's film as:

> a complex representation of the monstrous-feminine in terms of the maternal figure as perceived within a patriarchal ideology. She is there in the text's scenarios of the primal scene, of birth and death; she is there in her many guises

as the treacherous mother, the oral sadistic mother, the mother as primordial abyss ... and finally she is there in the chameleon figure of the alien, the monster as fetish-object of and for the mother. (1989: 73)

Creed's application of the Kristevan abject seems particularly appropriate to any discussion of the way del Toro explores issues of reproduction and alterity in *Mimic*. For example, a key aspect of Creed's work is the foregrounding of Kristeva's association of the abject with bodily wastes – shit, blood, urine and pus. This connects, in Creed's terms, with the way in which the horror film foregrounds these signs of the abject in order to satisfy an audience's desire for 'perverse pleasure (confronting sickening, horrific images, being filled with terror/desire for the undifferentiated) but also a desire, having taken pleasure in perversity, to throw up, throw out, eject the abject (from the safety of the spectator's seat)' (Creed 1989: 67). In line with other del Toro films, particularly *Pan's Labyrinth*, *Mimic* foregrounds such images of abjection as a key element in the representation of human and other, of 'I' and 'not I'. Del Toro characteristically uses this for comic as well as horrific purposes when the CDC investigator Josh (played by a laconic, dude-ish Josh Brolin) discovers massive piles of non-human excrement – here from the unproduced screenplay:

JOSH
Peter ...

PETER
Yeah ... ?

JOSH
There's some weird shit here.

PETER
Weird shit ... ?

JOSH
Take a look.

Leonard shines his flashlight ahead.

Revealed, quite literally, is a world of shit.

LARGE FECES scattered everywhere: on the floor, hanging
sausage-like from the ceiling. One can almost taste the
stench of old ammonia.
Peter puts on a rubber glove, inspects one of the fecal stalactites.

JOSH
> Fecal matter, unknown origin: weird
> shit.
> (Beat) Whatever it is, it's not human.

In the theatrical release Josh jokes here about his desire to be a dentist. Del Toro uses the physical signs of abjection continually through the film to underpin the convergence of human and insect other. At one point, whilst trapped like insects in the old subway car, the protagonists smear themselves with fluid from the insect's body in order not to be attacked, a new take on an old cinematic trope for disguising oneself as the 'other' or enemy. Tyler advises her partner, the rather obviously named Mann, not to sweat in order not to be recognized, which does indeed save his life at one point. Leonard's (Charles S. Dutton) seeping blood becomes an image of repulsion for the audience as well as a continual lure for the insects and finally leads to his demise. Crucially, the film repeatedly blurs or collapses the Kristevan sense of the border between selfhood and abjection. Creed suggests that 'a concept of a border is central to the construction of the monstrous in the horror film; that which crosses or threatens to cross the border is abject' (1989: 67). There is a clear relevance here to the Judas Breed who threaten to cross the border between species (a commonplace in other comparable films such as *The Fly* (1986), and the aforementioned 1950s B-movies). But it could be argued that the crossing of borders takes place in gendered/generic terms in both *Alien* and *Mimic*. *Alien* has been much discussed, along with other comparable films of the late 1970s and 1980s, for its apparent challenging of filmic gender norms – the action-hero 'final girl' taking the place of conventional male functions. The final scene of *Alien* became familiar territory for debate about the film's feminist credentials, as Ripley is cast very clearly in a sexualized/maternal/mythic role as a woman in the final scenes. In del Toro's later film there seems to be a similar confirming of Tyler's role as a good mother as opposed to a bad scientist, given the revelation that she is pregnant (although she does not know until the final moment). But this very Hollywood ending, with the expulsion of the abject insect Other involving characteristic del Toro elemental forces, especially fire and water, and the restoring of order, was not del Toro's original intention. His intended final image was of an alternative, broken family that did not conform to WASP normalities – the apparently autistic child Chuy, and the couple, with Tyler's husband originally conceived as African American. Hence the conventional human reproductive unit, the family, is here made abject and other in social, racial and psychological terms.

5

Trauma – Childhood – History: *The Devil's Backbone* and *Pan's Labyrinth*

This chapter considers del Toro's political horror films: *The Devil's Backbone* (*El Espinazo del Diablo*) and *Pan's Labyrinth* (*El Laberinto del Fauno*). If *Cronos* brought an alchemic touch to the vampire movie, re-politicizing the genre in its representation of US–Mexico economic and political relations, *The Devil's Backbone* and *Pan's Labyrinth* rework key Gothic motifs and fairy-tale conventions in order to explore the traumas of childhood and war, central concerns in del Toro's Spanish-language films that make use of the Civil War setting.

The Lost Boys: *The Devil's Backbone*

> Everybody in the movie is a ghost; the entire movie is about dead people. We are in 2001 and these are people who lived in 1939. Therefore the colours are amber, white, black and earth most of the time, and then we have the green and the very, very pale green-blue for night scenes. For the exteriors, we used a filter called chocolate that made all the light outside gold or amber. Everything in the movie was meant to look like a Goya painting because he is one of the great painters of war. (del Toro in Archibald 2001)

Cronos sees del Toro re-situating the vampire narrative as a metaphor for international dependencies which mirror border tensions between the U.S. and Mexico. *The Devil's Backbone* and *Pan's Labyrinth* similarly rework Gothic conventions and fairy-tale tropes act as vehicles for the exploration of trauma, childhood and war. Karen Lury has written extensively about the ways in which filmmakers have explored this kind of subject matter and her comments on Chris Marker's *La Jetée* (1962) could well be applied to del Toro's films: 'It demonstrates how the child figure and childhood enable film-makers to radically and creatively re-tell the past and, in particular, inform us about the strangeness, the murky ambiguities and the real trauma of war. It does this primarily because it is a film about memory' (Lury 2010: 112). Del Toro's use of the child's perspective in these films is a central element in their deconstruction and reconstruction of historical trauma, providing a disruptively individual and questioning approach to events. Rather like the Mexican del Toro approaching recent Spanish history, the child figure is both inside and outside the historical context, given their often invisible status within recorded history. As commentators have observed (Labanyi, Martin and Ortega 2012: 253), there is a certain irony in a contemporary Mexican director focusing so strongly in two major projects on the period of the Spanish Civil War (although the original setting for *The Devil's Backbone* was to be the Mexican Revolution). Both films were the result of transnational Spanish/Mexican and US production, but the Almodóvar brothers, Pedro and Augustin, were particularly instrumental in the backing of *The Devil's Backbone* through their production company El Deseo. The child figure is a key constituent of the 'dissonant elements' that Labanyi *et al.* see as key to del Toro's process of 'deconstruction rather than reconstruction of the past' (2012: 253). As a result del Toro's characteristically disruptive melding of diverse genres, filmic, literary and visual, creates a productively radical, dissonant and interrogative approach to the cinematic representation of history.

Both *The Devil's Backbone* and *Pan's Labyrinth* interrogate the historical and cultural trauma of the Spanish Civil War through the perceptions and reactions of child figures who are both victims of war and its impact (they are or become orphans) but also potential agents of resistance. Rather like the new Spanish democracy that followed on from Franco's death, they are inevitably shaped and damaged by the traumas of the past but may also represent future possibilities for change or transcendence. In del Toro's films this is an uncertain possibility: neither of his two Civil War films can offer the reassurance of an easy resolution or firm closure given that we obviously know the historical outcomes, but both suggest ongoing political and historical issues that are hitherto unresolved. Both seem to confirm the persistence of ghostly hauntological traces within the national psyche, as do the many Spanish films that have attempted to enact a similarly allegorical interrogation, from Erice's *Spirit of the Beehive* (1973) and Saura's *Cria Cruervos* (1975) (both of which appeared during the last years of Franco's rule) to Armendáriz's *Secrets of the Heart* (*Secretos del Corazón*) (1997), Cuerda's *Butterfly's Tongue* (*La lengua de las Mariposas*) (1999) and Bayona's *The Orphanage* (*El Orfanato*) (2007), amongst many others. All these films place children at their centre in ways that emphasize close links between personal trauma and unresolved family and/or national politics. Del Toro's involvement as Executive Producer in *The Orphanage* indicates his desire to foster new directing talent – this was the director J.A. Bayona's first major release – but also evinces his desire to revisit the ideas and implications of his own Spanish-language oeuvre in other contexts. The contemporary setting of *The Orphanage* underlines the persistent nature of an historical trauma that still shapes and undermines individual lives, and by implication, the national consciousness.

The centrality of children in these films is significant in a number of ways. As the above quotation from Lury's study implies, the child's point of view offers filmmakers a perspective on war and trauma that enables the emergence of the strange or uncanny – that which has been repressed or denied – given that children are often invisible in official accounts of war. Ellen Brinks has suggested that Freud's sense of children's susceptibility to the uncanny is key to del Toro's films: '*The Devil's Backbone* generates a number of recurrent uncanny images that efface the difference between death and life/survival, similar to the operations of traumatic memory' (2004: 296). The film's use of the child's point of view, both in its subject matter and also in its camerawork and cinematography by Guillermo Navarro, stresses the importance of child subjectivity and allows for this blurring of the borderlines between past and present, voice and silence, being and non-being. Ellen Brinks develops her point further by stressing the film's use of children as a kind of portal into other ways of seeing:

> By mediating the Spanish Civil War through the vocabulary of childhood trauma, however, the film also insists that this past is more 'accessible' through children's eyes, as beings whose underdeveloped egos (and weaker defence mechanisms) render them particularly susceptible and sensitive both to traumatic memory's durability and intrusiveness and to what escapes rational comprehension or control. It is with them that the audience is asked to identify. (2004: 294)

What is particularly distinctive about del Toro's treatment of trauma in these films is the characteristic use he makes of narrative genres that at first sight seem surprising in this context, yet which hinge crucially upon trauma and its effects. *The Devil's Backbone* is a vehicle for del Toro's fascination for the Gothic romance in its multiple guises and *Pan's Labyrinth* largely bases its narrative on a radical reworking of fairy tale and classic fiction from the literature of childhood. These familiar modes are echoed, re-configured and transformed in del Toro's narrative and aesthetic melting pot in a process that makes the audience think afresh about the form and the subject matter.

Despite the orphanage setting and the absence of actual families in the film (unlike Erice's *Spirit of the Beehive*), *The Devil's Backbone* is a version of Gothic family drama played out in an isolated setting that incongruously combines a recognizably Gothic locale, the castle-like orphanage with its darkly mysterious cellars and corridors, and the blinding heat of the shadowless plain which resembles the desert-like setting of a Spaghetti Western. Del Toro has highlighted this merging of contrasted genres that characterizes much of his film-making, suggesting that:

> the two main influences in the movie are the Gothic works of the Italian maestro of horror Mario Bava and the Western, especially classic Westerns like *The Searchers* or those directed by Anthony Mann, which are deconstructions of the Western, in a way. What I wanted to do was to meld these two things, seemingly so different, together. So I kept referring to the movie as my Mario Bava Western. (Chung 2002: 30)

The orphanage is characterized by shadowy, unknowable yet paradoxically domestic spaces (the kitchen is an important locale in the film) that conceal traces, secrets and ghosts of the past, emerging particularly from the seemingly unfathomable amber spaces of the watery cistern. In contrast, the desiccated and barren emptiness of the plain suggests the isolation of the orphanage and also the unforgiving brutality of the external world. Such physical contrasts serve some of the central dynamics in the film, between external reality and the unconscious, reason and superstition, violence and the imagination, child and adult worlds. These don't operate as simple binaries – the film is too nuanced for that – rather as aspects of an ongoing dialectic in del Toro's films about what it means to be human, especially a child, in extreme situations such as war. Just as the Spanish Civil War pitted family against family and even split families, so the film uses a central narrative template of a dysfunctional pseudo-familial structure – an orphanage – overseen by an adult 'family' that replicates aspects of Greek tragedy and Gothic perversity. In an interview with Mark Kermode in *The Guardian*, del Toro describes *The Devil's Backbone* as a 'microcosm of the Spanish Civil War … In trying to do that, I chose that war because it was a household war. People that shared beds, shared dining tables and shared lives ultimately killed each other' (Kermode 2006b). The impotent 'father' Casares is in love with the matriarchal Carmen, who in turn is locked in a quasi-incestuous relationship with the 'prince without a kingdom', her 'son' Jacinto. This set of incomplete relationships is also informed by questions of class (Casares and Carmen are bourgeois Republican intellectuals, Jacinto cast as working class and proto-fascist, although he does not overtly express political allegiances).

This personal as well as political site of conflict has its origins in the director's own experience of childhood, and del Toro has spoken in director's DVD commentaries and in interviews with Kimberly Chun and Jason Wood amongst others of the autobiographical elements of the film. These include specific paranormal incidents he experienced as a child, such as the Santi-esque sighs of a 'disembodied voice floating about half a foot from my face' (Chun 2002: 29), which was seemingly the spirit of his dead uncle – a major influence on del Toro's love for horror films (Chun 2002: 29). Other repetitions from del Toro's childhood which feature in the film included the design of the classroom which replicated those in the Jesuit school he attended and Carlos and Jaime's excursion for water, which originated from similar unnerving experiences in del Toro's grandmother's house. The characteristically oblique but significant use of religious imagery – as punishment three of the boys have to carry a heavy life-size figure of Christ on the cross into the central courtyard of the orphanage as a kind of Catholic window-dressing – suggests the relentless burden of the religion even for those who, like del Toro, rejected it early on in their lives. Del Toro has suggested on a number of occasions that his grandmother's fervent religious beliefs drew him towards atheism at an early age. Hence trauma and memory, personal, familial, political, become a rich source of inspiration for the film that del Toro describes as his 'first movie' (Chun 2002: 29).

Steven Bruhm has suggested that one of the functions of contemporary Gothic is to respond to 'social and national traumas … [that] have rendered humans unable to tell any kind of complete story about them. Thus the Gothic renders them in fits and starts, ghostly appearances and far-fetched fantasies, all attempting to reveal traumatic contradictions of the collective past that cannot be spoken' (Bruhm 2002: 271–2). *The Devil's Backbone* is replete with Gothic images that evoke the physical and mental landscape of traumas emanating from repressed memories of the Spanish Civil War. The film's visual palette develops the kind of vivid, almost lurid tonalities redolent of Mario Brava's Italian Gothic movies, with their neo-expressionist use of colour and violent contrasts. These filmic and visual characteristics are in turn underpinned in the narrative by the intertextual presence of Gothic fiction. The classic Gothic novel's dealings with internal family conflict, including incest and sexual repression, hidden secrets, unnatural, ghostly or monstrous manifestations, provide del Toro with a rich vocabulary of ideas and images which he then transforms and translates into the apparently incongruous context of the last days of the Spanish Civil War. The surprising appropriateness of Gothic conventions in this historical and political context can be linked to recent readings of modern Spanish culture that construct it as a 'ghost story'. As Jo Labanyi suggests, 'ghosts are the return of the repressed of history – that is, the mark of an all-too-real historical trauma which has been erased from conscious memory but which makes its presence felt through its ghostly traces' (2002: 6). Hence the ghostly child Santi is not only the orphan murdered by Jacinto (represented also as a kind of self-murder in the narrative) but is also an embodiment of the thousands who disappeared during the war itself and Franco's dictatorship – those buried in mass graves that are only recently being located. By extension Santi may also stand for every child lost in the chaos of modern war. As Enrique Ajuria Ibarra has pointed out, two objects central to the film's narrative, the ghost and the bomb, are invested with 'particular significance and meaning to fill a persistent historical gap in Spain. The ghost and the bomb voice the silenced horrors of the Spanish Civil War' (2012: 57).

Del Toro's interest in the English Gothic tradition from both eighteenth and nineteenth centuries is strongly evident throughout his work as director, producer and screen-writer. This even extends to producing his own neo-Gothic printed texts. As part of the background material supporting his contribution as producer and screen-writer for the 2010 chiller *Don't Be Afraid of the Dark*, del Toro published (with Christopher Golden and illustrator/director Troy Nixey) a pastiche of late nineteenth-century Gothic in the form of *Blackwood's Guide to Dangerous Fairies*, which purported to be the disturbing research diary of Emerson Blackwood, who makes a brief appearance at the beginning of the film. The book is replete with Gothic paraphernalia, including black edging to the paper and monstrous illustrations and images. In his director's commentary for *The Devil's Backbone*, del Toro explicitly references what was arguably the first Gothic novel, Horace Walpole's *The Castle of Otranto* (1764). He compares the melodramatic falling of the giant helmet which crushes Conrad, the weakling scion of the central family, in the novel's opening scene, with the landing of the bomb that sits in the central space of the orphanage and, by implication, the film itself. (The screenplay of *The Devil's Backbone* was developed by del Toro from an original story 'The Bomb' by Antonio Trashorras and David Muñoz and the original setting for the film was to be the Mexican Revolution. He changed the setting to Spain because 'Everything seemed to fit better'.) For the modern reader, Walpole's falling helmet may have its decidedly risible side, but the bomb in del Toro's film is deadly serious, although interestingly he inscribes it with a human dimension – the markings on the side make reference to his own address in Mexico and his and his wife's shared nicknames. This chimes with the way in which the bomb works as a kind of character in the action: other characters (Alma, Jaime, Carlos) talk about and to it anthropomorphically and one of the red streamers attached to it apparently becomes animate as it points the way for Carlos's search for the ghost Santi. *Bomba, ¿estás viva? Dime dónde está Santi* (Bomb, are you alive? Tell me where Santi is), asks Carlos. The bomb's association with Santi is reinforced by the fact that it dropped the night that he disappeared. As Ellen Brinks suggests:

> Like the helmet in *Otranto*, but more so, the bomb comes from and refers to an 'elsewhere', whose violence erupts into the boys' present and threatens the security of their future. *The Devil's Backbone's* premier scene thus underscores the film's gothic identification and raises an important question: why choose the gothic to remember and mediate a narrative of national, historical trauma? (2004: 292)

The bomb functions as a multiple signifier, a literal reminder of the presence of war even in this apparently isolated place (we see it dropping randomly from the bomb bay of a plane in a shot that has echoes of traditional black-and-white war movies and even Stanley Kubrick's 1964 black comedy *Dr Strangelove*) as well as an almost absurdly surreal phallic totem around which the narrative unfolds. It acts as a silent commentary on the arbitrary violence resulting from recurring human conflict, ticking inexorably even though it has apparently been 'defused' but cannot be moved. It's also a perhaps over-determined symbol of the hyper-masculinity embodied in Jacinto, the proto-fascist who finally enacts the explosive violence that the bomb itself fails to unleash in the orphanage, suggesting that the human is always more dangerous than the machine. As del Toro has said, '[a]s the movie progresses, you realize that the ones you have to fear are the living, not the dead' (Chun 2002: 31). The bomb also carries a symbolic payload of trauma as a signifier of the memory of war that can never fully be 'defused' or repressed, not only the 'silenced horrors of the Spanish Civil War' that have been supposedly 'dealt with' in Spanish political, historical and cultural memory, but also the spectre of ongoing twenty-first-century wars in which dead children are often the tragic but invisible collateral damage. As Brinks later argues, the Gothic's concern with the return of the repressed renders it a particularly appropriate narrative mode for the film, as it is 'a mode of symbolization that expressly seeks to explore what a culture prohibits, fears, or desires to the point of its repression, denial, or abjection' (Brinks 2004: 292).

In an alchemic combination that is symptomatic of del Toro's sometimes dizzying visual eclecticism (Maria Delgado has dubbed it 'comic-book-meets Goya') the other key literary inspiration for the film came from a very different genre from the high cultural matter of English Gothic fiction – the popular comic strip. Carlos Giménez's comic strip *Paracuellos*, the first series of which began in 1976 in the early stages of Spain's transition to democracy, deals with the artist's own traumatic experiences in the orphan homes (Hogares de Auxilio Social) established by the Franco regime after the Civil War, mainly for the children of Republicans killed during the conflict, and has been recognized as a significant text within its genre and beyond. As Carmen Moreno-Nuño Antonio suggests, '*Paracuellos* is part of the cultural production that tries to recover, through fiction, a collective (rather than historic) memory about the war, the post-war years, and the repression of the Franco regime, which had been ignored and silenced in Spain' (2009). Giménez collaborated with del Toro on aspects of storyboarding and design for the film, and a storyboard for this aforementioned scene involving Carlos and the bomb can be viewed on his website. (Giménez also designed the 'Pale Man' scene in *Pan's Labyrinth*.) By drawing on a popular cultural mode such as the comic book, del Toro not only reveals his great admiration for the form, which manifests itself in later films such as *Hellboy, Hellboy II* and *Blade II*, but also his willingness to meld and merge radically contrasted influences – from eighteenth-century Gothic fiction to twentieth-century graphic fiction. This splicing of film and comic book genres also stresses a key feature: the centrality of the child's experience; camera angles and movement mirror the children's perspective throughout, as do Giménez's storyboards and comic strips. As Karen Lury has noted: 'The structure, colour and composition of the comic strip are evident in both of del Toro's Spanish Civil War films' (2010: 114). These comic-strip techniques are employed from the outset – for example, in the scene where Carlos first sees the ghost, very early in the film. In a series of shots that seem to mimic the comic strip Carlos looks towards the archway where he sees the ghostly figure but is distracted by noise and looks away only to find the figure has vanished when he looks again.

In a discussion of the film's transnational credentials, Antonio Lázaro-Reboll has also emphasized the important role played by Giménez's personal experience in its creation:

> Giménez documents a reservoir of personal memories, having himself lived in one of these orphanages for several years. Giménez's collaboration extends from the casting of the children to the narrative, through the recreation of specific dialogues, episodes and themes reminiscent of *Paracuellos* (privation and suffering, fear and bullying, survival and solidarity), and to the *mise-en-scène*, in particular lighting, costume, props, and décor, which contributes to recreate the atmosphere of the Auxilio Social orphanages. Likewise, Giménez's aesthetic and rhetorical conventions are translated into other stylistic devices, for del Toro repeatedly draws links to the comic book syntax and grammar through framing and the position of the camera. (Lázaro-Reboll 2007: 48)

The trauma of lost and stolen childhoods that Giménez explores in *Paracuellos* gives the film its historical and cultural specificity which is underpinned by other cultural sources such as the Gothic and the classic literature of childhood, always an intertextual presence in del Toro's work. Del Toro's penchant for drawing on texts from the golden ages of English children's literature is evidenced by the persistent presence of Lewis Carroll's Alice books in *Pan's Labyrinth*. In *The Devil's Backbone* the reference point is perhaps more J.M. Barrie's tragic-comic *Peter Pan* story, with its 'lost boys', pervasive sense of childhoods that are forever missing or past, and children engaged with an ongoing battle with a dominant, unreadable and destructive adult world. For Del Toro, *The Devil's Backbone* is the boys' story – a companion piece to the female equivalent in the latter film. Interestingly, Barrie's classic story is used as a key intertext in Bayona's *The Orphanage*, which narrates a similar story of stolen childhoods. Just as the children in the orphanage represent the Spanish people, so the ghost Santi embodies both a traumatic past and a lost future – he is one of the disappeared, the 'desaparecidos' whose absent presence and lost childhood haunts not only Spanish and South American history but also the history of other ongoing sites of conflict, such as Northern Ireland and the Middle East.

The notion of haunting, of the return of the repressed as historical memory, encompasses another image used in *The Devil's Backbone* when defining spectrality. Del Toro characteristically uses a narrative framing device in the voice-overs that bookend *The Devil's Backbone* and that attempt to articulate the nature of a ghost and haunting. The reiterated voice-over, revealed at the end to be that of Dr Casares', talks of a ghost as 'an insect trapped in amber' which gives both visual and aural expression to a key aspect of trauma – the notion of repetition. Citing Freud, Enrique Ajuria Ibarra defines trauma as 'this persistent coming back of the unconscious to a site that has left a mark upon the subject; the unconscious attempts to develop an understanding of it, whilst the ego seeks to avoid it' (2012: 62). Roger Luckhurst has discussed the relationship between Gothic and trauma thus: 'Post-traumatic experience is intrinsically uncanny, finding cultural expression in ghostly visitations, prophetic dread, spooky coincidence or telepathic transfer ... ' (2008: 98). Santi repeatedly returns to the scene of his death, always attempting to draw his 'double' Carlos to the focus of his lost narrative, communicating mainly through sound rather than language. Carlos in turn acts as a messenger, a go-between negotiating real and other worlds in order to construct a narration of release (interestingly, his name echoes that of King Juan Carlos, Franco's chosen successor, who helped negotiate the transition from autocracy to democracy after the dictator's death). The older Jaime has attempted this through art (a hint here of Giménez's involvement and del Toro's own use of sketching as a source of imagination and inspiration) but will not share his responses, driven by the same kind of egotistical individualism that defines and destroys his 'double' Jacinto, until forced to by Carlos. Del Toro has talked about the film being constructed 'on a rhyme', which operates internally via the kind of doubling of characters and images noted by James Rose in his guide to the film, but which also permeates much of the director's corpus of work. His films 'rhyme' with each other to a greater or lesser extent, suggesting perhaps an uncanny return to repeated motifs and ideas that cannot be fully resolved.

Exploring the figure of the double in trauma narratives, Jacob Winnberg cites both Luckhurst and Cathy Caruth on the treatment of trauma in recent narrative. He notes Luckhurst's comment that recent trauma narratives in fiction have 'played around with narrative time, disrupting linearity, suspending logical causation, running out of temporal sequence, working backwards toward the inaugurating traumatic event, or playing with belated revelations that retrospectively rewrite narrative significance' (in Winnberg 2013: 233). Winnberg also relates this 'poetics of trauma' associated with narrative discontinuity to the figure of the double or doubling – another classic Gothic device. He cites Caruth's argument that trauma is always 'a double wound ... not available to consciousness until it imposes itself again repeatedly, in the nightmares and repetitive actions of the survivor' (233). These insights into narrative and trauma help locate and illuminate del Toro's narrative strategies in *The Devil's Backbone*, where a relatively sequential and realist central narrative is disrupted by framing sequences narrated by a ghost and the significant use of doubling, repetition and flashback. Indeed, the film begins with a bravura montage of flashbacks that narrate Santi's death in fragments. These strategies are taken further in *Pan's Labyrinth*, where the whole film is essentially a flashback as Ofelia apparently lies dying.

The question of release or liberation from trauma has been a crucial point of debate in analyses of del Toro's film. Some critics have focused more on the possibility of overcoming the traumatic legacy of war (Hardcastle 2005; Labanyi 2002) through the recognition of hauntological traces. Others, such as Lázaro-Reboll (2007), have suggested that this kind of approach may be in danger of becoming complicit with official state narratives of reconciliation and consensus that can produce what he terms 'collective amnesia' (2007: 47). Interestingly he is writing in 2007, the year of the passing of the Law of Historical Memory which officially condemned Francoism and inscribed state help in the tracing of lost victims of the Civil War and Franco's regime. Del Toro's film seems to resist notions of liberation and catharsis in that the haunting seems to continue beyond the end of the narrative, denying the possibility of any kind of full exorcism. Towards the end of the film we see Santi standing over the pool, despite the apparent achievement of his goal to pull Jacinto into his limbo state; the final voice in the film is Dr Casares, himself now a ghostly figure seen at a window, echoing the liminal spaces, in particular thresholds, where Santi is often seen as he shifts between worlds. In one of the film's many examples of uncanny repetition with slight variation, Casares repeats the opening lines of the film with one additional statement, 'A ghost, that is what I am', ironically affirming an identity he has lacked throughout the film. He observes the few remaining boys stagger in the unyielding sunlight on an unknown journey, possibly towards death.

The ambiguous nature of this ending where the trauma associated with the ghost figure is repeated, even doubled in the shots of Santi and Casares, is emphasized in a relevant example of del Toro's 'rhyming' between films. The actors playing Carlos and Jaime reappear in *Pan's Labyrinth* as young republican guerrillas fighting on after the end of the war who are killed in a raid by the fascist Vidal and his soldiers. The scene shows the Carlos figure dead and Jaime alive but badly wounded. Vidal aims his gun at him and the young guerrilla pushes it away. When Vidal realizes he is too badly wounded to be tortured into talking, his peremptorily shoots him through the hand, another rhyming image

which associates the resultant 'stigmata' with the martyred Christ. This is a kind
of reverse image of the monstrous Pale Man's hands, which feature prominently
in the imagery of *Pan's Labyrinth* and another example of the way in which
religious imagery pervades del Toro's film. Although the ending of *The Devil's
Backbone* depicts the boys successfully forming into a cohesive community that
can defeat Jacinto and avenge Santi, the implication here is that this is ultimately
an inadequate defence against the powerful political and military machinery
of state fascism. Characteristically in his movies, del Toro sets resistant and/or
alienated individuals in opposition to corporate or state power – a familiar aspect
of modernity that he treats in highly unusual ways. Although the double, even
triple endings of *Pan's Labyrinth* are more broadly positive, with some apparent
resolution of trauma, they exist paradoxically within a known historical context
that saw the triumph of Franco-ism and fascism in Spain. Despite Vidal's defeat
we know, of course, that what he represents is ultimately triumphant. The boys'
communal action in *The Devil's Backbone* also depicts their own reliance on
the kind of violence that has hitherto oppressed them. Their use of homemade
weapons with which to attack Jacinto recalls the pack behaviour in Golding's
Lord of the Flies (1954) and the casual violence of the boys in Buñuel's *Los
Olvidados*. As Ellen Brinks argues, '[w]hile this cathartic violence offers release,
a definite psychological pleasure for the boys and for the viewing audience,
the film avoids suggesting that it represents some kind of wish-fulfilment, a
fantasmatic republican triumph' (2004: 304). Del Toro has spoken of his careful
use of soundtrack music at this point in the film. In fact there is no climactic
scoring here, just the distant sound of the tango in order 'to avoid putting any
music there that would seem to approve the act of violence' (Chun 2002: 30).
Paul Julian Smith noted in his review for *Sight and Sound* (December 2001):

> [T]he conflict between brutal Spaniard Jacinto (played by matinee idol Eduardo
> Noriega, now hardened into a convincingly repellent macho) and kindly Casares
> (Luppi) is played out through their choice of music: the traditional Spanish
> songs of Imperio Argentina (Spanish collaborator with the Nazis) or the tangos
> of Argentine national hero Carlos Gardel.

In the film's obsessive doubling, Jaime is constructed as a younger potential
version of Jacinto. In the first shot we see of them they are closely juxtaposed
and Jacinto is ironically hammering a pole into the ground that has an uncanny
resemblance to the ones with which he is finally attacked by the boys. Jaime's
release from this particular trap of repetition is one of the more optimistic of

the film's outcomes. His trauma of guilt and repression is overcome by a kind of Freudian talking cure where Carlos acts as an intermediary.

The film's title places at its centre an image of the traumatized human body that particularly disturbs our sense of what childhood and, by implication, humanity can embody. If in Western culture we have traditionally projected onto childhood images of future hope and optimism, of innocence and purity, then the sick or dying child, the unborn or malformed foetus represents a traumatic reversal, a seeming denial of such cultural givens. Del Toro's films after *Cronos* repeatedly make use of such images as a key aspect of the narrative arc. Hence the plot of *Mimic* revolves around the saving of children's lives from a deadly disease and the film opens with scenes of children dead or dying in a hospital ward; *Pan's Labyrinth's* opening and closing shots include the depiction of a child bleeding to death. In the opening flashback of *The Devil's Backbone* we see a bleeding child who, as the ghost Santi, haunts the orphanage. Furthermore the title, title sequence and key image of the film reference the foetuses preserved in the amber liquid that Dr Casares sells as an aphrodisiac in the village to support the orphanage. Del Toro has explained the origins of the titular phrase in the DVD extra accompanying the Blu-ray edition of the film. El Espinazo del Diablo is a mountain range located near Durango in Mexico with a traditional mythic significance as a battleground between God and the Devil, where the latter is left defeated on earth after the triumphant God disappears. Hence El Espinazo emerges as a metaphor for the persistent presence of evil on earth and, by implication, in humans. In a central scene Casares explains to Carlos that the foetuses preserved in amber liquid limbo are superstitiously believed by the villages to be a product of sin. Rather like the orphans themselves they are believed to be 'nobody's children', supposedly a physical manifestation of human transgression, although ironically the liquid is thought to be curative for a number of ills, including impotence. Hence the rationalist Casares, though scorning such irrational beliefs, still takes the liquid for his own erectile problems, which are contrasted with the hyper-virility of the proto-fascist Jacinto. Victoria Nelson reads the significance of the foetuses through the lens of medieval alchemy, an approach that emphasizes the idea of personal and physical entrapment but that also stresses the ways in which ideas of alchemical transformation are undermined:

> [T]he foetus in a glass jar – an image the references alchemy's famous homunculus, a microcosmic 'little man', transformed within the alchemical retort in to a bringer of new life and possibilities – is the iconic opening image of *The Devil's Backbone*. As in *Cronos*, here the crucible imprisons rather than

transforms … Far from carrying hope of a new life, in the universe of this story
the dead babies are equivalent to … the lost souls, adults as well as children,
trapped in the orphanage … 'I think that's what the world does to kids, he said
to an Australian interviewer, 'You are born into your family jar, and you grow
into the shape of it, and the rest of your life you are limping like a motherfucker'.
(Nelson 2012: 229–230)

The uncanny, ghostly foetuses rhyme visually and thematically with the
traumatized body of Santi – another child preserved in the amniotic amber fluid of
time. The body horror associated with the foetuses (Carlos escapes from the room
as soon as possible, having refused some of the amber liquid) also references the
deforming impact of war and fascism on humanity and in particular children. In
this context the children are both the damaged detritus of war and Spain itself. The
film utilizes instances of body trauma throughout – children's bodies in particular
are cut, maimed and murdered, culminating in the climatic and explosive scenes
with which the film ends, foreshadowed by Santi's prophetic warning, 'Many will
die', and the final image of damaged children stumbling away from the orphanage.
Other adult bodies are sites of trauma or damage – notably Carmen's amputated
leg and Casares's sexual impotence (he is only able to exert power after his death).
Del Toro also exploits the irony that the outwardly most 'beautiful' body, that of
the superficially handsome Jacinto, is in fact the most deformed of all. In some
ways the film is an account of his tragedy, as he is another 'nobody's child' with
only a ghostly blurred photo of his parents to define his identity. Horror's obsessive
concern with the body is a critical commonplace but interestingly in *The Devil's
Backbone* the central obsession seems to be with wholeness. As del Toro says in
the opening quote above, all the characters are ghosts, and one of the ways in
which this is manifested is in their incompleteness, either physical, emotional
or psychological. Anna Powell has noted that '[h]orror film obsessively returns
to the trope of wholeness, its consequent graphic disintegration and its possible
renewal' (2006: 88). In *The Devil's Backbone* wholeness of a kind is re-established
by the communal actions of the children, but this is depicted with considerable
ambiguity and trauma endures beyond the boundaries of the narrative.

Ofelia's adventures underground(s)

Like *The Devil's Backbone*, *Pan's Labyrinth* is also heavily influenced by Spanish
cinematic traditions, particularly in its representation of Spanish history and the

concomitant issues of trauma, historical memory and political resistance. The film provides a stark and often disturbing representation of war alongside fantastic elements that parallel and blend with the violent realities of Franco's 'clean new Spain' as described by the film's fascist military. Once again Erice's *Spirit of the Beehive* provides del Toro with a powerful narrative template – a central girl figure who develops an imaginative space in response to the traumatic personal and political contexts that surround her, shaped by the dominant realities of the period after the end of the Civil War (Erice's film is set in 1940, four years earlier than *Pan's Labyrinth*). It is as though del Toro wants to tell the stories that are necessarily silenced or occluded in Erice's film, which was still subject to the dead hand of Francoism. For example, the single anonymous resistance fighter encountered by Ana in a brief, silent but, for her, profoundly disturbing relationship is extensively developed into the forest-dwelling guerrillas in *Pan's Labyrinth* who are drawn in some detail and whose final triumph over the fascist Vidal in claiming and naming his son offers a proleptic vision of a future democratic Spain post-Franco. The ultimately traumatized Ana, who ends Erice's film asserting an uncertain identity, becomes the older and assertively active Ofelia. The similarly named Ana in Saura's *Cría Cuervos* (1976) (played again by the wide-eyed Ana Torrent) is another filmic forerunner of Ofelia who attempts acts of rebellion against oppressive members of her family but is ultimately powerless – the film ends with her meekly going to school. In her persistent acts of resistance and disobedience Ofelia contradicts the image of female passivity and victimization implied in the literary connotations of her name and negotiates a path through the threatening trials of both real and fantastic worlds. The differences between the two films extend also into their visual and cinematographic qualities. Erice's film is characterized by a minimalist and austerely repressed aesthetic, shot in long, still sequences that are drained of colour and that evoke the apparently bleak emptiness of the lives portrayed. In contrast, *Pan's Labyrinth* revels in its use of distinctive colour palettes consisting of cool, dark blues and rich crimsons and golds that distinguish the different worlds that the film inhabits – fascist militarism, the forest and the realm of the fantastic. Although these are initially coded (for example, blue associated with the coldly inhuman Vidal and his brutal ideology) the film increasing blurs the distinctions between palettes in order to avoid overly simplistic binarism. The fantasy world of the labyrinth, from which the ambivalent and potentially sinister figure of the Faun emerges like some archaic figure frozen in time and nature, is also cast in blue, albeit with a green tinge appropriate to the natural world. In contrast to the deliberately static camerawork of the Erice, with its prevailing sense of an environment frozen in time and emotionally arrested, *Pan's Labyrinth* is shot by Guillermo Navarro with a restless fluidity that matches the questing and questioning nature of the central child figure. The camera twists and turns, continually moving above and around the characters. It acts as a witness to horror – early in the film we experience head-on the brutal summary 'execution' of a father and son by Vidal – and as an endorsement of the child's vision as it follows and traces the movements of Ofelia. Indeed, the film is permeated by images of sight and seeing, beginning with an almost Hitchcockian shot in the opening frame narrative that descends into Ofelia's eye and an early sequence in the 'main' narrative where Ofelia places a stone eye back into the totemic figure at the edge of the forest, thus releasing the fantastic, in the metamorphic shape of the insect, into the real. Paul Julian Smith (2006) has noted the echo here of an uncanny school-room scene in Erice's film, where Ana places the eyes on a mannequin figure, implying the child's capacity for seeing that which lies beyond the myopic vision of the adult. Erice depicts his shy, almost silent character struggling to move away from the physical and ideological confines of home, school and village. In doing so she internalizes the figure of the monstrous Other, Frankenstein's creature, which she has seen in a village showing of Whale's film, as an imaginative correlative for her own feelings. Del Toro's character, older and more confident, has the crucial benefit of imaginative fiction – we first see her tracing the outline of an Alice-type figure in her book as she travels with her sceptical mother – which provides her with an ongoing and evolving conceptual framework for her own experiences that transcends and transforms the real.

Another comparable Spanish film that employs fairy tale/mythic motifs in order to depict a transformation from dictatorship to democracy is Manuel Gutiérrez Aragón's *El Corazón del Bosque* (*Heart of the Forest* (1979)). The film depicts the conflict between the Resistance and the Civil Guards in 1942 and draws on many symbolic referents to portray the conflict as a mythic battle for heart of Spain. The film also draws upon fairy tale in order to invoke this struggle, and many familiar motifs are present. For example, food is used to suggest symbolically transformation and the formation of bonds; songs contain clues used to complete a journey; and a labyrinth is found in the depths of the forest. Like *Pan's Labyrinth*, Aragón's film creates a narrative where, as John Hopewell suggests, 'myth and ideology lend sense to an otherwise chaotic and valueless world' (1986: 174). Stranded in a traumatic world which makes little sense to her and where her continued safety is at risk, Ofelia gains access to a transformative world in which fantasy acts both as an escape and also as a means of transcendence. The ability to move between worlds does not solely offer an escape, though; it also begins to unify the two into a more consistent whole. She has the ability to flee from the realm of reality to fantasy, but perhaps more importantly, she is able successfully (but not painlessly) to shift between the estate and the forest, between childhood and adulthood and between dictatorship to democracy and in doing so gains a fuller perspective of the whole. The dialogic relation between the discourses of literary fairy tale and historic referents draws attention to the prominence of images and tropes in socio-political mythmaking. Gillian Rose refers to the ways in which language, images and symbolic referents dictate meaning 'and a particular knowledge about the world which shapes how the world is understood and how things are done in it' (2007: 136). Intertextual strategies which meld together loaded images of fascism and fairy-tale tropes deconstruct the fact/fiction dichotomy and suggest fantasy as a means of reading historical trauma. Isabel Santaolalla has identified the role of the forest as a motif symbolizing amongst other things an 'alternative to dictatorial oppression' (1999: 323). In another film by Carlos Saura, *The Hunt* (*La Caza* (1991)), a day of hunting rabbits acts as a motif of national conflict. During one particularly violent scene in *Pan's Labyrinth*, a starving father and son are caught hunting rabbits and killed by Vidal who assumes that they are part of the resistance. Vidal and his companions are depicted eating the rabbits in the next scene. This illustrates the unchecked brutality of Vidal's rule and employs the image of the rabbits as a symbol of rural Spain devoured by totalitarianism, drawing from existing cinema to tackle the Civil War and its legacies. In *Cría Cuervos* Saura uses another codified discourse for a film that was made right at the very end of the Franco era. Here the subject matter is a dysfunctional family headed by a patriarchal dictatorial and womanizing military figure who dies in the arms of his mistress at the beginning of the film. His oppressed wife, a talented pianist played by Geraldine Chaplin, is already dead of a painful cancer before the film begins and returns as a longed-for figure in the imagination of one of her three daughters, Ana. As Charles Derry suggests, she is representative of a 'Spain defeated and killed by Franco in the Civil War' (2009: 321). The film's shifts in time between a politically transitional mid-1970s, a later time (the 1990s) when the child Ana has grown up and a more distant personal and political past suggested by jumbled photographs that begin the film and with which the mute grandmother is obsessed. Here masculinity is associated with a rigid and emotionally barren fascism that has silenced women or made them invisible, although in both Erice's and Saura's films it is a female child who attempts to articulate, albeit haltingly, some resistance to a male hegemony. Del Toro develops this gender binarism further in both *The Devil's Backbone* and *Pan's Labyrinth*, both of which have female characters who attempt to exert agency.

The representation of Spain is dominated by a persistent traumatic duality and del Toro returns in *Pan' Labyrinth* to his interest in doubling and split identity, as Ofelia and her mother find themselves in a world deeply torn by factions. This is accentuated by the underworld, the alternate space where the conventions of the 'real' world are contrasted and revealed as fragile and often destructive constructs. Although it may seem the narrative takes place in two (increasingly interconnected) worlds, one real and one fantastic, another dual environment can be seen: the world of the estate and the forest. The estate, controlled by Captain Vidal and his Falangist forces, is ruled by fear and a fascistic insistence on order, rules, systems and control. This is symbolized by the pervasive presence of time-pieces, locks, keys – characteristic mechanical paraphernalia for a del Toro film – as well as uniformed soldiers who respond as automata to Vidal's orders. The forest is inhabited by the Resistance forces, a world symbolized by the organic and archaic, where the apparent timelessness of the forest is itself in resistance to the temporal rigidity enforced by Captain Vidal. This is powerfully visualized in the film by the transformation of the mill in which Vidal situates his headquarters. Victoria Nelson suggests that '[t]he mill's ancient cog-and-wheels innards, visible in the room where Captain Vidal is camped, are co-equal with the mechanism of the watch that he obsessively repairs, cleans, and rewinds, endlessly resuscitating it from mechanical death' (2012: 228). As Margaret Yolcom (2008) also notes, the mill has had its original purpose as a supplier of fundamental communal needs, the literal bread of life, perverted – the mill wheels lie abandoned at the rear of Vidal's study replaced by the wheels and cogs of his father's watch, symbolizing a relentless burden from the past to which even Vidal is subject. The mill's function as a source of life and sustenance is paralleled in its status as a generic fairy-tale setting, as del Toro emphasizes that we not only need bread (which arrives at one point in the film as a 'gift' from Franco's fascist regime) but also the psychological, emotional and cultural nourishment provided by stories and the creative imagination. The mill also carries a number of important Spanish cultural referents, from the windmills of Cervantes's *Don Quixote* to Velasquez, whose painting *Old Woman Cooking Eggs* (c. 1618) is evoked in the film's scenes of interior domestic life as Mercedes and the other women prepare food for Vidal. The masculine/ feminine binary that is constructed here and elsewhere serves to extend the film's exploration of duality into gender politics. For del Toro 'fascism is definitely a male concern and a boy's game' (Kermode 2006a: 24). Interestingly, the fascist Vidal, although brutal and vicious throughout, is shown also to be burdened by an oppressive masculinity and patriarchy that originates in the memory of his dead father, whose watch is such an obsessive object of attention for him. There are again echoes here of Erice's film as the father's pocket watch is found on the dead body of the guerrilla befriended by Ana, his daughter. Del Toro implies that Vidal's obsessive narcissism (we often see him gazing in the mirror) has its traumatized, self-destructive edge through a brief scene where Vidal appears to mime slitting his own throat whilst shaving. Hence, although he is cast as the villainous step-parent of classic fairy tale, Vidal enacts a more complex set of behavioural characteristics including a thoroughly perverse eroticism or homoeroticism as he lovingly handles his instruments of torture and talks of becoming intimate with his victims. Here, as in the figure of Jacinto in *The Devil's Backbone*, the externally handsome male body apparently exuding an uncomplicated, univocal masculinity is shown to be conflicted, perverse and potentially self-destructive. These powerful male bodies are violated or 'cut' by those deemed to be insignificant or invisible, notably women in the form of Mercedes in *Pan's Labyrinth* and the children in *The Devil's Backbone*. From their apparent positions of male supremacy they become both monstrous and other, akin to figures of horror such as the Pale Man, weighed down by a will to power that is expressed in the gold that contributes to Jacinto's drowning and the name of the father which Vidal evokes in a futile gesture before his death. He asks Mercedes to tell his son the time of his death in an uncanny repetition of the narrative surrounding his father's supposed heroic demise, recounted earlier by another officer – a tale, initially rejected by Vidal, in which his father fell in battle, breaking the mechanism so that his son will remember the moment of his death.

Time, along with sight, is a crucial metaphoric resource in *Pan's Labyrinth*. Indeed, all del Toro's films could be described as meditations on time and mortality – a theme initiated by his first major film, *Cronos*. In *Pan's Labyrinth* how a character constructs the meaning of time becomes a litmus test for selfhood. The fairy-tale story of Princess Moanna which is narrated at the beginning of the film tells of her father's pledge to wait to the end of time for her return, enacting the classic fairy-tale dislocation of temporal rigidity and sequentiality, but also offering a different vision of the paternal, one that is loving and loyal. From 'Once upon a time' to 'happily ever after' time is a pervasive element of stories for and about children and time is often subverted, reshaped and made inconsistent. Juliet Dusinberre states, 'Some writers for children realise[d] that the rejection of the moral and improving tale implied a rejection of cause and consequence, of destinies worked out in time. [They] recognised that the idea of a sequence was foreign to the young child' (1999: 151).

This view of time is in sharp contrast with the fascistic insistence upon rigid and recorded linear systems which can be seen in Vidal's near-obsession with maintaining correct and regimented temporal structures and his neurotic connection to the paternal watch, which as the homophone suggests exerts a continual watch or gaze over him. Here del Toro draws together elements of fascist propaganda concerning temporal 'efficiency' with the symbolic uses of timepieces in fairy-tale narratives, including of course a key intertext for del Toro's films such as Carroll's *Alice's Adventures in Wonderland*. Vidal seeks to control time in order to control his and others' destiny, attempting to 'fix' time and maintain the order and power of patriarchal law. Images of time and control are echoed in the hour-glass that Ofelia has to obey in her second quest, the encounter with that other monstrous vision of patriarchy, the Pale Man, as though the repressive temporal regime associated with Vidal has 'leaked' into the world of fantasy. Ofelia finds herself caught between the regimented here and now and the ancient world of the faun and the fantasy realm in which time moves slowly across aeons and can even be reversed – the nameless Faun visibly grows younger during the film and the viewer also witnesses time going backwards at the beginning of the film. This conversation between the ancient/mythic/historic and the present is a repeated trope in del Toro's oeuvre, recurring in his most recent film *Pacific Rim* in the battles between machine-led modernity and near-primordial monsters, the Kaiju. Ofelia finds herself caught in a critical moment in history and forced to make a decision between childhood reliance and adult independence which ironically sees her end the narrative as a perpetually young princess. Interestingly, Victoria Nelson finds a strong link here to the alchemic motif, suggesting that '[t]he prime alchemist in *Pan's Labyrinth* is none other than Ofelia, and most of the transformations in both worlds, material and supernatural, mirror her own moral development toward goodness' (2012: 230). Nelson uses the example of the transformation of the 'enchanted world' that takes place early in the film, as shown in the morphing of the stick-like insects into Rackham-esque fairies. Quoting del Toro's own description of it as 'a magical universe that's been left out in the rain too long', she suggests that '[t]hough mainstream audiences are quick to interpret this transformation as Ofelia's own make-believe fantasy, it also indicates that she has already gained the magical ability to change objects in her surroundings simply by focusing her awareness on them' (2012: 230).

Significantly, where films such as *El Corazón del Bosque* employ the adult male hero in its quest narrative, *Pan's Labyrinth* uses the female child. Children and particularly adolescents act as narrative agents in many fantasy narratives. *Pan's Labyrinth* is another text which uses fantasy as a means of commenting upon the troubled world of twentieth-century history. What is striking about the film is not the way in which the real and fantasy worlds are separate but interconnected by magical portals, but the way in which they are revealed as one chaotic yet interdependent environment. From the outset, where Ofelia sees a nymph in the outskirts of the forest, it is made clear that the fantasy world is not automatically an alternative to the strife of the real. Moreover, the fantasy world is a dangerous and terrifying place and the faun is by no means a benevolent guide; indeed he arguably entices Ofelia into danger and ultimately death and seeks to harm her newborn brother at the end of the narrative. Ofelia bears witness to a world in which death and conflict are impossible to escape and it is resilience rather than respite that keeps her alive for so long. Vicky Lebeau identifies a trend in cinema where the child acts as 'a figure through which to explore the legacy of war and genocide during the twentieth century' (2008: 141). She goes on to notice how such films are filled with 'painful iconography' where the child is a 'radically traumatised … participant in adult hostilities' (142). The opening montage which acts as a frame for the main narrative in a way that rhymes with the initial sequence of *The Devil's Backbone* reveals del Toro's take on this 'painful iconography'. After the production credits the film opens with a blank black screen over which the muted sound of a softly hummed lullaby can be heard along with a distant wind, joined by the sound of rapid breathing. The caption 'España 1944' (the lullaby an elegy for a lost nation?) is followed by nondiegetic material in the form of explanatory text setting the historical context for the film. Del Toro plays with viewer expectations here because instead of conventional military scenes or establishing shots of the Spanish landscape we see an indistinct dark screen, maybe rocks and stones. The shot then moves up to the apparently vertical form of a young girl lying horizontally on the ground with a bloodied hand outstretched in a position that references the crucifixion and stigmata of Christ. The camera spirals to show the girl in a horizontal position – accompanied by the continued humming of the lullaby supported by a simple rocking three-note musical accompaniment above, which can be heard by her continued rapid breathing. Her close-up face, filmed in a nocturnal grey-blue, fills the screen. It is at this very early point that there is a shift between reality and the fantastic as blood trickles back into the girl's nose as she apparently and impossibly returns to life. When this is complete the male voice-over begins with a classic fairy-tale opening 'A long time ago' in order to tell the story of Princess Moanna escaping into the 'real' world. When the Princess emerges into sunlight (seen as a brilliant blinding white light that fills the screen as the initial black had done) the first images of reality are of the remains of the village of Belchite near Zaragoza, the site of a key battle during the Civil War in 1937, the ruins of which have been left as a memorial. As the voice-over talks of the memory loss, sickness and pain that the fairy-tale princess experiences, so the empty shells of churches and buildings still standing appear but are somehow lost in the process of national forgetting that post-dated the war, a process that was beginning to be officially reversed as the film was released. The hollowed-out remnants of a Catholicism devalued by its complicity with violence and oppression rhymes with the passing references to defunct iconographies that occur throughout del Toro's earlier films. The sequence ends with a replay of the child in the car arriving at the place of trauma and transformation that del Toro used at the opening of *The Devil's Backbone*. In his DVD commentary, del Toro speaks of the problems he had with this opening which resolved once he had the image of the bleeding child and established the sense that the film is about a girl giving birth to herself 'the way she wanted to be'.

The juxtaposition and intersection of reality and fantasy often requires the use of non-fictional images and icons and this is also the case with *Pan's Labyrinth*. One of the most interesting and surprising of these is the way in which the appearance of the central child heroine of the film, Ofelia, mirrors that of Anne Frank, probably the most famous victim of twentieth-century wartime atrocities. The film is set in 1944, the year Anne and her family were taken from hiding in their house in Amsterdam by the Nazi SS – *Pan's Labyrinth* also contains other references to child victims of the Nazi death camps, most notably the pile of discarded children's shoes that Ofelia notices in the underground lair of the Pale Man monster. The striking facial resemblances in the film (even down to the parting of her hair) between the young actress who plays Ofelia, Ivana Baquero, and the famous remaining photographs of Anne Frank suggest that parallels can be drawn between the two. Both girls are on the verge of puberty, both create imaginative and creative spaces for themselves in order to deal with the traumatic experience of oppression and entrapment. Like Anne, Ofelia 'writes' herself into existence as an autonomous being, employing the realm of the imagination as a retreat from trauma as well as a space for self-actualization and resistance. There are, of course, major differences between the texts. Anne Frank's *Diary* explores her growing awareness of sexuality and her excitement at the changes taking place in her body; in contrast, Ofelia apparently remains in a state of pre-pubescent innocence, despite the traumatic images of the female body she encounters during her mother's difficult pregnancy, particularly when she nearly miscarries. *Pan's Labyrinth* is saturated with visual images that evoke the female body and in particular the womb (imagery that is used in a very different context in *Pacific Rim).* From the fig tree that models the shape of fallopian tubes, the visceral womb-like subterranean world that Ofelia explores as one of her trials and the womb-encased foetus that fills the screen as she 'talks' to her as yet unborn brother, del Toro repeatedly visualizes a process of birthing which is traumatic and painful. This, of course, relates paradoxically directly to the traumatic birth of a 'clean new Spain' that is the product of the fascist Francoist project which, in the context of the film, results in the death of two of the three main female characters. In this respect the film does construct a binarism based on gender – fascism grows from a sterile masculinity that does not 'see' women, who are barely visible and largely expendable constructs employed in the furthering of male hegemony in state and church. This is precisely the point that Mercedes makes in her confrontation with Vidal. Women are possibly seen as complicit with this. Ofelia's mother Carmen dies as a result of her compliance and there are vulture-like women in attendance at Vidal's banquet. However, set against this is the powerful narrative of Ofelia/Moanna giving birth to herself, which apparently ends in death for both figures but which also tells a crucial story of disobedience and the painful creation of autonomous selfhood.

As in the case of Carlos in *The Devil's Backbone*, Ofelia's trauma is also heightened by the fact as she is orphaned in the course of the film. Three potential substitute parental figures emerge in the form of Vidal, The Faun and Mercedes (the housekeeper and Resistance spy). However, each potential surrogate wants to take a part of Ofelia's innocence and power and ultimately place her in danger. Mercedes is far more of a caring figure than the callous Vidal or the manipulative Faun; however, her interest in Ofelia is not entirely benevolent and she too seems aware that in recruiting the child, she gains a stake in future power struggles. Rather than acting as a gentle protectress, a white witch of the forest illuminated by a maternal glow, Mercedes is fully aware that Ofelia faces a perilous trial of fire.

In comparison to the passivity of Ofelia's birth mother, she is therefore a more complex and layered representation of femininity. Ofelia's eventual sacrifice tips the balance of power and Mercedes becomes the custodian of Vidal's infant son and in doing so symbolically takes control of the future of Spain, but only after a fierce and hard fought battle where children perish. Del Toro is never afraid to implicate children in the potentially deadly politics of power. In this respect, the spectacle of children in the midst of trauma is itself scrutinized and the perverse nature of such spectacle revealed. What is constant in all of the potential paths that Ofelia is presented with is the inevitability of change and the pain that comes with this. Rosemary Jackson explores the ways in which metamorphosis reveals an unconscious desire/fear dichotomy and the impossibility and implausibility of escape:

> Metamorphosis in the modern fantastic suggests that the slipping of object into subject is no longer redemptive and that 'perverse' images of mutilation/ horror/monstrosity have taken precedence over superhuman or magical transformations of the subject. (1981: 82)

This is fundamental to *Pan's Labyrinth*. It is on the one hand a war narrative in which the child bears witness to the traumatic historic event and on the other a fantasy which draws on existing children's literature as vehicle for symbolic discourse. However, neither world takes precedence and as a result Ofelia dies between the two, torn apart by the apparent failure of each to work in symbiosis without destruction. Whereas (as the Faun explains) the fantasy dimension is ancient and slow moving, the swift and violent revolutions of the twentieth century make it impossible for both to coexist without violent consequences and Ofelia is a victim of these ultimately incompatible spheres, exiting at the end of the film and returning 'home' to her parents who are rulers of the fantasy realm.

Del Toro has spoken of the film's relationship to events of the early twenty-first century, in particular the attacks in New York on September 11th 2001. *The Devil's Backbone* first played at the Toronto Film Festival two days before and *Pan's Labyrinth* appeared exactly five years later, mirroring the difference between the periods of the two films, 1939 and 1944, respectively. The unresolved ambiguity of the earlier film is echoed in the latter as the disconnection between these incompatible spheres endures. Ofelia's apotheosis in the world of Princess Moanna has echoes of *The Wizard of Oz* (the camera dwells on Ofelia's shoes which echo Dorothy's silver ones that have given her magical power only here the shoes have become blood-red, stained perhaps by realities of war and death) and Hans Christian Anderson's 'Little Match Girl', with its sentimental vision of the poor and neglected finding their due place in heaven. The reassuring closure that is offered by these classics of children's literature is denied here – the cathedral-like scene of Ofelia's rebirth is saturated the gold and crimson of Catholic iconography, with her father (addressed as padre and featuring a vignette by Federico Luppi, latterly the ghostly Dr Casares of *The Devil's Backbone*) and mother ensconced on hugely elevated throne-like pinnacles. The effect is to widen the void that separates reality and imagination, rendering the final blooming of the fragile white flower of peace watched by the perennial del Toro insect all the more uncertain, dependent as it is on the human willingness to look beyond. The film's alchemic melding of modes is a direct invitation for the viewer to look beyond the aesthetic conventions and assumptions that underlie film genre as well as, crucially, to resist and challenge blind allegiance to repressive ideologies.

6

Gothic Superheroes: *Blade II, Hellboy* and *Hellboy II: The Golden Army*

Writing in 2002, the year in which *Blade II* appeared, John Whately summarized the then relation of the Gothic to high culture in the following way:

> The status of the Gothic text has then always been problematic; a form that is denied yet is influential, an exterior force impinging on a centre that rejects it, yet this centre uses many recognizably Gothic energies and imaginative potentials. (91)

The explosion in Gothic studies in the years since has blunted some of this apparent marginality as Gothic texts have become more and more respectably mainstream in terms of academic study. This chapter concerns del Toro's foray into the hugely popular superhero film genre, where in *Blade II* and his *Hellboy* films he fuses the superhero narrative with his own Gothic and comic sensibilities, with the results being characteristically accented and queer alternatives to the mainstream blockbusters.

Hollywood cinema has from its formative years embraced the vampire and monstrous Gothic figures and as a result horror has established itself as a key, if not always respected, genre in the film canon. This has been thoroughly documented in the work of critics such as David Skal, particularly in his *Hollywood Gothic* (2004). The vampire has also appealed to the auteur tradition in films that carry much greater cultural capital. Werner Herzog's remake of Murnau's *Nosferatu* (1979) was a particularly notable example in which the vampire becomes a vehicle for exploring a pervasive existential isolation and malaise in a film whose painterly aesthetic makes continual reference to the conventions of German expressionism and Romantic art. Films from the 1990s such as Neil Jordan's *Interview with a Vampire* (1994) and Francis Ford Coppola's *Bram Stoker's Dracula* (1992) continue this kind of thematic focus, bridging the gap between art-house sensibilities and Hollywood production values (both films had major stars in leading roles as well as luxuriously expensive design).

These later films cast the vampire in ways that evoke past representations but also introduce new elements; the vampire is eroticized and attractive yet sexually ambiguous, stylishly languid yet dangerous, a sometimes sympathetically drawn male wanderer through time, evoking the figure of the lone Romantic hero/anti-hero. This process of re-casting of the vampire as a sympathetic figure which began with these films continued in the twenty-first century with the hugely successful *Twilight* franchise which is aimed squarely at a teenage female audience, and in critically acclaimed TV shows such as *Buffy the Vampire Slayer* and HBO's *True Blood*. More generally, further shifts in the cultural and demographic location of horror took place around the millennium with the success of what has been dubbed 'quiet horror' with films such as Alejandro Amenábar's. *The Others* (2001) and M. Night Shyamalan's *The Sixth Sense* (1999).

Action vampires

Stephen Hantke sees this genre bending as part of a conscious demographic expansion of the genre away from cult consumption towards a mainstream audience. Hantke includes in this expansion 'the crossover of horror film into fantasy and action adventure, especially at the budgetary level of the summer blockbuster' (2010: xxi). The two *Blade* movies were clearly a product of this genre-busting evolution of the horror film into mainstream commercial cinema via the comic book. Interestingly, Hantke suggests that hardcore horror fans responded to this dilution of generic boundaries with a variety of strategies designed to keep the faith. These included a developing interest in foreign horror from sources beyond the US, such as the products of 'J' horror, and a renewed reverence for canonical films and directors from earlier eras. Hantke includes the two *Blade* movies in his discussion as examples of this commerce-led collapsing of the boundaries of horror and any discussion of del Toro's contribution to the franchise needs to take account of the multiple developments that were expanding the genre during this period. Other moves into the mainstream included so-called postmodern horror, most notably the *Scream* franchise, with its increasingly knowing and self-referential cinematic discourse. Another key development was the continued shift from, using Andrew Tudor's terms, 'secure' horror that offered reassuring narrative closure, usually embodied in the triumph of good over evil which the *Blade* franchise replicates, to 'paranoid' horror that offered little or no closure or certainty in reassuring moral outcomes (1989).

Hence the cinematic context into which *Blade II* emerges is one of considerable fluidity in which generic hybridity and boundary-crossing are increasingly common features.

The character of Blade as played by Wesley Snipes certainly offers a radically different reading of the vampire. His hybrid state – part human, part vampire (the latter kept in check by regular doses of anti-'thirst' serum which we see him injecting) – leads to a conflicted sense of identity that is more prevalent in the first of the two films. By *Blade II* he appears fully formed as a black avenger clothed in *Matrix*-like leather and wielding a range of technologically sophisticated weaponry as well as the samurai-inspired equipment that gives him his name. The doubled identity, technical hardware and often playful ambience, particularly in del Toro's film, reference the revamped *Batman* franchise which began with Tim Burton's 1989 film. Blade's duplicitous gizmo wizard Scud, possibly a kind of sexed-up, streetwise, joint-smoking version of Robin, accompanies one of Blade's entrances with the line 'The Dark Knight returns' in reference to Frank Miller's seminal graphic novel. *Blade II* revels in a kind of cyberpunk version of the caped crusader – his car is a vintage Dodge and Scud's workshop has a 'Scrapheap Challenge' feel to it as he creates formidable weapons out of what mostly look like spare parts. Like the *Batman* movies, *Blade II* acknowledges its comic book origins, but del Toro goes much further in creating a visual palette and pace that re-imagines the conventions of American comic book art through the lens of Japanese animated Anime in the service of a horror-led action film. The film does not dwell particularly on a version of the vampire as alienated being – indeed the relative paucity of screen dialogue renders character development seemingly minimal as the film depends largely on its breathless action-movie aesthetic of rapid visuals and pounding, eclectic soundtrack that mixes hip-hop and electronica. Indeed, David Goyer's original screenplay survives in the film in a stripped-down version that eschews any emotional and psychological complexity in order to sustain narrative pace; on their DVD commentary del Toro and producer Peter Frankfurt discuss somewhat gleefully the substantial cuts made to the original script at key points. Rather, the verbal emphasis is on significant one-liners that summarize situations or inaugurate conflict, such as Reinhardt's racist question to Blade, 'Can you blush?' This initiates an ongoing antagonism that is finally resolved in the fight between the two at the end of which Blade slices Reinhardt in two in a comic-ironic visual echoing of Blade's own bifurcated human/vampire selfhood – a moment which uncannily evokes the gladiatorial fight between Jesús and Angel at the end of *Cronos*, particularly since Ron Perlman plays both Angel and Reinhardt. That moment in *Blade II* is fairly typical of the film's enthusiastic engagement with B-movie as well as comic book conventions, carried off with a characteristic del Toro energy and inventiveness that offers intelligent pastiche but avoids parody. Interestingly, the film is framed by linked opening and closing establishing shots that attempt to evoke an external 'realist' setting for what is a narrative that is otherwise set in a shadowy, subterranean, claustrophobic world. A shot of a Prague tram is mirrored at the end by shots of a London bus as Blade pursues Rush, a vampire he spared at the beginning of the film, into the seedier depths of Soho. Rush is played by one of Spain's most famous comedian/actors, Santiago Segura, another aspect of the film's transnational approach to a well-established Hollywood genre, and the film ends with an almost throwaway comic moment as Rush, expecting girls in a strip joint, is confronted by the avenging Blade.

The film's hybridity and eclecticism can be traced in the number of intertextual visual and verbal references it makes to other movies. The Reapers' grotesquely projectile 'bite' visually alludes to Ridley Scott's *Alien* which had already been a key influence on del Toro's *Mimic*. The warrior-like 'bloodpack' references not only *The Magnificent Seven* (1960) and *The Dirty Dozen* (1967) but also James Cameron's *Aliens* (1986) (one unsympathetic reviewer suggested *Blade II* held much the same relationship to *Blade* as *Aliens* did to *Alien* – an all-action, muscle-bound retake of the more nuanced original). *The Matrix* provides a visual blueprint, not only in the mix of martial arts, black leather and cool shades, but also in scenes such as the early release of Abraham Whistler from his foetus-like stasis in an artificial womb. Blade's cutting of the umbilical cords that link his body to the vampire world echoes Neo's disconnection from the Matrix and rebirth into reality. It's also a characteristically perverse del Toro 'birthing' scene in which the son (Blade) facilitates the birth of the father-figure (appropriately named after the biblical father Abraham). Del Toro's film depicts the vampire world, with its obsessive pursuit of power and purity, as a corollary to late twentieth-century corporate America, visualized in the external ultra-modernity of its headquarters, replete with high-tech security, mood-lit lobbies and corridors and modernist sculptures (this idea would later be developed much more fully in the novels of *The Strain* trilogy). By contrast its interior suggests an ancient, neo-medieval civilization, ruled over by the red-cloaked Damaskinos whose marbled head recalls the skull-like visage of Murnau's Nosferatu, reprised in Herzog's film by Klaus Kinski. Elsewhere the screenplay oddly includes some lines from *The Godfather* (1972) and reworks one of the most notable scenes from Coppola's

Apocalypse Now (1979) as Wesley Snipes emerges revivified from a large pool of blood in a manner that strongly evokes Martin Sheen's most famous moment in that film. Finally, one of the more unlikely filmic intertexts is Derek Jarman's *Caravaggio* (1986), a masterly account of the painter's life that benefited from luminous cinematography by the distinguished Mexican Gabriel Beristain, who also filmed *Blade II*. Del Toro confirms on the DVD director's commentary that he wanted *Blade II* filmed with a similar *chiaroscuro*, the use of strong contrast in lighting that is characteristic both of the baroque painter and del Toro's visual imagination. The result is a familiar sustained juxtaposition of cool and rich colours: amber, gold and red set against a steely cold blue. The effect of this rich, if not random, intertextuality is to continually shift and de-stabilize the basis of the film's aesthetic, much as the camerawork maintains a continual fluidity and sense of movement. As in *Cronos* and, to a lesser extent, *The Devil's Backbone*, del Toro continually undermines generic expectations, in the process creating films that are both homages to his favourite literary, artistic and filmic modes, their makers and creators, as well as enactments of a much-quoted strategy notably explored by British novelist Angela Carter, another key figure in the late twentieth-century reworking of the Gothic, who wrote 'most intellectual development depends upon new readings of old texts. I am all for putting new wine in old bottles, especially if the pressure of the new wine makes the bottles explode' (1983: 69).

A sometimes neglected aspect of the 'new wine' that the *Blade* movies contain, hinted at in Reinhardt's aforementioned aggressive remark, is the fact of Blade's race. The figure of the black vampire can be traced back to films such as *Blacula* (1972), which in turn echoed the blaxploitation movies of the early years of that decade (*Shaft* 1971, *Superfly* 1972). The *Blade* movies utilize some of the cool urban machismo of the latter, but less is explicitly made of the combination of African American and vampire motifs. In reading *Blade II* it may be useful to consider the kind of subtexts that Gretchen Bakke has explored when discussing race and action-heroes in films such as this and *I Am Legend* (2007):

> When successful..., they not only save the world (the action hero's given task), but they set sickness right, they undo unfortunate mutation, and they purge the living of that most dangerous form of human corruption: white men who have lost control of their hungers. It turns out, or so these movies tell us, that the scourge of whiteness has an antidote and its essence is blackness. (2010: 419)

The vampires in *Blade II* are predominantly, if not exclusively, white, and they have at their service a non-vampiric white lawyer who cracks a del Toro joke about being barely human. This apparent reversal of conventional US racial politics manifests itself in a number of ways in *Blade II*, most notably in the scene where Blade is captured and pierced with multiple spikes in order to collect his blood as part of Damaskinos's genetic experiment to perfect the vampire race. Hence the black man's blood becomes the essence that will enhance the white vampires' genes and enable them to dominate the world. (The foetuses in this experimental laboratory are preserved in an amber liquid that recalls *The Devil's Backbone*, a motif resurrected in *Pacific Rim*.) In true del Toro style, traditional religious iconography is here reworked to allow for references to both the multiple piercing of St Sebastian and the stigmata of Christ. Blade clearly operates as a black Christ-like redemptive figure in the film, negotiating between the human and supernatural spheres of existence. He is filmed against an altar in a disused church after his first major fight with Nomak and following the death of Nyssa is seen in silhouette against the rising sun that has destroyed her, having held her in a mock-pietà during her slow, almost poetic and fairy-tale dissolution. Both *Blade* movies dwell with considerable attention on Blade's body as a signifier of wholeness and regenerative power that contrasts with the incessant images of bodily dissolution or damage that permeate both films. Yvonne Tasker has pointed to the contrasting use of white and black bodies in action movies:

> The naked display of the black body carries radically different meanings to the display of the body, which audiences are so frequently offered in big-budget action pictures. In their characterisation of the hero the action films of the 1970s reached for the stereotype of the confident hyper-sexualised black man. By contrast the exaggerated physical characteristics of the white hero tend to lead him into narrative situations in which he is subjected to torture and suffering. (1993: 39)

The *Blade* franchise interestingly illustrates the ways in which the representation of black masculinity may have developed in the post-Civil Rights years. The stereotypical black hyper-sexual hero of the 1970s becomes in *Blade II* a chaste figure who appears to repress any sexual identity, but who is also subjected to repeated torture and suffering in the manner previously applied to white heroes.

Blade's race and otherness as a 'Daywalker' also ironically aligns him with the film's antagonists, the Reapers, who are the products of Damaskinos's genetic experiments in creating pureblood vampires that also include aspects of Blade's genetic make-up. In particular, this links him closely to Jared Nomak, who takes on the role of avenging son in a manner that has affinities with Roy

Batty's ultimately destructive relationship with his father/creator Tyrell in Ridley Scott's *Blade Runner* (1982). Despite their voracious appetites and grotesque physiology, the Reapers operate as a kind of oppressed underclass, literally so as they inhabit the sewers in a manner that harks back to the mutating insects in *Mimic*. As in the earlier film, they are the product of bad science, of more perverse 'birthing' that rebounds on their creator, Damaskinos, as he attempts to play 'God' (a crime that aligns him with other del Toro creations such as De La Guardia in *Cronos*). The emphasis on achieving purity of blood through genetic experimentation also has clear Nazi connotations that have a sub-textual presence throughout the film, particularly in characters such as Damaskinos (played by a German actor, Thomas Kretschmann) and Reinhardt. These Nazi references re-emerge in *Hellboy* but also form part of an ongoing concern on del Toro's part with fascist ideology and its impact on the individual. Blade refuses a possible alliance offered by Nomak at the end of the film and instead engages in a final gladiatorial combat that is unlike any other of the film's many fight sequences. Del Toro apparently wanted each of these to be different in order to maintain variety, so the fight scenes had a number of different choreographers, including Wesley Snipes and one of the Bloodpack actors, Donnie Yen. As a result the sequences range from Ninja-style martial arts when the vampires come to Blade's warehouse lair to the hand-to-hand combat of the final fight between Blade and Nomak. This is choreographed almost as a World Wrestling Federation bout, with few if any weapons to hand. The result perhaps links the outcome to a more human dimension, a fight between 'brothers' that ends with Nomak himself pushing a blade into his near-invulnerable heart. Arguably the most important aspect of the Reapers is their decidedly unconventional bite. The vampire's 'kiss' has always conventionally carried a powerful erotic charge. As Gina Wisker suggests, '[a]t the end of the twentieth/start of the twenty-first century, as at the end of the nineteenth, vampirism has become an overwhelmingly popular metaphor for the erotic' (2005: 203).

In the first *Blade* film the most overtly erotic moment occurs when Karen Jenson the haematologist (another female scientist to feature in del Toro's work) is rescued by Blade and allows him to bite her in order to restore his potency. This is shot quite explicitly as an orgasmic sexual encounter that seals the developing relationship between the two characters. Elsewhere in the film the renegade vampire Frost apparently lives the clichéd lifestyle of a rich American gigolo/gangster, his uber-stylish penthouse apartment adorned by numerous attractive women. Essentially he is a young and upwardly mobile capitalist entrepreneur challenging the staid corporatism of the ageing vampire council. In general, Stephen Norrington's film follows a fairly conventional pattern in terms of the linkage between vampirism and sexuality, including the element of repression that is manifested in Blade's control of his vampiric/sexual 'thirst' (he becomes notably more animalistic after 'drinking' from Karen) as well as the quasi-oedipal perversity implied in the brief scenes between Blade and his flirtacious vampirized mother. Vampirism is conventionally identified with uncontrolled sexuality (as evidenced in the opening club bloodbath scene) and in the course of the film Karen explicitly identifies vampirism with sexual deviance, appropriately describing it in medical terms as a 'sexually transmitted disease'. However, the contrast between the designer/sexy world of Frost and that of Nomak, his rebellious counterpart in *Blade II*, could hardly be greater. Although he is played by a British ex-boy band star (Luke Goss), Nomak is a Nosferatu-like figure with a marbled skull and the grotesque expanding jaw characteristic of the Reapers. Despite his physical power he exudes an aura of sickness and genetic mutation again evoking the spectre of AIDS in contemporary vampire film (Gordon and Hollinger 1997).

The Reaper kiss appears entirely unerotic, satisfying a hunger for blood and power but in no way suggesting desire. There is no phallic puncturing here, rather a transference of toxins that paralyses the victim. In line with this process of de-eroticizing, there is no repeat in *Blade II* of the physical relationship between Blade and a woman. His relationship to Nyssa remains 'chaste' despite the exchange of blood that takes place after the battle with the Reapers – a situation that is confirmed by the pietà-like mise-en-scène of her willed death in the sunrise. Hence *Blade II* could well be described as one of the least sexually charged vampire movies ever made as the eponymous hero embodies the sexual continence of the samurai warrior or martial arts master, despite the overtly phallic implication of his name which references the earlier and highly sexualized black superhero Shaft. Del Toro's earlier reworking of the vampire myth, *Cronos*, could not be more different from *Blade II* (although the light bomb in the latter was apparently inspired by the Cronos device). However, the earlier film does give a brief nod to the association of vampirism and sex as the ageing central figure, Jesús, begins to awaken sexually as he uses the device. One might argue that sexuality is an absent presence in all del Toro's films. The one explicit sex scene, in *The Devil's Backbone*, is defined by the perverse power play operating between the young Jacinto and much older Carmen – a perversity that is mirrored in the fetishizing of his physical 'perfection' in contrast to her incomplete and partially mechanised body. His sexual potency and attractiveness in part allegorizes the powerfully seductive nature of fascist ideology, a pattern that is echoed in *Pan's Labyrinth* with the casting of the handsome Sergi Lopez as Vidal. In del Toro's films the body, in particular the male body, is subject to repeated physical traumas that disturb its borders and its integrity. *Blade II* conforms to the conventions of the action movie by fetishizing the apparently invincible male body of the central superhero, despite the continual attacks and invasions to which it is subject, although this is again subverted by his need to inject, identifying Blade with the abject figure of the habitual drug user. One way of reading this is to identify the ways in which del Toro repeatedly represents bodies against the conventional Hollywood grain in a process of genre queering that aligns his films with an influential trend at the end of the twentieth and beginning of the twenty-first century. This can be identified in female as well as male characters. There is little attempt in *Mimic* to exploit the female lead, Mia Sorvino, for any overt sexual purposes, despite the ongoing issue in the film of her uncertain pregnancy – throughout she is more potential mother/dedicated scientist than lover, a perhaps surprising situation in a mainstream Hollywood film. The casting of Maribel Verdú as the servant/housekeeper Mercedes in *Pan's Labyrinth* contrasted with her overtly erotic presence in Cuarón's *Y Tu Mamá También* (2001). In del Toro's film she is seen to be passionately fond of her brother, one of the guerrillas hiding in the forest, but is not otherwise portrayed in sexual terms. She sustains her cover of apparent submission to the regime of Vidal, until stabbing and slicing his much gazed-upon face with her kitchen knife, an appropriate method of revenge against a tyrannical and oppressive masculinity.

Del Toro's resistant representation of the body is most clearly expressed in his introduction of cyborgian imagery into the vampire myth. Both John J. Jordan and, more recently, Stacey Abbott have argued that the *Blade* films mark a radical re-imagining of vampire mythology that largely replaces legend with science (Jordan 1999; Abbott 2007). Hence there is little or no reference to the conventional pseudo-religious iconography of traditional vampire movies – crosses, wafers, holy water. Vampires are described as being 'allergic' to garlic, but this is now referred to using a scientific taxonomy, allium sativum, and has been incorporated into sophisticated weapon technology. Gone are the familiar strings of garlic flowers eagerly abandoned by willing victims of the vampire's kiss. Abbott identifies the origins of cyborgian discourse in *Blade II* in del Toro's first and highly unorthodox vampire film, *Cronos*, which begins with the historical placing of the Cronos device within hidden human time. The device is itself a cyborg, combining some of del Toro's key cinematic fetish objects – insects, clockwork machinery and monstrous creations that pulse with live, even after death. It 'gives birth' to its accidental user Jesús, who becomes another involuntary yet ultimately parasitic cyborg, dependent on the mechanism (and human blood) for continued life as his body becomes a site for insect-like metamorphosis (the shedding of layers of skin) as well as the blackly comic mechanical detritus of the undertaker's dark art. *Cronos* dwells particularly on the imperfections, malleability and progressive dissolution of the human body (expressed even in Angel's desire for cosmetic surgery on his nose). In *Blade II* the vampire body has effectively merged with technology and science, even Blade's serum dependency has a basis in scientific research, in contrast to Jesús's use of a transhistorical gold artefact. Indeed it is not only the vampire who has developed the neo-cyborg state, as other characters echo this – Whistler has a leg brace and Scud is almost an inseparable part of his machinery with his name evoking the infamous ballistic missile used in the wars of the 80s and 90s – as Silver and Orsini suggest 'his personal perfidy is tied up with the technology he represents' (2010: 152). Stacey Abbott makes the point that '[t]o fight vampires in the *Blade* universe is therefore to embrace a cyborg existence' (2007: 200). Even that most fundamental element of the vampire mythology, blood, has become subject to scientific discourse. The first *Blade* film features an early and highly memorable scene at a vampire rave where the revellers are ritualistically showered with blood – the 'blood bath' – as part of the evening's entertainment. Later in the film Blade's blood is used as part of an ancient ritual that will summon the vampire blood god and inaugurate a human Armageddon. So, despite the importance of technology in Stephen Norrington's film, vampire ritual and mythology still underpin the narrative. In contrast *Blade II* begins in a seedy underground scene of blood donation, as Nomak's blood is discovered to show anomalous DNA characteristics that align him with Blade. The eponymous hero's blood is later 'harvested', not as part of some ancient ritual but as a key factor in a genetic experimentation that will radically alter vampire bodies. This process of harvesting is carried out on a high-tech gurney-like machine made from shining steel, reflecting the coldly clinical efficiency of the vampire familiar (a sleek corporate lawyer) who operates it. The 'blood bath' scene in *Blade II* is literally that – a pool of blood that is a further part of the complex of machinery located in the depths of Damaskinos's laboratory into which Blade tumbles in order to regain his strength. Del Toro's film doesn't entirely abandon the folkloric aspects of vampire mythology – the cloaked, marbled figure of Damaskinos, who exudes green blood and crumbles to dust at his death, is seen in an inner sanctum redolent of more ancient vampire custom and myth, with its stone walls and castle-like interiors. However, although resembling Nosferatu, he is also a thoroughly modern geneticist, whose giant corporation operates well outside any ethical and moral concerns, which are ironically upheld by his daughter Nyssa. Millennial fears of bad science, of cloning, of dangerous DNA experiments that threaten the very basis of what it is to be human are very much to the fore here. These anxieties about the relationship between technology, science and progress re-emerge more specifically in other films with which del Toro has been involved as producer/executive producer, most notably the 2009 movie *Splice*, in which two renegade geneticists continue their work on multiple DNA splicing despite the termination of their funding by a large corporation. Their creation of a hybrid creature with human DNA, DREN, has predictably disastrous and cautionary consequences. Unlike such films, del Toro doesn't draw any overt moral or ethical conclusions about the merits or demerits of genetic experimentation in *Blade II*. The hero is himself a genetic splice who fights to preserve his own humanity whilst protecting the wider human population; he is also a Christ-like warrior with his own John the Baptist-like prophet/keeper, Whistler. Del Toro's fictional collaboration with Chuck Hogan in *The Strain* (2009) carries a more pronounced condemnation of human collaborators with the vampiric plague, in particular the corporate giant Eldritch Palmer who gleefully contemplates the spread of the vampire virus 'the strain spreading throughout New York City with the sure exponential force of compound interest, doubling and doubling itself every night – he hummed with the glee of a greedy banker' (245). In *Blade II* Damaskinos's company is named Caliban Industries, hinting at conflicted hybridity by evoking Shakespeare's *The Tempest*. In *The Strain* Palmer is head of the rather less ambiguously titled Stoneheart Group.

This sustained re-envisioning of vampirism through the lens of science and technology runs throughout *Blade II*. The 'Bloodpack' with whom Blade negotiates an uneasy alliance (they were initially formed to hunt him) are effectively clones of his cyborg status, right down to the black leather, shades, martial arts and heavy-duty weaponry. Only two of the Bloodpack, Reinhardt and Nyssa, are allowed any significant character development. The former sees Ron Perlman reprise a version of the thuggish Angel from *Cronos*, full of weary wise-cracking brutality. Nyssa's final demise where she disintegrates slowly in the sunrise is couched in a kind of visual lyricism that contrasts with the more immediate explosion of vampire bodies elsewhere – all fire and rapidly disintegrating skeletons – suggesting a human dimension to her that has shown itself in her expression of ethical concerns. As Alain Silver and James Ursini suggest '[for] del Toro...it is Nyssa who undergoes the human emotional transformation and who, after discovering her father's treachery, opts for self-immolation as a consequence' (2010: 252).

In contrast, the Reapers represent a genetic experiment gone badly wrong; their overheating metabolisms indicate their genetic flaws, although the prototype Nomak is exempt from this. There is a significant difference in the effects used to portray their deaths, though. Del Toro is at pains to distinguish these from the other vampires, particularly in the mass destruction that takes place in the wake of the Bloodpack's 'nuclear' weapon, the UV light bomb. On the DVD commentary del Toro compares the effect to the charred bodies of the dead of Pompeii – confirming the sense that the Reapers are ultimately victims themselves, in this case of technology that has run out of control just like their own bodies. This perhaps provides evidence for Silver and Ursini's belief that one of del Toro's most individual stylistic features is '[h]is defiant need to find an attractive aspect to monstrosities from his blood bug in *Cronos* to the lead figure in his *Hellboy* adaptations' (200). They dub him a 'vampire synthesist' who cannot finally succeed in shifting Blade from its comic book origins, stating that '[i]n the end, del Toro's style cannot transform *Blade* from comic book to epic drama. As a synthesist del Toro understands and defends those limitations' (252).

Ultimately, though, the term synthesist can't quite do justice to the kind of project that del Toro is engaged upon in a film such as *Blade II* which enacts a thoroughgoing generic transformation. The first *Blade* film is firmly set in the context of Los Angeles and makes plenty of visual references to this setting. In contrast *Blade II* begins in the old world of Eastern Europe so associated with vampire mythology, as we learn that Blade has pursued vampires in Moscow and Prague. The film's geographical trajectory from east to west underpins the transformative, alchemical processes with which del Toro re-energizes his chosen genres.

Hellboys and pyrogirls

The Devil's Backbone really liberated Guillermo in terms of his being able to discern between personal projects on the one hand and studio assignments on the other. Interestingly, *Hellboy* is a real synthesis of both. It's a really personal project, but one made within the Hollywood structure. It's amazing that they let him do this very personal film with a huge budget but no stars. (Bertha Navarro in Wood 2006a: 154)

I can tell you right now that my two favourite of my own films so far are *The Devil's Backbone* and *Hellboy*... *Hellboy* is ultimately what I think an atomic adventure book movie could be and is very different from the other comic-book franchise and has a huge heart and a lot of beauty in the horror ... it's a celebration of otherness and being different. It is a Beauty and the Beast story where at the end they kiss and they both turn to beasts. (del Toro in Wood 2006a: 155–156)

It's certainly tempting, if perhaps ironic, to view the two *Hellboy* films as del Toro's most personal to date, despite their comic-book origins and super-hero/fantasy subject matter. Apparently freed from the cultural and historical contextualizing of his Spanish films and, post *Blade II*, more at ease with the exigencies of the Hollywood production system, del Toro moulded the tent pole/ summer blockbuster and superhero genre to his own narrative and pictorial devices and in doing so trans-morphed the genre. He has widely acknowledged the autobiographical nature of the films '... the two *Hellboy* movies for me are semi-autobiographical. I do put a lot of details in from my life, which my wife recognizes' (Vulture 2008).

In a piece for *The Observer* newspaper he writes about how he 'made *Hellboy* in my own image' elaborating on the origins of much of the films' dense visual qualities in his personal notebooks: 'The first time an idea happens, it happens in these pages' (2008). Adapting the Mike Mignola stories from his Dark Horse comic series also allowed del Toro a great opportunity to indulge his 'fanboy' persona in no uncertain terms. The central Hellboy character that emerges in the films is certainly another in the line of liminal figures that feature in del Toro's movies who, like the director himself, have to negotiate often traumatic borderlines and find themselves isolated from the 'normal' world's assumptions about humanity and beauty. Hellboy has crossed the ultimate border, that between 'evil' and 'good', Hell/Chaos and Earth, life and death. In the first film his 'birth' out of Hell and Chaos is celebrated in touchingly traditional human ways – 'It's a boy' cries one of the GIs accompanying Bruttenholm/Broom (John Hurt) as though in the delivery room, and this opening prologue ends with the obligatory group photo of the happy 'family'. Hellboy's liminal status becomes crucial at the end of the film where he has to choose between saving humanity (and thus losing his girlfriend Liz) or unleashing the final apocalypse. We see him alarmingly develop into a fully fledged red devil as the FBI agent Myers (Rupert Evans) successfully attempts to remind him of his humanity. Despite being an FBI agent, Myers fulfils the role he has been given by Broom as the 'young knight who is inexperienced, but pure of heart', common in medieval tales, who will stand by Hellboy after his father's' death and help him 'in essence, become a man'. It's a scene that's mirrored towards the end of *Hellboy II: The Golden Army* where the beautifully sinister Angel of Death presents Liz with a similarly impossible decision, whether to save the wounded superhero and risk the prophecy that he will eventually lead to the destruction of the world (perhaps in a projected *Hellboy III*) or allow his death. Both scenes underscore the film's common thematic concern with moral and ethical choice as a crucial factor in the definition of humanity, one that they obviously share with *Pan's Labyrinth* in particular. Del Toro's introduction to *Hellboy II: The Art of the Film* provides further evidence for these links:

> As I worked on *Pan's Labyrinth* I wrote the *Hellboy II* script, multitasking for months as I always do. All the while I was reading and re-reading much of my Bettelheim, Tatar, Jung, Andersen and Grimm et al., and I thought of a small allegory about Hellboy's purpose on this earth. In the first film, Hellboy had to choose between becoming the All-powerful Beast of the Apocalypse or just a regular Joe. This second instalment could be about choices of a different kind. Which is more powerful, the capacity to destroy or the capacity to embrace? And what better to embody a lack of choice than a clockwork army, geared to kill anything and everything in its path? (del Toro et al. 2008: 6)

The first *Hellboy* film is framed by voice-overs that pose this fundamental, if somewhat clichéd, question 'what makes a man a man', answered by the assertion that it's 'the choices he makes'. This recurrent framing device clearly echoes the more interesting question 'what is a ghost' which inaugurates *The Devil's Backbone*. At one level this might seem to locate the film firmly in what Anna Powell calls 'the protectionist paranoid tradition of Hollywood sci-fi' (2012: 184) since this 'normative schmaltz … aligns him firmly with the idealised American male because of his freedom of choice' (184). However, as del Toro implies in the above quotation, the act of making choices becomes far more complex and problematic in the second film as the binary differentiation between good and evil so obvious in *Hellboy* becomes thoroughly ambiguous as the humanity to which Hellboy aspires is progressively revealed as the source of much destruction. In this context Myers's all-American imperative to 'remember who you are' becomes thoroughly ironized, since Hellboy's unresolved human/demon hybridity leads to his 'quitting' in the final frames of the film. So the director's own transnational status, combined with his negotiating a liminal position between corporate Hollywood ideologies and a more independent mode of film-making, suggests a distinctively personal dimension to what appears on the surface to be yet another developing superhero franchise.

The name given to Hellboy by Broom in the first film (his 'actual' name is Anung Un Rama meaning 'and upon his brow is set a crown of flame') encapsulates his borderline status – he is both devilish monster and boy, a 'thing' as the comically testy but ultimately intolerant government bureaucrat Manning designates him, and an (albeit 60 year old) adolescent with familiar issues concerning acceptable behaviour, sex, food, untidiness and so on. Hellboy's quarters at the BPRD (Bureau for Paranormal Research and Defense) combine high-tech security (which is generally unable to contain him) with the piled-high detritus of a teenager's bedroom. In this elaborate mise-en-scène music and TV screens play a significant commentative role – in the second film old horror movies such as *The Bride of Frankenstein* and *The Wolf Man* are playing and the former offers a particularly important intertextual moment as the Boris Karloff monster from Whale's 1935 film states that he and his mate 'belong dead'. As del Toro has suggested in an interview:

> It's as good as any other immortal line in cinema…. 'We belong dead.' The fact that the guy that is saying that is the monster and the fact that he is not stating the fate of the others but his own, it's a protean moment for the creature, because he is transforming into the most human of all the characters in the film. That is essentially what I tried to do with all the monsters in the movie. I tried to make them superhuman types. (Germain 2008)

Unlike other equivalent comic book superheroes turned into movie franchises (Spiderman, Batman, Iron Man and the Hulk, whose anger management issues he shares), Hellboy is not a 'man', nor is he a metamorphic figure with a split identity or alter ego. He has monstrous origins but has been raised by a loving human father, as evidenced throughout by his turbulent but ultimately close parent/ child relationship with Broom. The opening Christmas scenes of *Hellboy II* may take place in a military environment but also offer a self-consciously normative domestic scene between an excited child watching a classic post-war US TV puppet show (*Howdy Doody*) and a caring parent reading a bedtime story (which happens to be a proleptic version of the film's main narrative). Both films focus on the fragmented, constructed and provisional nature of identity and selfhood for the three central characters, Hellboy, Abe Sapien and Liz, but not in the bifurcated way beloved of superhero narratives. Their desire yet inability to fit into conventional modern American society (Hellboy somewhat forlornly files down his horns to do so) provides the basis for del Toro's exploration and celebration of an otherness and 'beautiful' monstrosity that is often contrasted with the intolerant and greedily destructive human world. The latter is all-too-ready to simply monetize the value of myth and antiquity (as in the opening auction scene of *Hellboy II*) or reject and demonize the othered Hellboy, even when he has saved kittens, babies and humanity in general from the apocalypse. Justin B. Schumaker argues that the contemporary superhero movie is fundamentally about a search for identity which results in a need for advocacy in a tumultuous world and Hellboy's journey concurs here (2011: 142). This journey is made all the more painful and profound considering how thankless Hellboy's mission is.

Both films feature the aforementioned government agency, the prosaically titled Bureau for Paranormal Research and Defense, which attempts to contain the abjected 'freaks' in a unit (ironically disguised as a waste management facility in Newark, New Jersey, which becomes Trenton N.J. in the second film) whilst at the same time relying on them to deal with extreme paranormal emergencies. Further confirmation of their abject status can be seen in the way Hellboy and the others are transported into the city in a garbage truck. In *Hellboy*, the pyrokinetic Liz is first seen as a depressed patient in a psychiatric hospital undergoing therapy and her misfit status is underlined by flashbacks to her unhappy childhood where she is ostracized as a freak. Her joy at being 'let out' when she is transferred back to the Bureau for Paranormal Research and Defense (BPRD) is displayed by her childlike enthusiasm for taking Polaroid pictures as she hangs out of the car in which Myers is escorting her, as though she can't quite believe the existence of the 'real' world. The super-intelligent amphibian telepath Abe Sapien, a highly cultured variant on *The Creature from the Black Lagoon*, is contemptuously called 'fishstick' by Manning and is fed on rotten eggs whilst listening to Vivaldi. His effete voice (provided by ex-*Frasier* star David Hyde Pierce in the first film and referencing R2-D2 from *Star Wars*) and high cultural tastes (a liking for Tennyson's poetry emerges in the second film) contrasts with Hellboy's blue-collar, 'ordinary Joe' persona, thus destabilizing any easy assumptions about heroism and American masculinity. There are clear references throughout to the *X-Men* franchise and its representation of rejected otherness, but there is little feeling of the kind of group solidarity which is engendered within the relatively opulent confines of the Xavier Institute, with its overtones of an expensive private school overseen by a benevolent Head teacher. The modified Beauty and the Beast romance between Liz and Hellboy traces a bumpy trajectory even when normalized by marriage and pregnancy in the second film and Abe and

Hellboy do share a homosocial 'buddy' moment together in *Hellboy II* as they drunkenly and somewhat surreally share six-packs whilst listening to Barry Manilow. However, despite the bookish glow of its library, the BPRD facility has some of the ambience of a high-tech prison/military installation with the Latin inscription 'In Absentia Luci Tenebrae Vincunt' – in the absence of light, darkness prevails (the correct Latin should be 'Lucis') in the entrance vestibule, underlining the irony that America fights the forces of darkness with some of their own. Hence the ambiguity surrounding Hellboy has much wider resonances – his 'birth' in late 1944 coincides with the final developmental stages of American atomic capability first tested in New Mexico in 1945, which ushered in a period of human history during which the threat of Armageddon becomes a first line of defence. (Following Mignola's narrative, *Hellboy II* begins on an American Air Base in New Mexico.) Furthermore, both *Hellboy* films appeared during a post-9/11 decade in which the superhero genre flourished, boosted by the success of Sam Raimi's *Spiderman* in 2002, a film like many others in this genre which is set in New York and depicts a morally simplistic system. At one level this re-emergence of the superhero seems to reflect the conservative ideology of the immediate post-9/11 period of the Bush administration (2001–2009) in which a Manichean good versus evil world view redolent of the Reagan years returned as a dominant form of American political rhetoric (DiPaolo 2011). However, the *Hellboy* films clearly resist and challenge such easy moral and political polarities, not only in the narrative centrality of their 'monsters', but also in the sheer imaginative exuberance of their celebration of difference. The choice of Ron Perlman, an actor with an unconventional portfolio of filmic personae, to play the lead confirms this sustained deviation from the superhero franchise norm. As Johannes Schlegel and Frank Haberman suggest:

[i]n Guillermo del Toro's pertinent films even the devil Hellboy (Ron Perlman) chooses to fight metaphysical evil – notwithstanding that he is not only a descendant from hell ('son of the fallen one'), a beast of the apocalypse whose destiny is 'to bring about the destruction of the earth' (*Hellboy II* 2008) but that he is also conjured by the Nazis with the help of the sinister, diabolical occultist Rasputin (Karl Roden). A greater disposition to evil could hardly be dreamt up – yet there is hardly any doubt as to which side Hellboy is actually on. The boundary between good and evil, therefore, seems to be at least permeable – and, consequently, the very distinction no longer absolute. (2011: 30)

This deviation from the norm comes to particular fruition in *Hellboy II*, with its more nuanced focus on unseen worlds that exist beyond the reach of twenty-first-century urban surveillance. Del Toro has distinguished between the films in suggesting that *Hellboy* depicted creatures on the loose in our world, whereas *Hellboy II* followed them into their own worlds, going to 'where the wild things are'. This reaches a climactic point in the second film with the Troll Market, possibly the most elaborate and wildly imaginative scene in all of del Toro's work.

The set for the Troll Market was constructed in a disused limestone quarry and transformed by production designer Stephen Scott into a kind of hallucinatory Moroccan bazaar populated by outlandish creatures, akin to those found in paintings by Hieronymus Bosch (and del Toro's own diaries and sketches), who stroll through streets that resemble the distorted expressionist landscape of Robert Wiene's *The Cabinet of Dr Caligari* (1920). The entrance to the Market, located under that most iconic of spaces, Brooklyn Bridge, is an elaborate clockwork door that was originally intended for a different underwater scene. The image of the door combines del Toro's love for such intricate yet low-tech mechanisms with some of the steampunk aesthetic that permeates the films – he has often expressed his dislike for high-tech. This door, with its sense of the ancient and enduring, acts as a kind of ironic riff on the space portals into other worlds beloved by science fiction. Above the door is another telling inscription 'Unus Mundus' (one world), which is a quote from the psychoanalyst and philosopher C.J. Jung, encapsulating his developing belief in a unified, unitary world that underlies the human (and animal) psyche and body. This Jungian concept relates directly to the market itself, which brings together images and creatures from multifarious myths and cultures. In a complex and allusive mise-en-scène, the Troll Market references the Gothic as well as images from eastern European, Indian and Arab cultures in its architecture and overall aesthetic. In his introduction to *Hellboy II: The Art of the Movie* del Toro talks of the need to avoid the Anglo-Saxon/Celtic magical universe that is common in mainstream films, 'as it would be impossible to surpass what's been established in scope or funding' (del Toro et al. 2008). The Market, with its proliferation of organic architectural shapes and labyrinthine alleyways, also acts as a wildly imaginative counterpart to the drab uniformity and soullessness of the proliferating shopping malls that *Hellboy II*'s main antagonist, Prince Nuada, cites as evidence for insatiable human greed – we earlier see him juxtaposed against a poster advertising just such a development: 'The humans have forgotten the gods, destroyed the Earth – and for what? Parking lots – shopping malls – greed has burned a hole in their chests that can never be filled. They will never have enough' (del Toro et al. 2008: 78).

Stephen Scott comments on a DVD extra that the Troll Market is conceived using curved lines and arches as a deliberate contrast to the human/urban world above, which is full of straight lines and grid systems. What the viewer sees is a kind of rhizomatic proliferation of forms and beings that stretch into the far distance, some only glimpsed momentarily. Although the scene seems to deliberately avoid the kind of more familiar fantasy images derived from Celtic myth and particularly redolent of Tolkien, Mike Mignola initially felt the idea was a little too close to the renowned Cantina scene in *Star Wars: Episode IV A New Hope*. However, the two moments ultimately have little in common. The Cantina scene is a far more conventional representation of human and alien other; in contrast, there are no conventional humans in the Troll Market, instead del Toro delivers a fully realized other world which very specifically does not include anything that smacks of science fiction – there are cobblers, musicians and other market sellers that have their origins in reality but that are transformed into the stuff of dreams. These fleeting figures combine characteristic cross-cultural influence, including the imagery of medieval cathedral gargoyles (del Toro has said were he a mason he would be carving these) with the grotesque *alejibres*, brightly coloured sculptures of fantastic creatures that feature in popular Mexican folk art. Indeed, Victoria Nelson has suggested that the Cathedral Head character, who gives Princess Nuala the map and whose head resembles the towers and rampart of a great Gothic church, is a 'Gothick emblem of its creator' (2012: 219) alluding to the centrality of medievalism and Catholicism in del Toro's universe. Hellboy immediately 'fits right in' since no-one is staring at him or Abe. The deliberate oriental otherness might seem to come dangerously close to the kind of patronizing Western attitude to the exoticism of the East that Edward Said explored in such works as *Orientalism* (1978). But as Dan Hassler-Forest has suggested, 'the overwhelming diversity grounds the scene first and foremost as the establishment of a thriving space of uncontrolled "otherness" in an unusually positive sense' (Hassler-Forest 2012: 204). He goes on to argue that the Troll Market can be seen as a version of Michel Foucault's concept of heterotopia – that is, a space in which the other can exist in a non-hegemonic environment that operates as a kind of counter-site to the socially and culturally normative. For him, *Hellboy II* in particular implicitly interrogates hegemonic norms:

> Del Toro's film uses alien beings and fantasy tropes to present a complex and ambiguous perspective on the modern city scape. Instead of acting as direct metaphors for specific social and ethnic groups the diverse beings are frequently hybrids that upset traditional representational clichés. The character of Hellboy

himself for instance unites the traditional performance of white working class American masculinity with a radically non-Caucasian skin colour and traditional Japanese hair style. (2012: 204)

Normative anxieties about the mixing of cultures and races are also hinted at in the brief but telling clips from classic black-and-white movies playing on Hellboy's TV screens after the Troll Market fight, where cross-cultural relationships are seen as threats to traditional US family life. This is reprised later in a CNN broadcast about the BPRD watched by Manning, affirming '[r]ecent polls show that a majority of Americans favor a congressional investigation into the BPRD and its promotion of inter-species marriage, seen by many as a threat to traditional families fuelled by federal funds'. Liz's pregnancy, with its odd echoes of the anxiety surrounding Susan's pregnancy in *Mimic* and as yet unrevealed to Hellboy, clearly represents a specific example of reproductive otherness existing outside the norm of the white American family; the film ends with her revelation that she will have twins. Superficially this could seem a rather sentimental conclusion, rounding the second film off with an apparently more 'normalized' birth than that which began the first film. But the rhetoric concerning all-American ideals of manhood and choice that frame the first *Hellboy* has undergone considerable slippage by the end of the second film as this decidedly non-normative family of 'freaks' walks into an unknown future. As Tony Vinci has argued, there are strong echoes here of *The Wizard of Oz*, the classic fantasy that also inflects the ending of *Pan's Labyrinth*:

> Like the cowardly Lion, the Tin Woodman, the Scarecrow, and Dorothy, Hellboy, Abe, Krauss, and Liz search to be human, yet, also like their counterparts, they already possess the qualities for which they search. However, instead of looking towards representation of cultural power for acceptance and approval, as Dorothy and company do, they treat those representations of traditional cultural power as forces to move away from and antagonize. (2012: 1056)

In the final shooting script, published in *Hellboy: The Art of the Movie*, del Toro includes a post-credit sequence that further disrupts any sense of closure. Proving too expensive to film, the sequence shows the resurrection of Kroenen and Rasputin from the first film, now aligned with corporate America in the form of Roderick Zinco 'billionaire, madman' (del Toro et al. 2008). Surely this is a possible forerunner of the sinister corporate magnate Stoneheart in del Toro and Hogan's vampire trilogy *The Strain* (2010–2012).

Throughout the Troll Market scene del Toro also seems characteristically interested in ironic juxtaposition and the question of visibility as the disparity between what is seen and not seen is always crucial in his work. Negotiating entrance to the Market involves the coercion of a Scottish troll (a fragglewump) which appears to normal vision as a sweet old lady with a liking for cats (the troll eats them, much to Hellboy's disgust). Yet she is mortally afraid of a canary in a cage. Inside the Market there's a constant trompe l'oeil effect that teases the eye – for example, we briefly see a street musician who apparently has a wizened corpse as an instrument. There's also a delightfully grim black joke when what appears to be a baby attached to a store holder who is being shaved with a cutthroat razor refuses to be petted and declares, 'I'm not a baby, I'm a tumour'. The fact that the Troll Market exists unseen within the heart of New York suggests that the 'other' is not separate or distant but essentially intrinsic and present, part of an 'Unus Mundus' in which easy Manichean polarities are far from stable. *Hellboy* does have its undead villains in the form of Rasputin and the cyborg SS officer Kroenen – but *Hellboy II* is deliberately more ambiguous. The antagonist Nuada is intimately equated to the 'heroine', his sister Princess Nuala with whom he has a telepathic connection and is also depicted as a kind of eco-warrior, the advocate of a irrefutable critique of the human race as destructive despoilers of nature.

Ultimately the significance of the Troll Market and *Hellboy II's* extensive gallery of monsters underscores del Toro's overt desire to celebrate heterogeneity and difference. Tony Vinci equates this to the ideas on fantasy explored in Rosemary Jackson's classic psychoanalytic study of the genre, *Fantasy: The Literature of Subversion* (1981). For Jackson, fantasy's function is to critique the status quo and question hegemonic, unitary perceptions of reality, and Vinci argues that the film 'exposes the anthropocentric privilege bestowed by an essentialized definition of "humanity", repositioning the human as an open signifier that functions on many registers simultaneously' (2012: 1044). Elsewhere Vinci argues that *Hellboy II* marks a significant shift from the first *Hellboy* film in that it moves from apocalyptic Lovecraftian cosmic horror, with its heady mix of human manifestations of evil (Rasputin, the Nazis) and ancient tentacled monsters (the Sammael, the Seven Gods of Chaos) to 'key elements of style, story and theme from a writer that expresses a more hopeful philosophy, J.R.R. Tolkien, indicating a shift in genre from cosmic horror to fantasy' (1041). This is interesting given del Toro's aforementioned statement about avoiding the 'Anglo-Saxon/Celtic magical universe' but perhaps the film is more influenced by another, less well-known fantasy writer Lord Dunsany, whose classic *The*

King of Elfland's Daughter (1924) involves a questing Prince, son of the King of Elfland, and which juxtaposes human and magical worlds. Dunsany is one of a number of writers of the supernatural referenced in the *Hellboy* films – others include Algernon Blackwood, whose surname is given to the auction house at the opening of *Hellboy II*, and Arthur Machen, after whom the museum in *Hellboy* is named, whilst the Troll Market itself evokes Christina Rossetti's dream/nightmare vision in 'Goblin Market' (1862). Del Toro has often acknowledged his love for Dunsany's writing and in *Hellboy II* recasts Elfland in a radically different environment. The film's opening narrative uses puppets to illustrate the story that Broom is telling the young Hellboy (whose would-be normative childhood ironically involves TV puppets and the imagined imminent arrival of a man in a big red suit, Santa Claus). The story is about the battle between human and elf, between 'human' and 'natural' worlds. Broom is constructed in both films as a mediatory figure between the worlds of rational scientific knowledge and belief in otherness, indicated most obviously in his decision to adopt Hellboy as his son, but hinted at throughout the first film prior to his death. For example, immediately after he is told of his terminal cancer he is seen turning tarot cards and refuses any other tests when confronted in the cards by a figure of death. In the opening passage of *Hellboy* he acknowledges his Catholicism to the soldier commanding the GIs and is shown facing a large and tortured crucifix in the cold blue light that suffuses the scene. This is a characteristic del Toro moment where a Christian-inflected view of the cosmos is juxtaposed with events that seem to question and undermine its power and relevance, although Broom's rosary plays a significant role in reminding Hellboy of his humanity much later as he chooses not to open the final lock to release the Gods of Chaos. As the crucifix burns a cross into Hellboy, Myers reminds him of the choice he has to remain human and reject his destiny, 'your father gave you that choice'. The conflation of human and divine fathers is not accidental here and although del Toro may have rejected the confining dogma of Catholicism, he continually explores questions of faith:

> I'm eager to explore themes that lend themselves easily to metaphor … The fantastic is the only tool we have nowadays to explain spirituality to a generation that refuses to believe in dogma or religion. Superhero movies create a kind of mythology. Creature movies, horror movies, create at least a belief in something beyond. (Breznican 2008)

In *Hellboy II* the figure of the rebel Prince Nuada becomes the conduit for a critique of the hegemonic world of human normality. After the opening 1944 framing sequence he is the first character we see, performing a dance-like, martial arts routine in a darkened space that is suddenly intruded upon by an image of modernity, the subway train that flashes past in the background, which offers a startling juxtaposition of ancient and modern that is recurrent throughout. Nuada himself embodies an uncanny mix of extreme physical energy with a facial appearance indicating age and antiquity. He also evokes a series of archetypal narratives in his relationship to his father Balor, from the Prodigal Son to Shakespeare's *Hamlet*. In a later scene the elfin court, ruled over by a horned Nature-figure King Balor, is seen to be located in a decayed industrial landscape, underscoring its anachronistic presence in a contemporary urban landscape – a condition that Hellboy shares on several occasions. When Hellboy emerges into the above ground world he is often either the object of frenzied tabloid fascination or rejected as a dangerous freak. This, as Tony Vinci argues, is a reversal of Dunsany:

> While in Dunsaby's *The King of Elfland's Daughter*, part of the human world is transformed into a parcel of Elfland and Lirazel and Alveoric live eternally in an earthly paradise, in del Toro's world, the opposite happens: family and lovers are separated and the elven qualities of the world disappear. (2012: 1046)

Nuada's character functions as an ongoing critique of Hellboy's comic but generally unsuccessful performance of normative working-class masculinity (he describes his body as 'an amusement park') and by implication the dominant ideologies of Western capitalist materialism. He challenges Hellboy to acknowledge his otherness, particularly in an extraordinary scene where Hellboy kills the 'Elemental', the forest god that, like the Prince, is the last of its kind. Del Toro wanted this to be 'scary and beautiful at the same time. And one of the things that he requested was that the monster be asymmetrical and also have a bit of a humanoid form' (del Toro et al. 2008: 140). The published script describes the forest god as 'five stories high and as fierce as untamed nature' (135). This elemental being is depicted throwing up 'burning oil drums and parked cars' as emblems of man's despoiling of the natural world. When Hellboy finally destroys it by shooting its 'glowing, cerebral heart' (ironically with his so-called Big Baby, a huge multi-barrelled monster of a gun), the destruction of the metamorphic green god results in a momentary Edenic greening of the city, '[m]oss and roots cover the pavement, walls, and abandoned vehicles. Hummingbirds flutter out from the newly grown moss mounds green grass overtakes the pavement. In the end, most of the building looks like the Garden of Eden' (del Toro et al. 2008: 150).

This scene of incongruous natural beauty spilling over the urban landscape is immediately followed by a *Frankenstein*-like moment where the crowd turns against Hellboy ('You damned freak' shouts one bystander) and Liz. To underscore this, the next scene between the two which takes place in Hellboy's room is punctuated by the aforementioned words uttered by Frankenstein's monster on the TV 'We belong –dead!!' The quotation has particular resonance at this point since Hellboy's destruction of the Elemental is also an act of self-destruction, given that he, Abe and Liz are closely associated with the elemental forces of fire and water. So this is a pivotal moment in his increasing estrangement from the human world, articulated for him by the Prince. Throughout Nuada is an antagonist rather than villain, and the empathetic doubling that exists between him and his sister Nuala suggests the possibility of an alternative, more sympathetic identity. However, his desperate methods seem in the end to replicate those of his human enemies. The comic/horrific tooth fairies (who re-appear in a somewhat different locale in the del Toro produced *Don't Be Afraid of the Dark)* only eat and defecate, thus mirroring capitalism's capacity to exploit, despoil and then move on. The Golden Army itself (the name apparently prompted by Roy Harryhausen's *The Golden Voyage of Sinbad* (1973)) replicates the inexorable and uncontrollable destructive power of nuclear weaponry. However, the Prince's final words reiterate his belief that humans are the root cause of the natural holocaust:

> In the end – the humans – will tire of you – how much longer do you have? They've turned against you already…them or us – which holocaust should be chosen? We die – and the world will be poorer for it. (del Toro et al. 2008: 206)

Hellboy's reaction is to agree: 'He's right - the prince – ho *do* we fit into this world?' His attempts to 'mimic' hegemonic normative humanity and this moment of awareness lead him and the others to 'quit' in the last moments of the film, whose final emphasis is on birth and the construction of a nuclear 'family' (including Krauss and Abe) that challenges the 'essentialized, anthropocentric humanity that…Hellboy aspires to become' (Vinci 2012: 1044). Like so many of del Toro's central figures, they choose not only to reject any attempt at assimilation into the dominant norm but actively take an oppositional stance. Hellboy's epiphany also has an appropriate geographical location, taking place as it does close to the Giant's Causeway in County Antrim, Northern Ireland. The Causeway's associations with the mythic stories of Finn MacCool and the battles of giants have obvious resonances with the film's main narrative, but they also confirm Hellboy's acknowledgement and espousal of the kind of oppositional ideology associated with Nuada, whose name derives from Nuada Airgetlám, the first king of the Tuatha De Danann, mythic early settlers of Ireland. Airgetlám mean 'silverarm' and refers to the story of the mythic Nuada losing one arm in battle – in the film his father King Balor is missing an arm. So myth and fairy tale are validated as a necessary prophylactic against the materialist contemporary.

In an essay that appeared in the same year as *Hellboy II*, Jack Zipes commented on the necessity of fairy tale and fantasy narratives:

> [u]nlike reality, they allegedly open the mysteries of life and reveal ways in which we can maintain ourselves and our integrity in a conflict-ridden world. They compensate for the constant violation of nature and life itself and for the everyday violation of our lives engendered through spectacle. (2008: 2)

Zipes further defines the role of fantasy in the contemporary world thus, '[w]e do not need fantasy to compensate for dull lives, but, I want to suggest, we need it for spiritual regeneration and to contemplate alternatives to our harsh realities. More than titillation, we need the fantastic for resistance' (2008: 3).

In its movement towards this position of resistance, the narrative arc of *Hellboy II* traces a similar trajectory to del Toro's other films, whether it be the boys' rejection of neo-fascist power in *The Devil's Backbone*, Ofelia's rejection of patriarchy and fascism in *Pan's Labyrinth* or Blade's battle with corporate hegemony in *Blade II*. It is the characteristic generic hybridity in his work that creates its particular power and resonance. When questioned on the differences between fairy tale and monster movies, del Toro replies:

> It's a very, very thin difference. I think that horror stories come from fairy tales, in a way. They share a lot of similarities. I think the difference is tonal. You know, the fairy tale contains a lot more elements of magic and whimsy and the horror story contains a lot more, sort of, almost existential feelings – sort of dread, and ultimately they are similar melodies, played at a very different key. (del Toro 2012a)

Recently the *Hellboy* films have attracted a number of critical analyses (Powell 2012; Hassler-Forest 2012) which have found their 'existential feelings' and espousal of strategies of resistance a particularly fruitful subject for readings informed by contemporary theory. As previously indicated, Hassler-Forest locates del Toro's films within a wider discussion of the intersection between American politics and popular film culture, particularly in relation to the post-9/11 intensification of neo-liberal late capitalism. Hassler-Forest reads the *Hellboy* films through the lens of Michel Foucault's work in particular, highlighting its engagement with issues of surveillance and power:

> [r]ather than presenting the superhero as a figure who uses panoptic devices to enforce his own brand of normative power, the Hellboy films develop a very different perspective on the topic of surveillance and control. Both films present narratives and imagery that instead revolve around issues of difference, marginalization and minority groups' right to forms of visual representation. (2012: 194)

In particular, the *Hellboy* films can be distinguished from other more traditional American superhero franchises as they 'disavow the nostalgic values of patriarchal capitalism, presenting instead a superhero figure who embodies the values of otherness, self-determination and postmodern bricolage as most vital to identity' (Hassler-Forest 2012: 205). One might imagine Hellboy's response to this assessment – 'Man …' or 'Mmmh', or perhaps a characteristic 'Holy crap!' particularly given his 'redneck' appearance and demeanour, but in general this is a revealing and helpfully provocative account of the films' deviation from the Hollywood norm.

In a contribution to a collection of essays on Deleuze and Film, Anna Powell reads the first *Hellboy* film through the lens of Gilles Deleuze and Félix Guattari's highly influential re-conceptualization of postmodern philosophy, stemming in particular from the former's writing on cinema (2012). Although Deleuze broadly rejected 'popular' film culture and focused much of his film commentary on art-house classics and auteur movies, for Powell *Hellboy's* richly layered hybridity renders it available to Deleuzian readings. For her *Hellboy* '[i]s, in Deleuze and Guattari's terms, a mixer of planes, in that it mixes film and literature, science and philosophy, and humour and horror. The film's generic planes are also a mix of science fiction, gothic horror and comedy. Its science-fiction elements include high-tech weaponry and gadgets, and an earth under threat from alien invasion' (173). This heterogeneous mix is compounded and deepened by the use of further motifs from other hybrid forms such as retro Steampunk, inspired perhaps by films such as *The City of Lost Children* (1995) in which Perlman also starred:

> Along with the Tesla-style generator form the opening scene…*Hellboy's* Steampunk credentials include retro nostalgia and elaborate clockwork such as the concealed traps of Rasputin's mausoleum, and Baron von Kroenen's (Ladislaav Beran) metal prosthetics. Even Abe Sapien's goggles are a Steampunk fashion item. (Powell 2012: 178)

Powell usefully equates *Hellboy's* heterogeneity with the production of 'a new working assemblage [which]…refuses to be fixed in signifying codes and representational equations, but rather proceeds via the open-ended conjunction "and…and…and"'. Here she quotes from Deleuze and Guattari's seminal text *A Thousand Plateaus: Capitalism and Schizophrenia* (1988) where they assert that this open-ended conjunction 'carries enough force to shake and uproot the verb "to be"' (179). Powell limits her focus to the first film but it's arguable that the second film, with its greater open-endedness, further mix of planes and celebration of heterogeneity, is even more available to this kind of reading. In fact, it could be argued that this challenging and disturbing of given signifying codes represent the most fundamental aspect of del Toro's work as a writer and director thus far.

7

From Development Hell to the Pacific Depths:
The Strain and *Pacific Rim*

The period between 2008 and 2013, the end of which marks the appearance of del Toro's next film as a director, *Pacific Rim*, was characterized by an almost feverish stream of projects that did not materialize or were shelved. We discuss this period and their potential to extend del Toro's involvement in the world of cinema as producer. We also explore del Toro's excursion into the literary world, which sees him return once more to the vampire genre in the three novels that comprise *The Strain Trilogy*. Finally, we turn our attention to *Pacific Rim* – a film that has so far divided critical opinion but which we argue displays many of del Toro's thematic and artistic sensibilities, albeit re-packaged for a younger audience.

In production…

Two major directorial projects did not reach fruition for different reasons. Since 2006 del Toro had been trying unsuccessfully to obtain studio backing for an adaptation of H.P. Lovecraft's 1931 novella *At the Mountains of Madness*, which he had read as a teenager and that had evidently made an enormous impression on him. Del Toro had already written a screenplay in collaboration with Matthew Robbins, but studio intransigence appeared to stem from the 150-million-dollar potential cost of the project and the likelihood of an 'R' rating for the film's content. In 2010 the prospects for the film's creation appeared to improve with the involvement of James Cameron as producer and the engaging of Tom Cruise as leading actor. Del Toro was quoted as saying, 'I first talked about it with Jim Cameron 20 years ago when we first met and began our friendship, with *Cronos*, when it was still in the editing room. He came in and he knew the project but his fresh perspective and the right questions from him has made the project take a huge leap' (Lyttlelton 2010). However, a year later the project again foundered and by 2012 del Toro was announcing on his official website that the release of Ridley Scott's *Prometheus* (2012) would prove a problem for his project given the relative similarity of the *Prometheus* plot to the Lovecraft novella.

The Lovecraft adaptation would have been a labour of love for del Toro, given the importance of its source material to him. In contrast, his involvement from 2008 in the making of *The Hobbit: An Unexpected Journey*, which he agreed to direct as well as contribute to the writing of the screenplay, was more surprising given his claim in an interview with *Salon* staff:

> I was never into heroic fantasy. At all. I don't like little guys and dragons, hairy feet, hobbits – I've never been into that at all. I don't like sword and sorcery, I hate all that stuff. C.S. Lewis was another thing. I really enjoyed him as a kid, but he's too Catholic for me. It's not something as an adult I can feel comfortable relating to. (Salon Staff: 2006)

After 18 months of planning and writing, he announced his withdrawal from the project, which was taken over by Peter Jackson, although del Toro is still mentioned in the screenplay credits. This action inevitably resulted in considerable speculation as to its cause, although the main reason given by del Toro was the lengthy delay in getting the go-ahead for filming from the financially troubled studio MGM. After del Toro's departure, the original plan for two films based on Tolkien's novel extended to three and production finally began in 2010. There has also been much speculation about what kind of film *The Hobbit: An Unexpected Journey*, which finally appeared in 2012, would have been had del Toro continued as director.

Del Toro's work as writer and/or producer has been as varied, in terms of genre and content, as his directorial oeuvre. He has been closely involved with a number of high-profile animated films, including *Kung Fu Panda 2* (2011), *Puss in Boots* (2011) and *Rise of the Guardians* (2012). This commitment to animation is destined to continue in planned future projects such as *Pinocchio* (date unknown). In contrast he has also continued to support Spanish-language film in projects such as *Biutiful* (2010), directed by his friend and fellow Mexican Alejandro Gonzalez Iñárritu, and *Julia's Eyes* (2010), directed by Guillem Morales and starring one of del Toro's favourite actors Belén Rueda in the title role. The latter film explicitly explores one of del Toro's favourite tropes, that of seeing and visibility, given that the central figure is a woman losing her sight and gradually needing to visualize what she cannot actually see. This theme is further explored in *Don't Be Afraid of the Dark*, a remake of one of del Toro's favourite TV movies originally screened in 1973 which he has said 'freaked him out as a child' (Bradshaw 2011). *Guardian* film critic Peter Bradshaw saw *Don't Be Afraid of the Dark* as a 'minor del Toro', despite being a 'labour of love' for the director, who co-wrote the screenplay with Matthew Robbins and produced the film, although its director was Troy Nixey (Bradshaw 2011). The film uses a similar trope to *Pan's Labyrinth* – the child that sees worlds that adults cannot – but despite making effective use of the tooth fairies that first appeared in *Hellboy II: The Golden Army*, the film seemed ultimately to lack tension, 'an *Amityville Horror* with delusions of grandeur' in the words of *Observer* critic Philip French (2011). Del Toro's absolute commitment to the project manifested itself further in the publication of *Don't Be Afraid of the Dark: Blackwood's Guide to Dangerous Fairies* (del Toro and Golden 2011), which was billed as a companion piece to the film. Characteristically, del Toro takes a familiar publishing phenomenon, the movie tie-in, and transforms it; the book is a lavish facsimile of the fictional narrator's journal of discovery, complete with ink-stained edging, sections on black paper and elaborately ghoulish illustrations by the film's director Troy Nixey. The journal traces the travels of the biologist Emerson Blackwood (who makes a very brief appearance at the beginning of the film) and tells his Pandora-meets-Frankenstein story about the dangers of the secret worlds that lie beyond science and rational perception. This is interwoven with detailed accounts of the fairy worlds of different nations and cultures that form a kind of encyclopaedia of dangerous fairies. In many ways the book is more interesting than the film, which seems to follow a familiar Hollywood narrative trajectory.

From tombs to tomes

Perhaps the most interesting project brought to final fruition during this interim period is another book or series of books – the three novels that del Toro co-authored with novelist Chuck Hogan and that are generally known as *The Strain Trilogy*, from the title of its first volume. Del Toro is no stranger to collaborative working on screenplays, so it is perhaps not surprising that he should embark on a jointly written work of fiction, unusual though that generally is in novel publishing. In many ways *The Strain Trilogy* enacts the kind of alchemic transformation of genre that has guided all of del Toro's film work. It reacts against the kind of over-romanticized, somewhat tortured depiction of vampires that had become dominant in the later twentieth and early twenty-first century through, for example, the novels of Anne Rice, Stephenie Myers' *Twilight Saga* (in both book and film form) as well as other, less sentimental, TV series such as *True Blood*. Nina Auerbach suggests:

> Individual vampires may die; after almost a century even Dracula may be feeling his mortality; but as a species vampires have been our companions for so long that it is hard to imagine living without them. They promise escape from our dull lives and the pressure of our times, but they matter because when properly understood, they make us see that our lives are implicated in theirs and our times are inescapable. (1995: 9)

In *The Strain Trilogy* del Toro and Hogan focus not on romanticized escape but on the pressure of 'our times' and the metaphoric potential of the vampire myth, as evidenced in statements such as this from del Toro:

> [T]hematically and socially the monsters in *The Strain* are social monsters. They're creatures that are born out of everything we do wrong and the reasons we cannot fight them is because we are incredibly fallible as a social entity. *The Fall* begins by saying that it took the world 60 days to end and we're basically accountable for that because of our arrogance and pride. That's exactly how I feel: you can apply that to eco-tragedies, viral outbreaks or any kind of disaster. It's a miracle that society functions at all because it is such an imperfect model. (Jewell 2010)

Taking a lead from Stoker's original, the novels combine recent history, ancient myth and contemporary actuality in an entirely dystopic vision of the fall of humankind. The second volume has *The Fall* as its title and traces the 60 days it takes to undermine human society – a kind of reverse creation that sees the earth overtaken by the vampire 'plague'. In order to reclaim the vampire narrative del Toro goes back to its fictional origins in Stoker's 1897 novel – hence the plane that lands at JFK airport carrying its deadly payload harks back to Dracula's ship arriving in England, whilst at the same time echoing the events of September 11, 2001 (much of the initial action takes place near to Ground Zero). Similarly, the chief vampire hunter in the novels is Abraham Setrakian, named after Abraham Van Helsing of the original, but also referencing Professor Broom of the *Hellboy* films, another of del Toro's academic figures pitting their knowledge against seemingly omnipotent forces. Indeed, it could be argued that the trilogy offers a kind of summation of many of the key tropes from del Toro's films to date. As the former professor who has become the proprietor of Knickerbocker

Loans and Curios, a Spanish Harlem pawnshop, Setrakian also re-evokes the antiquarian Jesús Gris from *Cronos*. Both men are implicated, in different ways, in the crossing of centuries of time – Jesús with his use of the Cronos device and Setrakian in his search for the *Occida Lumen*, the ancient text that holds the key to the history of the vampires. Jesús's antagonist, the capitalist La Guardia, re-emerges in *The Strain* in the form of Eldritch Palmer, owner of the corporate Stoneheart Group. Like La Guardia, Palmer relies on artificial means to keep him alive and is searching for immortality – he attempts to do a deal with the vampires in order to gain eternal life. He and his organization represent another opportunity for del Toro's critique of neo-liberal late capitalism's vampiric hold on Western society. Palmer boasts to Ephraim that he and his like 'have taken those basic human drives and advanced our own selves through their exploitation. We have monetized human consumption, manipulated morals and laws to direct the masses by fear or hatred, and, in doing so, have managed to create a system of wealth and remuneration that has concentrated the vast majority of the world's wealth in the hands of a select few' (del Toro and Hogan 2010: 275). This represents an uncanny prefiguring of the Occupy movement's fundamental objections to late capitalism's concentration of power and wealth in the hands of the top one per cent. Perhaps referencing the world financial turmoil of 2007 and 2008, Palmer envisages the viral strain in terms of money and power – 'the strain spreading throughout New York City with the sure exponential force of compound interest doubling and doubling itself again every night – he hummed with the glee of a greedy banker' (245).

Much of the later action in the novels takes place underground, the natural territory of the figure who becomes the unlikely hero of the narrative, Vasiliy Fet, the vermin exterminator. He is another of del Toro's 'ordinary Joe' heroes (we first see him at Ground Zero), who in some ways is redolent of a human Hellboy using his detailed knowledge of the underground world beneath New York as a vital tool in the resistance. As he says towards the end of the first novel, 'Everything connects underground, one way or another' (456) – an assertion that might be used as a motto for many of del Toro's films. The involvement of the Centre for Disease Control (CDC), two epidemiologists (Nora and Ephraim are central protagonists), the use of underground Manhattan locations, the post-apocalyptic viral epidemic, all hark back to *Mimic* as an intertext, although in the trilogy the freedom that imaginative fiction allows results in a dystopic ending that resembles del Toro's original ideas for *Mimic*, before studio intervention enforced a conventional form of Hollywood closure. The role of the child as an extra-social lens that has been central to much of del Toro's cinema recurs here in the figure of Zack, the heroic resistance fighter Ephraim's son by a now defunct marriage. Pursued throughout by his monstrous mother Kelly, who is 'turned' at an early stage, the still-human Zack becomes a surrogate son and vessel for the telepathic Vampire Master. Here again, the dominant dystopic mode of the trilogy renders the trope of the child as moral compass, familiar from *Pan's Labyrinth* and *The Devil's Backbone*, as blurred and unstable. History becomes circular and repetitive as Setrakian's memories of Treblinka as a survivor of the Nazi holocaust are rewound in the concentration camps set up by the vampires with the aid of human collaborators. Throughout, the vampires echo Nazi ideology as well as contemporary white capitalist power.

One of the few published analyses of *The Strain Trilogy* foregrounds a rather different aspect that develops ideas first explored in *Cronos*. Simon Bacon situates the novels within a specifically Mexican cultural identity which 'utilizes a very particular form of self-derogatory national identity that is particular to the Mexican sense of identity in terms of its relationship to larger more wealthy countries around it' (2012). Bacon relates this to the work of the Mexican artist and performer Sergio Arau, who 'knowingly delights in the derogatory identification placed upon him by colonial rulers and subsequently builds a negatively positive identity that is uniquely his, and Mexico's own, trespassing upon externally enforced categories through a mocking self-reflexivity which destabilizes its original identity' (2012). This he describes as 'a process that is alchemical in nature for it takes what is base, or what imperialism categorizes as worthless and demeaning, and through the fires of embracing it and making it one's own to excess, it becomes the gold of a true and individual identity' (2012). *The Strain Trilogy* works, therefore, as a transgressive reinterpretation of Stoker's classic Dracula narrative that:

> [r]eorientate[s] its intent, seeing the vampire as the embodiment of white capitalist consumer culture and the crew of light as a band of immigrant 'cucarachas' that fight to save a world that vilifies them. This enacts a wilful inversion of narrative and cultural expectation where anti-heroes, such as gang members and Santo-esque ex –wrestlers replace the 'defenders of the faith' and are turned into heroes. (2012)

These narrative tropes look back to the exiled and abjected anti-heroes of the *Blade* and *Hellboy* franchise and forward to the resistance saviours of the world in *Pacific Rim*.

The popcorn perverse

It is curiously ironic that the further del Toro's films move away from narratives that focus on predominantly and recognizably human characters in relatively identifiable situations, the more personal they become. For del Toro, the *Hellboy* films were his most 'personal' to date in terms of the ways in which they reflected his own take on the world, on the position of the outsider figure and the exiled character. Despite its summer blockbuster credentials, robots versus monsters plotline and broadly, not to say sketchily drawn human characters, *Pacific Rim* carries an even more distinctly del Toro-esque fingerprint. There are some incidental clues to this in the plot details. For example, it is five years since the washed-up Jaeger pilot Raleigh Becket (Charlie Hunnam) has operated one of these monstrous Mecha machines, following the death of his brother Yancy. This exactly matches the length of time that had elapsed since the director's last film – a period filled with major projects that were frustratingly unfulfilled for various reasons. In one sense, *Pacific Rim*, the summer blockbuster movie, is analogous to the giant Jaegers – a complex and massive technical structure that relies on interdependency and co-operation as well as a relentless driving force doing battle with studio backers, film critics and financial expectations for the opening weekend. In his introduction to David Cohen's tie-in book *Pacific Rim: Man: Machines and Monsters* (2013), del Toro talks of how the film:

> came at a crucial time in my life and, basically, saved it … This movie came from the heart. In fact, it came from the youngest, freshest part of my heart. In making this film, my craft, experience and rigor were those of a forty-eight-year-old man, but my heart was that of an eleven-year-old. This was playtime boot camp. (Cohen 2013: 9)

Elsewhere he has described his experiences of seeing Kaiju films as a young teenager in seedy Mexican 'one brick' cinemas, the name deriving from the brick audience members were given to throw at rats inhabiting the cinema. The child as witness is a central facet of del Toro's earlier film-making, in particular the Spanish films and *Mimic*. This trope does seem to become more buried within the more recent films, although arguably both *Hellboy* films have a man/child as the main figure. Interestingly, in *Pacific Rim* it seems that del Toro himself is the implied child/witness figure as borne out by the film's status as testimony to the director's childhood experience of film. One of *Pacific Rim's* most successful moments features Mako's childhood memory of the Kaiju attack on Tokyo, where she is saved by the intervention of the Jaeger piloted by Stacker Pentecost.

This scene switches the film's perspective from an omniscient overhead camera angle to a ground-level point of view. The focus on the destruction of a major Japanese city clearly references the 1945 attacks on Hiroshima and Nagasaki which underlie Honda's *Gojira* (*Godzilla*) (1954). Del Toro layers on to these other references that locate the scene in relation to his own oeuvre and other key intertexts in his film-making. The red shoes that the child Mako is wearing evokes the final fairy scenes of *Pan's Labyrinth*, when Ofelia/Princess Moanna is reunited with her parents, which in turn references the ur-text *The Wizard of Oz*. The rescue of little Mako has a Princess/George and the Dragon/ fairy-tale motif behind it, underpinned by the *Oz* reference, as well as a narrative function that establishes Mako's indebtedness, to be repaid to the patriarchal figure of Pentecost. The perhaps incongruous *Oz* motif also locates the band of misfit fighters who populate the film within an archetypal narrative that stresses the need for collective action to overcome individual weakness.

Pacific Rim expresses in almost every frame the director's love for what he sees as underrated source materials – the fiction of H.P. Lovecraft and Japanese Mecha, Kaiju and Anime. These sources are framed within other del Toro favourites, the blockbuster sci-fi/fantasy/horror, particularly the classic B-movies of this genre from the mid-twentieth century. In this respect, the film is in conversation with shining-steel contemporary franchises such as *Transformers* (2007–). If the discourse of *homage* is a feature of all del Toro's films, then its centrality to *Pacific Rim* needs to be recognized if the film is to be fully appreciated. Even the credits sequence contains reference to two very significant dedicatees from earlier film-making – the 'master monster makers' Ray Harryhausen (who died in May 2013) and Ishirō Honda. Harryhausen was perhaps the pre-eminent figure in the world of stop-motion animation. As del Toro told US *Entertainment Weekly*: 'To my generation, and every generation of monster lovers to come he will stand above all. Forever. His monsters made millions of lonely children smile and hope for a better world – a world populated by Cyclops and griffons and the children of the Hydra' (Boucher 2013). The second key figure is Ishirō Honda, whose seminal mega-beast movie *Godzilla* has provided a constant reference point for del Toro. In an introduction to the Criterion Collection edition of the film, del Toro has spoken of his deep love and affection for what he describes as a darkly poignant film made in the shadow of the Second World War destruction of Japanese cities with atomic weapons (del Toro 2013). Honda's film inaugurates the Kaiju monster tradition in Japanese film and del Toro acknowledges his debt by calling his own monsters in *Pacific Rim* Kaiju. Honda's much-quoted statement that '[m]onsters are born too tall, too strong, too heavy. That is their tragedy' sums up his lifetime belief that the monstrous could be complex and interesting.

These two figures represent the two main deities in the pantheon of pre-digital monster moviemaking and embody a kind pioneering creativity that is always visible in del Toro's work. However, a third possible dedicatee and major influence on *Pacific Rim* (and other del Toro films as noted elsewhere in this book) can be identified. This is Ridley Scott, two films by whom, *Alien* and *Blade Runner*, are significant intertextual presences in *Pacific Rim*. The former film's extensive use of uterine imagery in its exploration of monstrosity and gender has been widely discussed since it first appeared in 1979, most notably in Barbara Creed's *The Monstrous Feminine, Film, Feminism, Psychoanalysis* (see our earlier discussion of *Mimic*). Creed outlines the ways in which the uterine, fallopian and phallic mise-en-scène of Scott's film, which originated in the designs and artwork of the Swiss Surrealist artist H.R. Giger, underpins a sexual/reproductive subtext in which the alien monster becomes an embodiment of the all-consuming archaic mother against whom the central figure, Ripley, has to battle. For the most part the monsters in *Pacific Rim* owe more to the Gojira creature in Honda's *Godzilla* than to Scott and Geiger's metamorphic *Alien*, and the film locates their origin in a slightly more familiar primordial setting than *Alien*'s deep space – the deep ocean and then the bowels of the earth itself. However, this setting inaugurates a strand of comparably uterine imagery that pervades *Pacific Rim*'s final act. The Kaiju appear from a split in the ocean bed named 'The Breach' which itself leads, through a tubular passage called 'The Throat', to a womb-like space in which the Kaiju are bred like slaves by a master race of colonizing alien beings. The Breach is described as 'dilating' when the Kaiju emerge from it. Prior to this is a scene set in the body of a dead Kaiju in which the camera observes the work of the carpet-bagging Hannibal Chau's scavengers, in the course of which a baby monster is born. The key to the destruction of the Kaiju is the placing of a 'seed' – a massive explosion – in the womb-like 'terrible place' of Gothic imaginings in order to close the Breach. The film prepares for this through an almost relentless drenching of numerous scenes in water and rain. The battles between Jaegers and Kaijus take place in water, geographically appropriate given the Pacific Rim location, but also metaphorically telling as a symbolic fight for domination of the sea as the origin of the very human life that is threatened with the apocalypse. The rain that pervades elsewhere also suggests, as in Scott's *Blade Runner*, a world in which ecological change is leading to or has led to potential disaster. We are in fact told explicitly in *Pacific Rim* that the pollution of the ocean, amongst other ecological disasters, has made it easier for the Kaiju to develop – indeed the geeky scientist Geiszler says that 'we have practically terraformed it for them'. The dystopic setting of Scott's *Blade Runner*, dubbed as 'Hong Kong on a very bad day', despite being set in a future Los Angeles, re-emerges in *Pacific Rim*'s final act as Hong Kong is specifically referenced as the place for a heroic last stand against the Kaiju. The mise-en-scène here owes much to the dystopic vision of the urban environment in the earlier film – streets are crowded and rain-soaked, lit by an artificial daylight of neon and location for Hannibal Chau's black-market dealings in Kaiju parts. (The scene in his shop is a kind of comic/grotesque, almost wild-west (gunslingers included) version of a comparable but sinister scene in *Blade Runner* which takes place in Chew's prosthetic eye lab). Hong Kong's status as geographical, cultural and economic hub, historically colonized and re-colonized, is also appropriate in other ways. As is the case in *Pacific Rim*, both *Alien* and *Blade Runner* have colonization as a central theme – the former involving central characters who are part of the corporate colonization of space as well as the literal and violent colonization of the human body as a process of alien reproduction, the latter depicting the colonization of the human by the artificial (replicant) to the point that they are indistinguishable from one another. Memory, as a key aspect of identity, becomes deeply problematic and uncertain in both central characters in *Blade Runner* and it is significant that memory plays a key role in *Pacific Rim*, only here del Toro offers the hybrid dualized memory of the Drift as a powerful force for good. *Blade Runner* is also set in a world so environmentally polluted and dominated by corporate power that colonized 'off worlds' are advertised as (falsely) utopian alternatives from the polluted Earth. Its ambiguous ending and endemic pessimism played badly with audiences at the time – it appeared in the same year as Spielberg's resolutely feel-good *E.T. the Extra-Terrestrial*. Scott's film was notoriously subject to studio intervention – a situation del Toro could very well empathize with post *Mimic, At the Mountains of Madness* and even *The Hobbit: An Unexpected Journey*.

Pacific Rim melds a dizzyingly wide range of intertextual material but also makes numerous meta-textual references to del Toro's own oeuvre, most notably via images of colonization and resistance. This begins at the level of the body in *Cronos* (although wider issues of transnational invasion are hinted at throughout). Perlman's performance as the thuggish Angel de la Guardia is re-channelled in his brief cameo as the dangerous Hannibal Chau. Vampiric invasion re-occurs in both *Blade II* and *The Strain Trilogy*, in both cases associated with a pandemic form of disease. In *The Devil's Backbone* and *Pan's Labyrinth* colonization by fascism of both real bodies and the body politic is at the centre of the narratives and both deal with the politics of resistance and choice. The decommissioned Jaeger pilots become, as Pentecost suggests, 'the resistance' working against the grain of international bureaucracy which puts its faith in the so-called 'Wall of Life'. Again, images self-reflexively re-occur in *Pacific Rim*, notably the preserved foetuses which give *The Devil's Backbone* its title and which prefigure the pickled Kaiju organs that Chau markets and the resultant parasitic capitalism. Del Toro even reprises the Hitchcockian keyhole shot as Mako spies on Becket's room and body. *The Devil's Backbone* depends for its narrative arc on movement from individuality to community as the boys learn to work collectively in order to combat Jacinto, and del Toro explores a similar kind of movement in the idea of the Drift's neural handshake as well as the supranational philosophy behind the Pan Pacific Defence Corps.

Although del Toro has thus far been thwarted in his attempts to adapt H.P. Lovecraft's *At the Mountains of Madness*, due in part to the fact that Ridley Scott's *Prometheus* draws so heavily from this tale, he does manage to include a good deal of Lovecraftian elements into *Pacific Rim*, albeit in a way which is filtered through slapstick comedy and video game 'beat-em-ups'. Consider for instance the Kaiju species in the film, which are cloned beings altered by a creator species intent on colonizing the Earth. These increasingly large and vicious generations (Category 3, Category 4, etc.), which finally come to resemble huge Cthulhu species, are arguably 'Shoggoths' to their creator species's 'Elder Things' and continue the filmic tradition of mining the canon of Lovecraft. In addition, we have the character of Dr Newton Geiszler, a scientist who drifts (mind melds) with the consciousness of the Kaiju monsters. This puts an extraordinary mental pressure on Geiszler and he spends much of the movie in a semi-psychotic state, mirroring the psychological trauma that many of Lovecraft's protagonists experience after encountering his beasts. In contrast to Lovecraft's nihilistic sensibilities, where protagonists often lose their minds after gazing into the monstrous abyss, it is through fraternity and camaraderie that Geiszler prevails after he joins forces and drifts with his rival Gottlieb. This continues del Toro's consistent moral message that it is through the power of combination that redemption is possible. In the context of *Pacific Rim*, this involves a post-national world shake-up which seeks to undo the petty rivalries of the past and refigure humanity as a unified transnational conglomeration. In an interview del Toro has highlighted this intention:

> I wanted not to make a jingoistic war movie, where one country saves the entire world. I wanted to make it about the world saving the world … I tried to have a language that would allow kids, rather than identify with firepower and testosterone to identify with a band of losers, I didn't want to make a movie about winners and firepower (where) everything was shiny and glossy and new, I wanted to make a movie where everything was dented and rusty and off kilter and our heroes are incomplete unless they come together. So, rather than one hero I made quiet a choral movie where all ten or so characters have almost the same amount of time and each of them represents a different side to humanity: intelligence, ingenuity, self-sacrifice and so forth. (http://www.youtube.com/watch?v=B4amXT0sztA)

Part of this 'off-kilter' used-future style involves references to ecological damage; it is mentioned that pollution in the oceans make ideal conditions for the monstrous invasion and there is a reference to water damaging a nuclear reactor. This evokes the post-tsunami crisis at Fukushima and follows in the tradition of the Kaiju film as nuclear anxiety allegory. In many ways the transnational 'band of losers' are attempting to atone for the sins of the past where humanity has ignored environmental concerns and has instead remained in nation-specific self-serving silos. The Jaeger squad represent a kind of post-empire tag team and their instantly recognizable physical stereotypes draw upon Cold War propaganda visuals filtered through a video-game narrative simplicity. Del Toro has repeatedly referred to the film as a movie for kids as envisioned through his own 12-year-old self and the simplicity of the film has clearly irritated some who long for his earlier work. One review provides this scathing assessment: 'Mexican director Guillermo del Toro (*Pan's Labyrinth*) has made a regrettable switch from the art-house to the out-house. *Pacific Rim* is a special-effects behemoth, a toy franchise with a deafeningly loud movie attached – *Transformers* with an A-level' (Quinn 2013).

In some ways, the simplicity and reliance on visual symbolism of the film's narrative is both its driving force (there are no final act plot twists and deconstructions here) and what connects it to his earlier output. For instance, many of del Toro's films involve characters coming to terms with a subterranean/supernatural force which is initially terrifying and mysterious and eventually liberating (in, for instance, *The Devil's Backbone* where Carlos eventually realizes his bond with Santi), and in this respect there is an overarching plea for open-mindedness which binds his oeuvre. In *Pacific Rim*, characters need to be *literally* open-minded in order to have any chance of survival because of the psychic bonding technology. Similarly, in *Pan's Labyrinth* there is an exploration of what is monstrous and what is noble in a manner which is ambivalent to binary opposites and fundamentally extrapolative as to the human condition. No such ambivalence is evident in *Pacific Rim* where the monstrous features literally in the Kaiju and the noble in the good humanitarians who control the Jaegers. On this level, it is perhaps a misguided endeavour to seek out complex elements of del Toro's earlier work in a film which intentionally includes these elements distilled for a young audience.

What is absolutely in keeping with del Toro's method is the blending together of discrete genres to create a hybrid text. Yomota Inuhiko draws attention to the importance of the 'popular and mythical imagination of Japan' to the Kaiju genre where 'the south seas has always been an ambivalent space which possesses both utopian charm and sacred qualities' (Inuhiko 2007: 107). This charm was harnessed by the government in pre-war policies of colonial and military expansion. Considering this, the *Gojira* creature from Ishirō Honda's original film can be seen as much as a ghostly embodiment of soldiers lost during the war and through the folly of colonial territorialism as it can be as a spectre of atomic power. The Kaiju of *Pacific Rim* are themselves part of a colonial invasion, almost as a warning that if you play the colonial game you will eventually meet your match. The human race is eventually defended by a band of Mechas which appear to be manifestations of propaganda from the superpowers of Earth which so dominated the twentieth century. On this level, the film can be seen as a counter-text to the *Transformers* series which has been criticized by many as being deeply ideological, conservative, culturally hegemonic and fundamentally cynical.

Another key Japanese genre that del Toro employs is Mecha, which often features hyper-commodified powerful mechanical structures controlled by or fused with human pilots. On one level, the Mecha genre can be seen as an exercise in visual excess action and spectacle. This is typically seen in Manga and Anime but has its origins in early science-fiction writing. After Japan's re-engagement with the outside world in 1868, a popular writer translated for a Japanese audience was Jules Verne. Verne's stories often involve human beings given enhanced capacities of speed and power due to technological prowess. Books such as *Around the World in Eighty Days* (1873) illustrate a fascination with the harnessing of technology and *The Steam House* (1880) includes a colonial adventure with a group travelling through India in a huge steam-powered elephant. Verne's influence saw Mecha storylines incorporated into the popular 'boken shosetu' (adventure novel) genre which was prevalent in the first half of the twentieth century. The post-war period saw the massive growth in popularity of Manga comic books and later Anime where the Mecha sub-genre flourished. Sharalyn Orbaugh locates a strong element of technophilia in the images of the fighting human/robot hybrid and they can be read as pop-cultural fantasies which respond to the military defeat of the Second World War (Orbaugh 2005). We may be forgiven for assuming that these mechanically focused narratives work purely on a visual, action-orientated level of spectacle and that the human elements of the stories are relegated (a claim that some negative reviews of *Pacific Rim* back up). However, some have contended that at their core, Mecha narratives are about humans and their relation to technology and that fundamentally they question the nature of humanity in a technologically advanced society. Susan J. Napier explores this tendency:

> While the image in Mecha *anime* is strongly technological and is often specifically focused on the machinery of the armoured body, the narratives themselves often focus to a surprising extent on the human inside the machinery. It is this contrast between the vulnerable, emotionally complex and often youthful human being and the ominously faceless body armour or power suit and the awesome power he/she wields vicariously that makes for the most important tension in many mecha dramas. (2005: 205–206)

The creation of a hybrid Mecha genre continues del Toro's fascination with humanity's relationship with technology which began with *Cronos* and continued up to the Golden Army in the second *Hellboy* film, a symbol of the vast potential of technology to dominate and destroy as well as assist and enhance. Whereas *Cronos* and *Hellboy II: The Golden Army* have their origins in Gothic and horror genres, Mecha narratives are more firmly rooted in science fiction and as such tend towards some of the patriarchal conventions of the genre. The science-fiction writer Samuel Delaney has said of the genre:

> The flashing lights and the dials and the rest of the imagist paraphernalia of Science Fiction functioned as social signs-signs that people learned to read very quickly. They signalled technology. And technology was like a placard on the door saying 'Boys club' "Girls keep out!" (Delaney quoted in Barr 2008: 9)

Napier extends this observation in relation to Mecha fiction and the climactic third act saying that:

> [i]n contrast to the abjected feminine worlds of the gothic and the occult, which privilege women's bodies and their terrifying potential to engulf the male inside dark, organic spaces, the worlds of Mecha might be seen as stereotypically masculine in their emphasis on hardedged, thrusting, outward orientated power. (206)

In this respect, the blending of the Kaiju and Mecha genres for what del Toro considers to be the first time may be more than a simple homage to both. It can also be seen to fuse together feminine Gothic and the masculine technophilic, fundamentally queering each element along the way.

Typical of a del Toro project, the locating of a woman as a central character in a film drawing on genres not noted for their gender balance serves to disturb narrative assumptions and conventions. However, the character of the orphaned Mako Mori (Rinko Kikuchi), who becomes a Jaeger pilot against the wishes of her surrogate parent Stacker Pentecost (Idris Elba), is the only woman drawn in any detail in an otherwise male-dominated cast. As one critic noted, the film would fail the Bechdel Test requiring two female characters to talk about something other than a man. Mako's look seems to reference the visual conventions of Anime whilst adopting the active roles (including piloting giant robots) that some examples of the genre give to female characters. As Tom Shone notes in his blog/review, her bobbed hairstyle and androgynous appearance also references early (and unconventional) Hollywood stars such as Louise Brooks. Throughout the film del Toro actively avoids casting her as an object for the male gaze, even when she is stripped down to martial arts combat gear when proving her eligibility as a Jaeger pilot. In fact the leading young male character Raleigh Becket fulfils the role of gaze object as Mako observes him (on two occasions through a keyhole) stripped to the waist. Their relationship is portrayed more in the vein of a 'bromance', given their tag partnership in operating Gypsy Danger. Only at the very end of the film does the relationship edge towards overt sexuality when, having successful planted the device that will destroy the Kaiju and their makers, they come together on a dinghy in a scene that bizarrely resembles the end of a Bond movie, in particular *The Spy Who Loved Me* (1977). There is only one other named woman character, Sasha Kaidanovsky – the female half of the husband and wife Russian Jaeger team who are killed in the final denouement. Both Russians are played as cartoon characters by del Toro – as he says, 'They are incredibly fierce, they are unafraid, they are very much hardcore' (Cohen and del Toro 2013: 35). They are also made to look very similar, with cropped white/ blond hair and dark eyes. Perhaps the most mysterious female characters are the nuns who are briefly seen in a shot prior to the final attack on Hong Kong. They are part of a religious cult that worship in the skeletal remains of a Kaiju and who represent a reverse image of the resistance Jaeger fighters in their apparently willing acceptance of the apocalypse and their reported belief that humanity is being punished by displeased Gods.

The film offers an apparently binarized view of masculinity. On the one hand there are the Jaeger pilots whose conventional male physicality plays out a kind of *Star Wars* meets *Top Gun* (1986) machismo, complete with appropriate accoutrements (the bulldog that the Australian Chuck Hansen somewhat incongruously trails around, which seems like an ironic reference back to Sam's feminizing bling-laden Chihuahua in *Transformers*). Other occasional intertextual flickers suggest some level of parody here – during the long flashback sequence that begins the film, Becket's older brother and co-pilot Yancy echoes Han Solo's remark to Luke in *Star Wars Episode IV: A New Hope* when he tells him 'Don't get too cocky, kid'. Physical or emotional vulnerability is to be quickly hidden or denied (as in the case of the blood that seeps from Pentecost's nose, signifying his terminal cancer) or ruthlessly exposed if seen as threatening or inadequate (exemplified in the aggressive Hansen junior's attitude to Becket). The iron will of masculine repression is particularly evidenced in the character of Stacker Pentecost (Idris Elba), the outwardly severe Marshall, who leads the Jaeger pilots, self-described in the film thus, '[a]ll I need to be to you and everyone in this place is a fixed point. Last man standing'. This includes his adopted child Mako, their relationship hidden until it is revealed to Becket during his 'drift' with her. His body is an interesting site of tension in the film. Outwardly statuesque and imposing, he is largely seen in non-military costume but is always finely tailored in blue double-breasted suiting when not in combat gear. According to the film's costume designer Kate Hawley, '[h]is clothes are almost holding him up' (Cohen and del Toro 2013: 35). In another scene he twice tells Becket (who has just grabbed him) 'Never touch me again.' This constructs an important paradox that is essential to the film – his near-cyborgian status as the most experienced pilot and military strategist is engaged in an uneasy symbiosis with his human fallibility. The implications of his name also seem to embody essential contradiction – the more mundane Stacker sitting uneasily with the numinous and charismatic implications of Pentecost, which are ultimately fulfilled in his self-sacrificial death. *Pacific Rim* also focuses on another problematic parent/child father/son relationship (a recurrent del Toro motif) in the two Australian characters, the Hansens. Ostensibly included to serve the film's internationalist agenda (and also to provide a memorable shot of the Sydney Opera House juxtaposed with a similarly finned Kaiju) the pair's full-on, apparently unequivocal masculinity is portrayed as being beset by oedipal tensions: the son Chuck is described by Pentecost (in one of the film's snappier lines) as an 'egomaniac with daddy issues'. In another cherishably parodic moment when, during a Kaiju battle, their Jaeger has been disabled, the father suggests they exit the machine in order to 'do something really stupid', that is fire flares at the ravening, rampant monster. In contrast, the two geeky odd-couple scientists who provide the film's intended comic relief are small and physically inept but intellectually brilliant, thus apparently following genre conventions. Dr Gottlieb (Burn Gorman) references Kubrick's *Dr Strangelove* (1964) and also appears to have issues with personal space, indeed with his own humanity as he declares numbers to be 'the closest we will get to the handwriting of God'. The more developed Dr Geiszler (Charlie Day), whose body is tattooed with Kaiju images as a sign of his obsession with the beasts, is a continuation of the kind of incorporation of the monstrous into normality demonstrated in the opening section of the film, where we see ironic fleeting images, inter alia, of children's toys and TV game shows based on the Kaiju, all part of the assimilation and 'moving on' process that the emotionally bereft Becket wearily narrates. Capitalism's greedily monstrous and amoral capacity to swallow, assimilate and profit from any eventuality re-emerges in Geiszler's dealings with the one-eyed and cynically piratic Hannibal Chau (Ron Perlman), another human/monster who deals in black-market Kaiju parts. Both Geiszler and Chau provide Spielbergian moments of comic drama as they are pursued and/or devoured by Kaiju. A key intertextual source here is *Jurassic Park* (1993), which arguably, along with the earlier *Jaws* (1975), established the grammar of the modern monster movie. Del Toro's spin is to reprieve both of these less-than-heroic characters. Geiszler and Gottlieb finally develop a way of defeating the Kaiju by mind-melding with remnants of monster brains and in doing so prefigure the film's final denouement where Mako and Becket physically enter the beasts' lair. The geeks have already done this, appropriately using their minds which, in a very Lovecraftian moment, nearly sends them mad, but does save the world. Hannibal Chau, having been swallowed by a baby Kaiju, re-emerges in the film's credit sequence cursing the loss of one of his trademark silver shoes.

The third genre traditionally filled with male protagonists which *Pacific Rim* evokes is the war movie or more specifically, the resistance war movie. The director has said in interview that he is 'obsessed' by the period which embodied the 'last bout of heroism' and that *Pacific Rim* is thematically and visually inspired by the period (http://www.youtube.com/watch?v=B4amXT0sztA). Certainly, the broadly drawn characters such as Becket's reticent hero and Chau's profiteering uber-spiv, represent figures familiar to fans of the war movie. Stacker Pentecost's rousing speech is part Winston Churchill, part Henry V and the battles are reminiscent of bomber squad missions. The Jaegers themselves are also designed with key propaganda/ideological features in mind (the main one (Gypsy Danger) is designed as a cross between the Empire State Building and John Wayne) and embody ideas associated with the Second World War through a kind of mechanoid hypostasis.

Robert McLaughlin (2006) notices how key war movies set in the Pacific such as Howard Hawkes' *Air Force* (1943) dwell on the notion of interdependence as key to survival and that the bomber crew scenario acts as a highly suitable metaphor for the notion of unity in the face of attack which is the prevailing moral message of *Pacific Rim*. The film is not the first to draw upon Second World War images of crew as symbols of unity in a monster-movie rendition. Steven Spielberg's *Jaws* employs a similar strategy and there are key similarities to be found in del Toro's film. Robert Wilson contends that *Jaws* echoes the submarine movie and that we can read the shark's attacks on the beaches of Amity to the attacks on Pearl Harbour and the resulting counter-mission from Brody and his crew as the US Pacific campaign, saying that '[S]pielberg was depending on his audience's experience with sub-war movies to provide a thematic context in which to dramatize both the Shark's obvious disdain for the rules of the Geneva Convention and Quint's desire for a personal revenge against it' (1977: 32–33).

Other readings of *Jaws* have worked along Freudian lines and have drawn attention to the somatization of sexual anxieties and desires in the film. According to these readings, the libertine sexual activity of the young party kids at the beginning of the film triggers terrible retribution. The shark, a phallic monster powered by the aqueous feminine, attacks the children of the community which has allowed such sexual transgressions and the men of the community must band together to hunt the vengeful threat and drive it back to its oceanic abyss (Morris 2007: 55–56). Others have identified the primal horror of *Jaws* to be 'oral sadism' 'regression to the womb', and in an interview Spielberg has said that the film is 'a raw nerve movie, it's just baring your nerves and saying this is about the birth sac, you swim around in yourself' (Gordon 2008: 38). *Pacific Rim* can be read in similar terms, with the Kaiju representing creatures spawned from the ocean from a symbolic vaginal fissure and combated by the phallic Mechas. In a typically idiosyncratic take on this psycho-sexual fantasy, del Toro adds Mako Mori to the drama, and it is a woman who is the pivot for the humans' success. In a key moment, she must cut her umbilical bond with Pentecost, her father figure, in order to penetrate the inter-dimensional fissure. In this context, the denouement of *Pacific Rim* is symbolically extremely violent, in a film that is aimed in a large part to a teenage audience. In order to close the rift, Mori and Becket must penetrate it and release their nuclear payload into the utero-tube to complete the mission of the Mecha fleet. What we are left with is an almost gleefully immature and bombastic film which on further inspection involves a complex, intriguing and disturbing symbolic discourse. If we are to acknowledge the influence of Scott's *Alien* on much of del Toro's work including *Pacific Rim*, the fact that the humans name the inter-dimensional rift 'the throat' is pertinent. The finale of the film can be seen as a counter-re-enactment of Kane's horrific encounter with the alien 'face hugger' which penetrates his throat and impregnates him with the alien spawn. In this case, vengeful humans penetrate the throat of the alien invaders and plant their explosive seed. Whatever the reading of *Pacific Rim*, be it a *homage*, popcorn adventure spectacle, Freudian psycho-sexual fantasy or intertextual mash-up, it continues del Toro's alchemic schema and adds to a body of work which is as complexly layered as it is entertaining.

Filmography

A.I. Artificial Intelligence (2001) Dir. Steven Spielberg.

Air Force (1943) Dir. Howard Hughes.

Alien (1979) Dir. Ridley Scott.

Aliens (1986) Dir. James Cameron.

Alligator (1980) Dir. Lewis Teague.

Apocalypse Now (1979) Dir. Francis Ford Coppola.

Biutiful (2010) Dir. Alejandro González Iñárritu.

Black Sabbath (1963) Dir. Mario Bava.

Black Sunday (1960) Dir. Mario Bava.

Blade (1998) Dir. Stephen Norrington

Blade II (2002) Dir. Guillermo del Toro.

Blade Runner (1982) Dir. Ridley Scott.

Blue Velvet (1986) Dir. David Lynch.

Bram Stoker's Dracula (1992) Dir. Francis Ford Coppola.

Bride of Frankenstein (1935) Dir. James Whale.

Caravaggio (1986) Dir. Derek Jarman.

Carrie (1976) Dir. Brian De Palma.

Children of Men (2006) Dir. Alfonso Cuarón.

Cinema 16: World Short Films (2008) Dir. Guillermo del Toro et al.

Creature from the Black Lagoon (1954) Dir. Jack Arnold.

Cría Cuervos (1976) Dir. Carlos Saura.

Cronos (1993) Dir. Guillermo del Toro.

Cruising (1980) Dir. William Friedkin.

Dark City (1998) Dir. Alex Proyas.

Deep Red (1975) Dir. Dario Argento.

Dial M for Murder (1954) Dir. Alfred Hitchcock.

Don't Be Afraid of the Dark (2010) Dir. Troy Nixey.

Doña Lupe (1985) Dir. Guillermo del Toro.

Dr. Strangelove (1964) Dir. Stanley Kubrick.

Eastern Promises (2007) Dir. David Cronenberg.

Edward Scissorhands (1990) Dir. Tim Burton.

El Corazón del Bosque (*Heart of the Forest*) (1979) Dir. Manuel Gutierrez Aragon.

El Espinazo del Diablo (*The Devil's Backbone*) (2001) Dir. Guillermo del Toro.

El Fantasma del Convento (*The Phantom of the Convent*) (1934) Dir. Fernando de Fuentes.

El Laberinto del Fauno (Pan's Labyrinth) (2006) Dir. Guillermo del Toro.

El Spíritu de la Colmena (The Spirit of the Beehive) (1973) Dir. Victor Erice.

El Topo (The Mole) (1970) Dir. Alejandro Jodorowsky.

Empire of the Sun (1987) Dir. Steven Spielberg.

E.T. the Extra-Terrestrial (1982) Dir. Steven Spielberg.

eXistenZ (1999) Dir. David Cronenberg.

Fantasia (1940) Dirs. Various.

Fort Apache: The Bronx (1981) Dir. Daniel Petrie.

Frankenstein (1931) Dir. James Whale.

Frenzy (1972) Dir. Alfred Hitchcock.

Friday the 13th (1980) Dir. Sean S. Cunningham.

Gattaca (1997) Dir. Andrew Niccol.

Geometria (1987) Dir. Guillermo del Toro.

Gods and Monsters (1998) Dir. Bill Condon.

Gojira (Godzilla) (1954) Dir. Ishirō Honda.

Gone With the Wind (1939) Dir. Victor Fleming.

Goya in Bordeaux (1999) Dir. Carlos Saura.

Grindhouse (2007) Dir. Robert Rodriguez.

Halloween (1978) Dir. John Carpenter.

Hancock (2008) Dir. Peter Berg.

Hellboy (2004) Dir. Guillermo del Toro.

Hellboy II: The Golden Army (2008) Dir. Guillermo del Toro.

A History of Violence (2005) Dir. David Cronenberg.

Hook (1991) Dir. Steven Spielberg.

Hulk (2003) Dir. Ang Lee.

I Am Legend (2007) Dir. Francis Lawrence.

Indiana Jones and the Temple of Doom (1984) Dir. Steven Spielberg.

Interview With the Vampire (1994) Dir. Neil Jordan.

Iron Man (2008) Dir. Jon Favreau.

Jaws (1975) Dir. Steven Spielberg.

Julia's Eyes (2010) Dir. Guillem Morales.

Jurassic Park (1993) Dir. Steven Spielberg.

Kick-Ass (2010) Dir. Mathew Vaughn.

Kung Fu Panda 2 (2011) Dir. Jennifer Yu.

Kuroneko (1968) Dir. Kaneto Shindō.

L'Arcano Incantatore (*Arcane Sorcerer*) (1996) Dir. Pupi Avati.

La Caza (1966) Dir. Carlos Saura.

La Haine (1995) Dir. Mathieu Kassovitz.

Lady from Shanghai (1947) Dir. Orson Welles.

Logan's Run (1976) Dir. Michael Anderson.

Lord of the Flies (1963) Dir. Peter Brook

Los Olvidados (The Forgotten) (1950) Dir. Luis Buñuel.

Mama (2013) Dir. Andrés Maschietti.

Mimic (1997) Dir. Guillermo del Toro.

Minority Report (2002) Dir. Steven Spielberg.

Munich (2005) Dir. Steven Spielberg.

My Own Private Idaho (1991) Dir. Gus Van Sant

Naked Lunch (1991) Dir. David Cronenberg.

North by Northwest (1959) Dir. Alfred Hitchcock.

Nosferatu (1922) Dir. F.W. Murnau.

Nosferatu: Phantom der Nacht (*Nosferatu*) (1979) Dir. Werner Herzog.

Notorious (1946) Dir. Alfred Hitchcock.

On the Town (1949) Dirs. Stanley Donen and Gene Kelly.

Onibaba (1964) Dir. Kaneto Shindō.

Pacific Rim (2013) Dir. Guillermo del Toro.

Prometheus (2012) Dir. Ridley Scott.

Psycho (1960) Dir. Alfred Hitchcock.

Puss in Boots (2011) Dir. Chris Miller.

Rear Window (1954) Dir. Alfred Hitchcock.

Rise of the Guardians (2012) Dir. Peter Ramsey.

Saving Private Ryan (1998) Dir. Steven Spielberg.

Schindler's List (1993) Dir. Steven Spielberg.

Scream (1996–2011) Dir. Wes Craven.

Se7en (1995) Dir. David Fincher.

Shadow of a Doubt (1943) Dir. Alfred Hitchcock.

Silent Running (1972) Dir. Douglas Trumbull.

Sleeping Beauty (1959) Dir. Clyde Geronimi.

Soylent Green (1973) Dir. Richard Fleischer.

Spider-Man (2002) Dir. Sam Raimi.

Splice (2009) Dir. Vincenzo Natale.

Star Wars Episode IV: A New Hope (1977) Dir. George Lucas.

Star Wars: Episode I – The Phantom Menace (1999) Dir. George Lucas.

Strange Days (1995) Dir. Katherine Bigelow.

Superman (1978) Dir. Richard Donner.

Superman Returns (2006) Dir. Brian Singer.

Sukiyaki Django Western (2007) Dir. Takashi Miike.

Suspiria (1977) Dir. Dario Argento.

Taxi Driver (1976) Dir. Martin Scorsese.

Terminator 2: Judgement Day (1991) Dir. James Cameron.

The Cabinet of Dr. Caligari (1920) Dir. Robert Wiene.

The Creature from the Black Lagoon (1954) Dir. Jack Arnold.

The Devils (1971) Dir. Ken Russell.

The Dirty Dozen (1967) Dir. Robert Aldrich.

The Fly (1986) Dir. David Cronenberg.

The Godfather (1972) Dir. Francis Ford Coppola.

The Hobbit: An Unexpected Journey (2012) Dir. Peter Jackson.

The Innocents (1961) Dir. Jack Clayton.

The Lost World: Jurassic Park (1997) Dir. Steven Spielberg.

Them! (1954) Dir. Gordon Douglas.

The Magnificent Seven (1960) Dir. John Sturges.

The Matrix (1999) Dirs. Andy Wachowski and Lana Wachowski.

The Orphanage (El Orfanato) (2007) Dir. J.A. Bayona.

The Others (2001) Dir. Alejandro Amenábar.

The Sixth Sense (1999) Dir. M. Night Shyamalan.

The Spy Who Loved Me (1977) Dir. Lewis Gilbert.

The Terminator (1984) Dir. James Cameron.

The Twilight Saga (2008–2012) Dirs. Various.

The Wicker Man (1973) Dir. Robin Hardy.

The Wizard of Oz (1939) Dir. Victor Fleming.

Top Gun (1986) Dir. Tony Scott.

Transformers (2007) Dir. Michael Bay.

Twelve Monkeys (1995) Dir. Terry Gilliam.

Vertigo (1958) Dir. Alfred Hitchcock.

War of the Worlds (2005) Dir. Steven Spielberg.

Watchmen (2009) Dir. Zack Snyder.

Wuthering Heights (1939) Dir. William Wyler

X-Men (2000) Dir. Bryan Singer.

Y Tu Mamá También (2001) Dir. Alfonso Cuarón.

TV programmes

Angel (1999–2004) Dirs. Joss Whedon et al.

Buffy the Vampire Slayer (1997–2003) Dirs. Joss Whedon et al.

Dickens on Film (2012) Dir. Anthony Wall, BBC, 13 January 2012.

Goya Crazy like a Genius (2008) Robert Hughes, BBC, 15 February 2008.

La Hora Marcada (1986–1990) Dirs. Various, including Guillermo del Toro, Alfonso Cuarón, Emanuel Lubezki.

Sex and the City (1998–2004) Dirs. Various.

The Big Bang Theory (2007–) Dirs. Mark Cendrowski et al.

The Night Gallery (1970–1973) Dir. Rod Sterling.

The Outer Limits (1963–1965) Dirs. Various.

True Blood (2008–) Dirs. Alan Ball et al.

DVDs

Blade II. Eiv. (2002).

Cronos. The Criterion Collection. (2010).

Hellboy (Director's Cut). Sony Pictures Home Entertainment. (2004).

Hellboy II: The Golden Army (2 Disc Special Edition). UCA. (2008).

Los Olvidados (60th Anniversary Edition). 3DD/*inD*. (2010).

Mimic (Director's Cut Blu-ray). Miramax/StudioCanal. (2011).

Spirit of the Beehive. Optimum Home Releasing. (2003).

The Guillermo del Toro Collection: Blu-ray Special Edition (*Cronos*, *The Devil's Backbone*, *Pan's Labyrinth*). Optimum Releasing. (2010).

Comicography

Giménez, C. (2007), *Paracuellos*, Random House Mondadori.

Jodorowsky, A. (1966), *Anibal 5*, Editorial Novaro.

Mignola, M. (1993–), *Hellboy*, Dark Horse Comics.

Mignola, M. and Augustyn, B. (1989), *Gotham by Gaslight*, DC Comics.

Mignola, M. and Starlin, J. (1988), *Cosmic Odyssey*, DC Comics.

Bibliography

Abbott, S. (2007), *Celluloid Vampires: Life after Death in the Modern World*, Austin: University of Texas Press.

Acevedo-Muñoz, E. R. (2003), *Buñuel and Mexico: The Crisis of National Cinema*, Berkeley: University of California Press.

Ackroyd, P. (1990), *Dickens*, New York: HarperCollins.

Adamou, C. (2011), 'Evolving Portrayals of Masculinity in Superhero Films', in R. J. Gray and B. Kaklamanidou (eds.), *The 21st Century Superhero: Essays on Gender, Genre and Globalization in Film*, Jefferson NC: McFarland.

Anderson, J. (2013), '*Pacific Rim* Cinematographer Guillermo Navarro goes digital on del Toro's Gargantuan Monster Epic'. *Indiewire*, accessed 13 July 2013 from http://blogs.indiewire.com/thompsononhollywood/pacific-rim-cinematographer-navarro-goes-digital-on-del-toros-gargantuan-monster-epic

Applebaum, S. (2006), 'Guillermo del Toro: "The violence in this movie is calculated to be absolutely, realistically, unpleasant." ' *Stephen Applebaum Culture Web*, May 2006, accessed 24 August 2012 from http://stephenapplebaum.blogspot.co.uk/2006/12/guillermo-del-toro-violence-in-this.html

Archibald, D. (2001), 'Insects and violence'. *Guardian*, 28 November 2001, accessed 17 November 2012 from http://www.theguardian.com/culture/2001/nov/28/artsfeatures?INTCMP=SRCH

Armitt, L. (2000), 'The Magic Realism of the Contemporary Gothic', in D. Punter (ed.), *A Companion to the Gothic*, Oxford: Blackwell.

Atkinson, M. (2007), 'Moral Horrors in Guillermo del Toro's *Pan's Labyrinth*: The Supernatural Realm Mirrors Man's Inhumanity to Man', *Film Comment*, 1: 50–53.

Auerbach, N. (1995), *Our Vampires, Ourselves*, Chicago: University of Chicago Press.

Bacon, S. (2012), 'Las Cucarachas in Transylvania: Trespassing and Identity in Guillermo Del Toro's *The Strain Trilogy*'. *Hispanet Journal* 5, accessed 2 February 2013 from http://hispanetjournal.com/LasCucarachas.pdf

Badger, G. (1999), 'Towards a Moral Pornography: Joel-Peter Witkin', in D. Brittain (ed.), *Creative Camera: Thirty Years of Writing*, Manchester: Manchester University Press.

Bakke, G. (2010), 'Dead White Men: An Essay on the Changing Dynamics of Race in US Action Cinema', *Anthropological Quarterly*, 83(2): 400–428.

Barlow, A. (2005), *The DVD Revolution: Movies, Culture And Technology*, Santa Barbara: Praeger.

Barr, M. S. (2008), *Afro-future Females: Black Writers Chart Science Fiction's Newest New-wave Trajectory*, Columbus: Ohio State University Press.

Bell, J. (2012), 'Directors' Poll'. *Sight & Sound*, 62–71, accessed 6 January 2012 from http://explore.bfi.org.uk/sightandsoundpolls/2012/

Benshoff, H. M. (1997), *Monsters in the Closet: Homosexuality and the Horror Film*, Manchester: Manchester University Press.

Benshoff, H. M. and Griffin, S. (eds.) (2004), *Queer Cinema: The Film Reader*, London: Routledge.

Berger, V. and Komori, M. (eds.) (2010), *Polyglot Cinema: Migration and Transcultural Narration in France, Italy, Portugal and Spain*, Vienna: Lit Verlag.

Boucher, G. (2010), 'Guillermo del Toro on Frank Franzetta'. *Los Angeles Times*, 11 May 2010, accessed 4 April 2012 from http://herocomplex.latimes.com/uncategorized/guillermo-del-toro-on-frank-frazetta-he-gave-the-world-a-new-pantheon-of-heroes/

——. (2013), 'We Lost a Legend'. *Entertainment Weekly*, accessed 5 April 2012 from http://insidemovies.ew.com/2013/05/07/jj-abrams-damon-lindelof-guillermo-del-toro-ray-harryhausen/

Bourdieu, P. (2010), *Distinction: A Social Critique of the Judgement of Taste*, Abingdon: Routledge.

Bovberg, J. (2003), 'DVD Talk Interview: Guillermo del Toro'. *DVD Talk*, accessed 3 June 2013 from http://www.dvdtalk.com/guillermodeltoro.html

Bradshaw, P. (2011), 'Don't Be Afraid of the Dark'. *Guardian*, 6 October 2011, accessed 10 October 2011 from http://www.theguardian.com/film/2011/oct/06/dont-be-afraid-of-the-dark-review

Brereton, P. (2005), *Hollywood Utopia: Ecology in Contemporary American Cinema*, Bristol: Intellect.

Breznican, A. (2008), '*Hellboy II* director del Toro takes his demons seriously'. *USA Today*, 7 July 2008, accessed 3 October 2012 from http://usatoday30.usatoday.com/life/movies/news/2008-07-07-del-toro-hellboy_N.htm

Brinks, E. (2004), '"Nobody's Children": Gothic Representation and Traumatic History in *The Devil's Backbone*', *JAC*, 24(2): 291–312.

Bruhm, S. (2002), 'The Contemporary Gothic: Why We Need It', in J. E. Hogle (ed.), *The Cambridge Companion to Gothic Fiction*, Cambridge: Cambridge University Press.

Bruns, A. (2008), *Blogs, Wikipedia, Second Life, and Beyond: From Production to Produsage*, Bern: Peter Lang, Publishing.

Brunvand, J. H. (1981), *The Vanishing Hitchhiker: American Urban Legends and Their Meanings*, New York: W. W. Norton.

Burleson, D. R. (1990), *Lovecraft: Disturbing the Universe*, Lexington: University Press of Kentucky.

Calautti, K. (2012), 'Guillermo del Toro on *Pacific Rim, Rise of the Guardians* and More'. *Spin Off Online*, accessed 4 February 2013 from http://spinoff.comicbookresources. com/2012/11/12/guillermo-del-toro-talks-pacific-rim-rise-of-the-guardians-and-more

Callaghan, G. (2013), *H. P. Lovecraft's Dark Arcadia: The Satire, Symbology and Contradiction*, Jefferson NC: McFarland.

Camino, M. (2007), 'Women, War and Wounds: The Spanish Civil War in Victor Erice's *El espíritu de la colmena* and David Trueba's *Soldados de Salamina*', *International Journal of Iberian Studies*, 20(2): 91–104.

Carrier, D. (2003), *Writing about Visual Art*, New York: Allworth Press.

Carter, A. (1983), 'Notes from the Front Line', in M. Wandor (ed.), *On Gender and Writing*, London: Pandora Press.

Case, S.-E. (1993), 'Tracking the Vampire', *The Journal of Feminist Cultural Studies*, 3(2): 1–20.

Chun, K. (2002), 'What Is a Ghost? An Interview with Guillermo del Toro', *Cineaste: America's Leading Magazine on the Art and Politics of the Cinema*, 27(2): 28–31.

Clark, N. and Boucher, G. (2010), 'Guillermo del Toro reflects on scares (*Cronos*) and scars (*The Hobbit*)'. *Los Angeles Times*, 10 December 2010, accessed 3 May 2012 from http://herocomplex.latimes.com/movies/guillermo-del-toro-reflects-on-scares-cronos-and-scars-the-hobbit/

Clark, R. and McDonald, K. (2010), 'A Constant Transit of Finding': Fantasy as Realisation in Pan's Labyrinth', *Children's Literature in Education: An International Quarterly*, 41(1): 52–63.

Clover, C. J. (1993), *Men, Women and Chainsaws: Gender in the Modern Horror Film*, London: British Film Institute.

Cohen, R. (1997), *Global Diasporas: An Introduction*, London: UCL Press.

Cohen, D. and del Toro, G. (2013), *Pacific Rim: Man, Machines and Monsters*, London: Titan Books.

Coleman, L. (1996), 'Alligators in Sewers', in G. Bennett and P. Smith (eds.), *Contemporary Legend: A Reader*, New York: Garland.

Contreras, J. P. (2009), 'The New Master of Horror Movies', *Americas (English Edition)*, 16(2): 60–61.

Cooper, L. A. (2012), *Dario Argento*, Urbana: University of Illinois Press.

Corliss, R. (2008), 'Sci-Fi's No. 1 Fanboy, Forrest J Ackerman, dies at 92'. *Time*, 6 December 2008, accessed 12 February 2013 from http://www.time.com/time/magazine/article/0,9171,1865977,00.html

Creed, B. (1989), 'Horror and the Monstrous Feminine: An Imaginary Abjection', in J. Donald (ed.), *Fantasy and the Cinema*, London: British Film Institute.

———. (1993), *The Monstrous-Feminine: Film, Feminism, Psychoanalysis*, London: Routledge.

Cruz, G. (2009), 'Guillermo del Toro on vampires'. *Time*, 3 June 2009, accessed 6 June 2013 from http://www.time.com/time/arts/article/0,8599,1902395,00.html

Davies, A. (2006), 'The Beautiful and the Monstrous Masculine: The Male Body and Horror *in El Espinazo del Diablo* (Guillermo del Toro 2001)', *Studies in Hispanic Cinemas*, 3(3): 135–147.

———. (2008), 'Guillermo del Toro's *Cronos*: The Vampire as Embodied Heterotopia', *Quarterly Review of Film and Video*, 25(5): 395–403.

———. (2012), *Spanish Spaces: Landscape, Space and Place in Contemporary Spanish Culture*, Liverpool: Liverpool University Press.

Davies, L. (2011), 'Guillermo del Toro's *Cronos* or the Pleasures of Impurity', in S. Wasson and E. Alder (eds.), *Gothic Science Fiction 1980–2010*, Liverpool: Liverpool University Press.

Deleyto, C. and Azcona, M. M. (2010), *Alejandro González Iñárritu*, Urbana-Champaign IL: University of Illinois Press.

Dennison, S. and Lim, S. H. (eds.) (2006), *Remapping World Cinema: Identity, Culture and Politics in Film*, London: Wallflower.

DePalma, A. (1994), 'From a Mexican Grave Comes "Cronos"'. *The New York Times*, 20 March 1994, accessed 8 January 2013 from http://www.nytimes.com/1994/03/20/movies/film-from-a-mexican-grave-comes-cronos.html

Derrida, J. (1994), *Spectres of Marx: The State of the Debt, the Work of Mourning, and the New International*, London: Routledge.

Derry, C. (2009), *Dark Dreams 2. 0: A Psychological History of the Modern Horror Film from the 1950s to the 21st Century*, Jefferson NC: McFarland.

Dery, M. (ed.) (1994), *Flame Wars: The Discourse of Cyberculture*, Durham NC: Duke University Press.

De Ros, X. (2005), '*El Espíritu de la Colmena*', in A. Mira (ed.), *The Cinema of Spain and Portugal*, London: Wallflower.

del Toro, G. Official website accessed 13 January 2012, from http://deltorofilms.com/wp/

———. (2006), *El Laberinto Del Fauno*, Madrid: Ocho y Medio, Libros de Cine.

———. (2008a), 'Director Guillermo del Toro on how he made Hellboy in his image', *Observer*, 27 July 2008, accessed 8 September 2012 from http://www.theguardian.com/film/2008/jul/27/guillermodeltoro

———. (2008b) *Hitchcock*, Madrid: Editorial Espasa Calpe, S.A.

———. (2012a), 'Guillermo del Toro on villains, horror and fairy tale'. *Breezes from Wonderland*, accessed 4 May 2013 from http://blogs.law.harvard.edu/tatar/2012/11/20/guillermo-del-toro-on-the-villains-horror-and-fairy-tales/

———. (2012b), 'The Genius of Hitchcock: Lessons of Darkness', *Sight and Sound*, 22(8): 38–42.

———. (2012c), 'Guillermo del Toro's Top Ten'. *Criterion Collection*, accessed 21 February 2013 from http://www.criterion.com/explore/125-guillermo-del-toro-s-top-10

———. (2013) 'Guillermo del Toro on *Godzilla*'. *Criterion Collection*, 11 July 2013, accessed 15 July 2013 from http://www.criterion.com/current/posts/2830-guillermo-del-toro-on-godzilla

del Toro, G. and Golden, C. (2011), *Don't Be Afraid of the Dark: Blackwood's Guide to Dangerous Fairies*, New York: Hyperion.

del Toro, G. and Hogan, C. (2010), *The Strain*, London: Harper.

———. (2011), *The Fall*, London: Harper.

———. (2012), *The Night Eternal*, London: Harper.

del Toro, G., Mignola, M., Sandoval, S. and Ruiz Velasco, F. (2008), *Hellboy II: The Art of the Movie*, Milwaukie: Dark Horse Books.

Dickstein, M. (2004), 'The Aesthetics of Fright', in B. K. Grant and C. Sharrett (eds.), *Planks of Reason: Essays on the Horror Film*, Oxford: Scarecrow Press.

Diehl, L. A. (2008), *Estranging Science, Fictionalizing Bodies: Viral Invasions, Infectious Fictions, and the Biological Discourses of 'the Human,' 1818–2005*, Ann Arbor: Proquest.

DiMare, P. C. (2011), *Movies in American History: An Encyclopedia*, Santa Barbara: ABC-Clio.

DiPaolo, M. (2011), *War, Politics and Superheroes: Ethics and Propaganda in Comics and Film*, Jefferson NC: McFarland.

Dixon, W. W. (2007), 'Night World: New York as Noir Universe', in M. Pomerance (ed.), *City That Never Sleeps: New York and the Filmic Imagination*, New Brunswick NJ: Rutgers University Press.

Dusinberre, J. (1999), *Alice to the Lighthouse: Children's Books and Radical Experiments in Art*, Basingstoke: MacMillan Press.

Earles, S. (2009), *The Golden Labyrinth: The Unique Films of Guillermo del Toro*, Hereford: Noir.

Eisenstein, S. (1949), *Film Form: Essays in Film Theory* (ed. J. Leyda), New York: Harcourt, Brace.

Elder, R. K. (2013), *The Best Film You've Never Seen: 35 Directors Champion the Forgotten Or Critically Savaged Movies They Love*, Chicago: Chicago Review Press.

Elliott, D. (2010), 'Queering the cult of Carrie: appropriations of a horror icon in Charles Lum's Indelible'. *Scope*, (15), accessed 12 December 2012 from http://www.scope.nottingham.ac.uk/cultborr/chapter.php?id=12

Ellis, J. and Sánchez-Arce, A. M. (2011), ' "The Unquiet Dead": Memories of the Spanish Civil War in Guillermo del Toro's *Pan's Labyrinth*', in A. Sinha and T. McSweeney (eds.), *Millennial Cinema: Memory in Global Film*, New York: Wallflower.

Elsaesser, T. (2013), 'Specularity and Engulfment: Francis Ford Coppola and Bram Stoker's *Dracula*', in S. Neale and M. Smith (eds.), *Contemporary Hollywood Cinema*, London: Routledge.

Ezra, E. and Rowden, T. (eds.) (2006), *Transnational Cinema: The Film Reader*, London: Routledge.

Falconer, R. (2008), *The Crossover Novel: Contemporary Children's Fiction and Its Adult Readership*, London: Routledge.

Fiske, J. (2008), 'The Cultural Economy of Fandom', in E. Mathijs and X. Mendik (eds.), *The Cult Film Reader*, Maidenhead: Open University Press.

French, P. (2011), '*Don't Be Afraid of the Dark* review', *Observer*, 9 October 2011, accessed 3 January 2012 from http://www.theguardian.com/film/2011/oct/09/dont-be-afraid-dark-review

Fry, C. L. and Craig, J. R. (2002), 'Unfit for Earth, Undoomed for Heaven', *The Genesis of Coppola's Byronic Dracula*', *Literature Film Quarterly*, 30(4): 271–278.

Fuery, K. (2009), *New Media: Culture and Image*, Basingstoke: Palgrave Macmillan.

Gelder, K. (ed.) (2000), *The Horror Reader*, London: Routledge.

George, S. A. (2001), 'Not Exactly "of Woman Born": Procreation and Creation in Recent Science Fiction Films', *Journal of Popular Film and Television*, 28(4): 176–183.

Germain, D. (2008), '*Hellboy II's* Del Toro obsessed with his demons'. *Houston Chronicle*, 8 July 2008, accessed 6 May 2012 from http://www.chron.com/entertainment/movies/article/Hellboy-II-s-Del-Toro-obsessed-with-his-demons-1787187.php

Gies, D. T. (ed.) (2007), *The Cambridge Companion to Modern Spanish Culture*, Cambridge: Cambridge University Press.

Gilbert, C. (2011), '10 Questions for Guillermo del Toro'. *Time*, 5 September 2011, accessed 4 March 2013 from http://www.time.com/time/magazine/article/0,9171,2090370,00.html

Gilchrist, T. (2013), 'Ron Perlman discusses *Pacific Rim*, Guillermo del Toro, and His Bucket List'. *Spinoff Online*, accessed 14 July 2013 from http://spinoff.comicbookresources.com/2013/07/11/ron-perlman-discusses-pacific-rim-guillermo-del-toro-and-his-bucket-list/

Glendinning, N. (1977), *Goya and His Critics*, New Haven: Yale University Press.

Gordon, A. (2008), *Empire of Dreams: The Science Fiction and Fantasy Films of Steven Spielberg*, Lanham MD: Rowman & Littlefield.

Gordon, J. and Hollinger, V. (eds.) (1997), *Blood Read: The Vampire as Metaphor in Contemporary Culture*, Philadelphia: University of Pennsylvania Press.

Gottlieb, S. B. (ed.) (2002), *Framing Hitchcock: Selected Essays from the Hitchcock Annual*, Detroit: Wayne State University Press.

Grant, C. and Kuhn, A. (eds.) (2006), *Screening World Cinema: The Screen Reader*, London: Routledge.

Haggerty, G. E. (2006), *Queer Gothic*, Urbana: University of Illinois Press.

Hairston, A. (2010), 'Stories Are More Important Than Facts: Imagination as Resistance in Guillermo del Toro's *Pan's Labyrinth*', in T. L. Duchamp and E. Gunn (eds.), *Narrative Power: Encounters, Celebrations, Struggles*, Seattle WA: Aqueduct.

Hanley, J. (2007), 'The Walls Fall down: Fantasy and Power in *El laberinto del Fauno*', *Studies in Hispanic Cinemas*, 4(1): 35–45.

Hansen, R. (ed.) (2011), *Roman Catholicism in Fantastic Film: Essays on Belief, Spectacle, Ritual and Imagery*, Jefferson NC: McFarland.

Hantke, S. (ed.) (2010), *American Horror Film: The Genre at the Turn of the Millennium*, Jackson: University of Mississippi Press.

Hardcastle, A. E. (2005), 'Ghosts of the Past and Present: Hauntology and the Spanish Civil War in Guillermo del Toro's *The Devil's Backbone*', *Journal of the Fantastic in the Arts*, 15(2 [58]): 119–131.

Harris, E. (1994), *Goya (3rd edition)*, London: Phaidon Press.

Hassler-Forest, D. (2012), *Capitalist Superheroes: Caped Crusaders in the Neoliberal Age*, Alresford: John Hunt Publishing.

Hauptman, J. R. O. (2005), *Beyond the Visible: The Art of Odilon Redon*, New York: Museum of Modern Art.

Higbee, W. and Lim, S. H. (2010), 'Concepts of Transnational Cinema: Towards a Critical Transnationalism in Film Studies', *Transnational Cinemas*, 1(1): 7–21.

Hjort, M. and Mackenzie, S. (eds.) (2000), *Cinema and Nation*, London: Routledge.

Hodgen, J. (2007), 'Embracing the Horror: Tracing the Ideology of Guillermo del Toro's *Pan's Labyrinth*', *Velox: Critical Approaches to Contemporary Film*, 1(1): 15–30.

Hoffman, A. R. (2010), '"This Movie Is Like a Rorschach Test": Disrupted Allegory and the Image of the Child in *Pan's Labyrinth*', *Genre*, 43(1/2): 137–162.

Hopewell, J. (1986), *Out of the Past: Spanish Cinema after Franco*, London: British Film Institute.

Hubner, L. (2010), 'Pan's Labyrinth, Fear and the Fairy Tale', in S. Hessel and M. Huppert (eds.), *Fear Itself: Reasoning the Unreasonable*, Amsterdam: Rodopi.

Hughes, R. (2003a), 'The Unflinching Eye'. *Guardian*, 4 October 2003, accessed 24 October 2012 from http://www.guardian.co.uk/artanddesign/2003/oct/04/art. biography

———. (2003b), *Goya*, London: Harvill.

Hughes, W. and Smith, A. (eds.) (2009), *Queering the Gothic*, Manchester: Manchester University Press.

Hunt, N. (2003), 'The Importance of Trivia: Ownership, Exclusion and Authority in Science Fiction Fandom', in M. Jancovich (ed.), *Defining Cult Movies: The Cultural Politics of Oppositional Tastes*, Manchester: Manchester University Press.

Ibarra, E. A. (2012), 'Permanent Hauntings: Spectral Fantasies and National Trauma in Guillermo del Toro's *El Espinazo del Diablo (The Devil's Backbone)*', *Journal of Romance Studies*, 12(1): 56–71.

Inuhiko, Y. (2007), 'The Menace from the South Seas', in A. Phillips and J. Stringer (eds.), *Japanese Cinema: Texts and Contexts*, Abingdon: Taylor & Francis.

Jackson, R. (1981), *Fantasy, the Literature of Subversion*, London: Methuen.

Jaffe, I. (2008), *Hollywood Hybrids: Mixing Genres in Contemporary Films*, Lanham MD: Rowman and Littlefield.

Jameson, F. (1995), *The Geopolitical Aesthetic: Cinema and Space in the World System*, Bloomington: Indiana University Press.

Jenkins, D. (2008), 'Guillermo del Toro'. *Time Out*, August 2008, accessed 8 November 2012 from http://www.timeout.com/london/film/guillermo-del-toro-interview-3

Jenkins, H. (2006), *Fans, Bloggers, and Gamers: Exploring Participatory Culture*, New York: New York University Press.

Jenkins, H. (2009), *Confronting the Challenges of Participatory Culture: Media Education for the 21st Century*, Cambridge MA: MIT Press.

Jewell, S. (2010), 'In the vein of Dracula'. *New Zealand Herald*, 30 November 2010, accessed 2 June 2013 from http://carnageandculture.blogspot.co.uk/2010/12/in-vein-of-dracula.html

John, J. (2003), *Dickens's Villains: Melodrama, Character, Popular Culture*, Oxford: Oxford University Press.

———. (2013), *Dickens and Mass Culture*, Oxford: Oxford University Press.

Jordan, J. J. (1999), 'Vampire Cyborgs and Scientific Imperialism: A Reading of the Science-Mysticism Polemic in *Blade*', *Journal of Popular Film and Television*, 27(2): 4–15.

Kantaris, G. (2007), 'Cyborgs, Cities and Celluloid: Memory Machines in Two Latin American Cyborg Films', in C. Taylor and T. Pitman (eds.), *Latin American Cyberculture and Cyberliterature*, Liverpool: Liverpool University Press.

Kaveney, R. (2008), *Superheroes!: Capes and Crusaders in Comics and Films*, London: I. B. Tauris.

Kearns, K. (1996), *Nineteenth-Century Literary Realism: Through the Looking*, Glass, Cambridge: Cambridge University Press.

Kehr, D. (2006), 'A director digs deep to escape from reality'. *The New York Times*, 5 November 2006, accessed 8 September 2012 from http://www.nytimes.com/2006/11/05/movies/moviesspecial/05kehr.html?pagewanted=print&_r=0

Keller, J. R. (2002), *Queer (Un)Friendly Film and Television*, Jefferson NC: McFarland.

Kenway, J., Bullen, E., Fahey, J., and Robb, S. (2006), *Haunting the Knowledge Economy*, Abingdon: Routledge.

Keough, P. (2007), 'Guillermo del Toro interview, part I'. *The Phoenix*, 11 January 2007, accessed 10 December 2012 from http://blog.thephoenix.com/blogs/outsidetheframe/archive/2007/01/11/guillermo-del-toro-interview-part-i.aspx

Kermode, M. (2006a), 'Girl Interrupted', *Sight and Sound*, 16(12): 20–24.

———. (2006b), 'Guillermo del Toro'. *Guardian*, 21 November 2006, accessed 21 May 2012, from http://www.theguardian.com/film/2006/nov/21/guardianinterviewsatbfis outhbank?INTCMP=SRCH

Khan, O. (2001), 'El fantasma más hermoso. "El espinazo del Diablo"', *Cinemanía*, May 2001 (68): 62–65.

Kolker, R. P. (2009), *The Altering Eye: Contemporary International Cinema*, Cambridge: Open Book.

Kotecki, K. (2010), 'Approximating the Hypertextual, Replicating the Metafictional: Textual and Sociopolitical Authority in Guillermo del Toro's' *Pan's Labyrinth',* *Marvels & Tales*, 24(2): 235–254.

Koven, M. J. (2003), 'The Terror Tale: Urban Legends and the Slasher Film'. *Scope*, May 2003, accessed 2 February 2013 from http://www.scope.nottingham.ac.uk/article.php?issue=may2003&id=259&section=article

Kraniauskas, J. (1998), 'Cronos and the Political Economy of Vampirism: Notes on a Historical Constellation', in F. Barker, P. Hulme and M. Iversen (eds.), *Cannibalism and the Colonial World*, Cambridge: Cambridge University Press.

Krämer, P. (1996), 'Steven Spielberg', in L. R. Williams and M. Hammond (eds.), *Contemporary American Cinema*, New York: McGraw Hill International.

Labanyi, J. (ed.) (2002), *Constructing Identity in Contemporary Spain: Theoretical Debates and Cultural Practice*, Oxford: Oxford University Press.

Labanyi, J., Martin, A. and Rodriguez Ortega, V. (2012), 'Melodrama and Historical Film', in J. Labanyi and T. Pavlović (eds.), *A Companion to Spanish Cinema*, Chichester: Wiley.

Laezman, R. (2002), 'Beautiful Horror', *Latino Leaders*, 3(1, February–March 2002): 38.

Lambie, R. (2011), 'Guillermo del Toro interview'. *Den of Geek*, 22 October 2011, accessed 22 September 2012 from http://www.denofgeek.com/movies/18225/guillermo-del-toro-interview-the-director%E2%80%99s-cut-of-mimic-hp-lovecraft-and-more

Landis, J. (2011), *Monsters in the Movies*, London: Dorling Kindersley.

Lázaro-Reboll, A. (2001), 'Goya in Bordeaux'. *Scope*, November 2011, accessed 12 December 2012 from http://www.scope.nottingham.ac.uk/filmreview.php?issue=nov2001&id=847&section=film_rev

Lebeau, V. (2008), *Childhood and Cinema*, London: Reaktion Books.

Lerer, S. (2009), *Children's Literature: A Reader's History, from Aesop to Harry Potter*, Chicago: University of Chicago Press.

Lewis, L. A. (ed.) (2002), *The Adoring Audience: Fan Culture and Popular Media*, Abingdon: Taylor & Francis.

Linden, S. J. (1996), *Darke Hierogliphicks: Alchemy in English Literature from Chaucer to the Restoration*, Lexington: University Press of Kentucky.

Lippard, C. (1996), *By Angels Driven: The Films of Derek Jarman*, Trowbridge: Flicks Books.

Lovecraft, H. P. (2009), *At the Mountains of Madness: And Other Weird Tales*, New York: Barnes & Noble.

Luckhurst, R. (2008), *The Trauma Question*, Abingdon: Routledge.

Lucy, N. (2008), *A Derrida Dictionary*, Oxford: Wiley-Blackwell.

Lury, K. (2010), *The Child in Film: Tears, Fears, and Fairy Tales*, London: I.B. Tauris.

Lázaro-Reboll, A. (2007), 'The Transnational Reception of *El Espinazo del Diablo* (Guillermo del Toro 2001)', *Hispanic Research Journal: Iberian and Latin American Studies*, 8(1): 39–51.

————. (2008), "Now Playing Everywhere': Spanish Horror Film in the Marketplace', in
J. Beck, V. Rodríguez Ortega and R. Sklar (eds.), *Contemporary Spanish Cinema and Genre*, Manchester: Manchester UP.

————. (2012), *Spanish Horror Film*, Edinburgh: Edinburgh UP.

Lyttlelton, O. (2010), 'Guillermo Del Toro updates on *At The Mountains of Madness*,
Aiming for A June 2011 shoot'. *Indiwire*, 3 December 2010, accessed 9 November
2012 from http://blogs.indiewire.com/theplaylist/guillermo_del_toro_updates_on_
at_the_mountains_of_madness_confirms_a_june_s

McDonald, K. (2002), 'Review of *Artificial Intelligence: AI.*' *Scope*, May 2002, accessed
22 June 2013 from http://www.scope.nottingham.ac.uk/filmreview.php?issue=may20
02&id=775&section=film_rev

McLaughlin, R. (2006), *We'll Always Have the Movies: American Cinema during World
War II*, Lexington: University Press of Kentucky.

McLaughlin, J. (2009), 'All in the Family: Alfred Hitchcock's *Shadow of A Doubt*', in M.
Deutelbaum and L. Poague (eds.), *A Hitchcock Reader (2nd edition)*, Oxford: Wiley-
Blackwell.

Meerzon, Y. (2012), *Performing Exile, Performing Self: Drama, Theatre, Film*,
Basingstoke: Palgrave Macmillan.

Miles, R. J. (2011), 'Reclaiming Revelation: *Pan's Labyrinth* and *The Spirit of the Beehive*',
Quarterly Review of Film and Video, 28(3): 195–203.

Monahan, M. (2004), 'Guillermo del Toro on Luis Buñuel's *Nazarin*'. *Daily Telegraph*, 13
September 2004, accessed on 12 December 2012 from http://www.telegraph.co.uk/
culture/3623878/Guillermo-del-Toro-on-Luis-Bunuels-Nazarin-1959.html

Monegal, A. (1998), 'Images of War: Hunting the Metaphor', in J. Taléns and S. Z. Díez,
(eds.), *Modes of Representation in Spanish Cinema*, Minneapolis: University of
Minnesota Press.

Moore, R. (2007), 'Orphanage director inspired by *Peter Pan*'. *Seattle Times*, 31
December 2007, accessed 22 August 2012 from http://seattletimes.com/html/
movies/2004097254_orphanage31.html

Morefield, K. R. (2008), *Faith and Spirituality in Masters of World Cinema*, Cambridge:
Cambridge Scholars Publishing.

Moreno-Nuño, C. (2009), 'The comic-strip of historical memory: an analysis of
Paracuellos by Carlos Giménez, in the Light of Persépolis by Marjane Satrapi
and Maus by Art Spiegelman.' *Vanderbilt e-Journal of Luso-Hispanic Studies*,
Vol. 5, accessed 10 December 2012 from http://www.homiletic.net/index.php/
lusohispanic/article/view/3231/1440

Morris, N. (2007), *The Cinema of Steven Spielberg: Empire of Light*, London: Wallflower Press.

Mraz, J. (2009), *Looking for Mexico: Modern Visual Culture and National Identity*,
Durham NC: Duke University Press.

Naficy, H. (ed.) (1999), *Home, Exile, Homeland: Film, Media, and the Politics of Place*,
Abingdon: Taylor & Francis.

———. (2001), *An Accented Cinema: Exilic and Diasporic Filmmaking*, Princeton NJ: Princeton University Press.

Napier, S. J. (2004), *Ghosts and the Machines: The Technological Body*, London: Wallflower Press.

———. (2005) 'Ghosts and the Machines: The Technological Body', in Redmond, S. (ed.), *Liquid Metal: The Science Fiction Film Reader*, Columbia: Columbia University Press.

Nelson, V. (2012), *Gothicka: Vampire Heroes, Human Gods, and the New Supernatural*, Cambridge MA: Harvard University Press.

O'Brien, B. (2007), 'Fulcanelli as a Vampiric Frankenstein: The Frankenstein and Dracula Myths in Guillermo del Toro's *Cronos*', in R. J. Hand and J. McCoy (eds.), *Monstrous Adaptations: Generic and Thematic Mutations in Horror*, Manchester: Manchester University Press.

O'Connor, L. (2010), 'The Corpse on Hellboy's Back: Translating a Graphic Image', *Journal of Popular Culture*, 43(3): 540–563.

O'Malley, P. R. (2006), *Catholicism, Sexual Deviance, and Victorian Gothic Culture*, Cambridge: Cambridge University Press.

Orbaugh, S. (2005), 'The Genealogy of the Cyborg in Japanese Popular Culture', in K. Wong, G. Westfahl and A. Kit-sze Chan (eds.), *World Weavers: Globalization, Science Fiction, and The Cybernetic Revolution*, Hong Kong: Hong Kong University Press.

Orme, J. (2010), 'Narrative Desire and Disobedience in *Pan's Labyrinth*', *Marvels & Tales*, 24(2): 219–234.

Palmer, P. (2012), *The Queer Uncanny: New Perspectives on the Gothic*, Cardiff: University of Wales Press.

Perlich, J. (2010), 'Rethinking the Monomyth: *Pan's Labyrinth* and the Face of a New Hero(ine)', in J. Perlich and D. Whitt (eds.), *Millennial Mythmaking: Essays on the Power of Science Fiction and Fantasy Literature, Films and Games*, Jefferson, NC: McFarland.

Perriam, C. (2008), '*El espíritu de la colmena*': Memory Nostalgia Trauma (Victor Erice, 1973)', in J. R. Resina (ed.), *Burning Darkness: A Half Century of Spanish*, Cinema, New York: State University of New York Press.

Pilcher, T. and Brooks, B. (2005), *The Essential Guide to World Comics*, London: Collins and Brown.

Pomerance, M. (ed.) (2007), *City That Never Sleeps: New York and the Filmic Imagination*, New Brunswick: Rutgers University Press.

Powell, A. (2006), *Deleuze and Horror Film*, Edinburgh: Edinburgh University Press.

———. (2012), 'The Daemons of Unplumbed Space: Mixing the Planes in *Hellboy*', in D. Martin-Jones, and W. Brown (eds.), *Deleuze and Film*, Edinburgh: Edinburgh University Press.

Quinn, A. (2013), 'Toy franchise with a deafeningly loud movie attached: *Pacific Rim* film review'. *Independent*, 11 July 2013, accessed 12 July 2013 from http://www.independent.co.uk/arts-entertainment/films/reviews/toy-franchise-with-a-deafeningly-loud-movie-attached-pacific-rim-film-review-8703541.html

Rabiger, M. and Hurbis-Cherrier, M. (2013), *Directing: Film Techniques and Aesthetics*, Abingdon: Taylor & Francis.

Rawle, S. (2011), 'Transnational, Transgeneric, Transgressive: Tracing Miike Takashis Yakuza Cyborgs to Sukiyaki Westerns', *Asian Cinema*, 22(1): 83–98.

Resina, J. R. (ed.) (2000), *Disremembering the Dictatorship: The Politics of Memory in the Spanish Transition to Democracy*, Amsterdam: Rodopi.

Rose, G. (2007), *Visual Methodologies: An Introduction to the Interpretation of Visual Materials*, London: Sage.

Rose, J. (2010), *Studying the Devil's Backbone*, Leighton Buzzard: Auteur Publishing.

Ruffles, T. (2004), *Ghost Images: Cinema of the Afterlife*, Jefferson NC: McFarland.

Rulfo, J. (1994), *Pedro Páramo (transl. M. Sayers Peden)*, London: Serpent's Tail.

Salkowitz, R. (2012), *Comic-Con and the Business of Pop Culture: What the World's Wildest Trade Show Can Tell Us About the Future of Entertainment*, New York: McGraw-Hill.

Salon Staff. (2006) 'Conversations: Guillermo del Toro'. 13 October 2006, accessed 9 November 2012 from http://www.salon.com/2006/10/13/conversations_toro/

Sammon, P. (1997), *Future Noir: The Making of Blade Runner*, London: Orion.

Santaolalla, I. C. (1999), 'Julio Medem's *Vacas* (1991): Historicizing the Forest', in P. Evans (ed.), *Spanish Cinema; The Auteurist Tradition*, Oxford: Oxford University Press.

Savage, J. (2002), 'The Object(s) of Interpretation: Guillermo Del Toro's *El Espinazo del Diablo* (*The Devil's Backbone*), *Senses of Cinema: An Online Film Journal Devoted to the Serious and Eclectic Discussion of Cinema*, 21.

Schlegel, J. and Haberman, F. (2011), 'You Took My Advice About Theatricality a Bit … Literally": Theatricality and Cybernetics of Good and Evil in *Batman Begins*, *The Dark Knight*, *Spider-Man*, and *X-Men*', in R. J. Gray and B. Kaklamanidou (eds.), *The 21st Century Superhero: Essays on Gender, Genre and Globalization in Film*, Jefferson NC: McFarland.

Schumaker, J. B. (2011), 'Super-Intertextuality and 21st Century Individualized Social Advocacy in *Spider-Man* and *Kick-Ass*', in R. J. Gray and B. Kaklamanidou (eds.), *The 21st Century Superhero: Essays on Gender, Genre and Globalization in Film*, Jefferson NC: McFarland.

Searle, J. R. (1969), *Speech Acts: An Essay in the Philosophy of Language*, Cambridge: Cambridge University Press.

Shaw, D. (2003), *Contemporary Cinema of Latin America: Ten Key Films*, London: Bloomsbury.

Shohat, E. and Stam, R. (eds.) (2003), *Multiculturalism, Postcoloniality, and Transnational Media*, New Brunswick NJ: Rutgers University Press.

Shone, T. (2013), '*Pacific Rim*, a trilling bit of blockbuster sublimity'. *Guardian*, 12 July 2013, accessed 13 July 2013 from http://www.theguardian.com/film/filmblog/2013/jul/12/pacific-rim-guillermo-del-toro-blockbuster

Sienkiewicz, M. and Marx, N. (2009), 'Beyond a Cutout World: Ethnic Humor and Discursive Integration in South Park', *Journal of Film and Video*, 61(2): 5–18.

Silver, A. and Ursini, J. (2010), *Vampire Film from Nosferatu to Twilight (4th Edition)*, Montclair NJ: Limelight.

Skal, D. J. (2004), *Hollywood Gothic: The Tangled Web of Dracula from Novel to Stage to Screen*, New York: Faber & Faber.

Smith, G. (2003), *Dickens and the Dream of Cinema*, Manchester: Manchester University Press.

Smith, P. J. (2001), 'Ghost of the Civil Dead: *The Devil's Backbone*', *Sight and Sound*, December 2001, accessed 5 June 2012 from http://old.bfi.org.uk/sightandsound/review/1904

———. (2006), '*The Spirit of the Beehive*: Spanish Lessons'. *The Criterion Collection: Current*, accessed 22 February 2012 from http://www.criterion.com/current/posts/447-the-spirit-of-the-beehive-spanish-lessons

Smith, A. and Hughes, W. (eds.) (2009), *Queering the Gothic*, Manchester: Manchester University Press.

Sontag, S. (1993), 'Foreword', in J. Rulfo, *Pedro Páramo (transl. M. Sayers Peden)*, London: Serpent's Tail.

Staff, S. (2006), 'Conversations: Guillermo del Toro'. *Salon*, 13 October 2006, accessed 30 November 2012 from http://www.salon.com/2006/10/13/conversations_toro/

Steenberg, L. (2010), 'Guillermo del Toro', in Y. Tasker (ed.), *Fifty Contemporary Film Directors (2nd Edition)*, Abingdon: Routledge.

Stewart, G. (2003), 'Dickens, Eisenstein, Film', in J. Glavin (ed.), *Dickens on Screen*, Cambridge: Cambridge University Press.

Stock, A. M. (2006), 'Migrancy and the Latin American Cinemscape: Towards a Post-National Critical Praxis', in E. Ezra and T. Rowden (eds.), *Transnational Cinema: The Film Reader*, London: Routledge.

Sutton, T. and Benshoff, H. M. (2011), 'Forever Family" Values: *Twilight* and the Modern Vampire', in A. Briefel and S. J. Miller (eds.), *Horror After 9/11: World of Fear, Cinema of Terror*, Austin: University of Texas Press.

Tasker, Y. (1993), *Spectacular Bodies: Gender, Genre and the Action Cinema*, London: Routledge.

Thomas, S. (2011), 'Ghostly Affinities: Child Subjectivity and Spectral Presences in *El Espíritu de la Colmena* and *El Espinazo del Diablo*', *Hispanet Journal*, 4, 1–23, accessed 5 April 2012 from http://www.hispanetjournal.com/GhostlyAffinities.pdf

Thompson, J. O. (2000), 'Reflexions on Dead Children in the Cinema and Why There Are Not More of Them', in G. Avery, K. Reynolds, P. Yates and J. Goodall (eds.), *Representations of Childhood Death*, Basingstoke: Macmillan.

Tudor, A. (1989), *Monsters and Mad Scientists: A Cultural History of the Horror Movie*, Oxford: Wiley-Blackwell.

Van Elferen, I. (2011), 'Music That Sucks and Bloody Liturgy', in R. Hansen (ed.), *Roman Catholicism in Fantastic Film: Essays on Belief, Spectacle, Ritual and Imager*, Jefferson NC: McFarland.

Verne, J. (2007), *Around the World in Eighty Days*, London: Penguin Classics.

———. (2008), *The Steam House: Tigers and Traitors*, Rockville: Wildside Press.

Vinci, T. M. (2012), 'Remembering Why We Once Feared the Dark: Reclaiming Humanity Through Fantasy in Guillermo del Toro's *Hellboy II*', *The Journal of Popular Culture*, 45(5): 1041–1059.

Vulture (2008) accessed 28 June 2013 from http://www.vulture.com/2008/07/guillermo_del_toro_on_why_hellboy_ii.html

Walkuski, E. (2012), 'Hulk' TV Show on hold says Guillermo del Toro'. *Screen Crush*, accessed 3 March 2013 from http://screencrush.com/hulk-tv-update/

Whatley, J. (2002), 'Gothic Cults and Gothic Cultures 1: Modern and Postmodern Gothic', *Gothic Studies*, 4(2): 91–212.

White, E. (2008), 'Insects and Automata in Hoffman, Balzac, Carter, and del Toro', *Journal of the Fantastic in the Arts*, 19(3): 363–378.

Willson, R. (1977), '*Jaws* as Submarine Movie', *Jump Cut*, 15: 32–33.

Winnberg, J. (2013), 'Redeemed Now and Forever" Traumatic and Therapeutic Realism in Peter Ackroyd's *The House of Dr Dee*', in J.-M. Ganteau and S. Onega (eds.), *Trauma and Romance in Contemporary British Literature*, Abingdon: Taylor & Francis.

Wisker, G. (2005), *Horror Fiction: An Introduction*, New York, NY: Continuum.

Wolfreys, J. (2002), *Victorian Hauntings: Spectrality, Gothic, the Uncanny and Literature*, Basingstoke: Palgrave.

Wolk, D. (2007), *Reading Comics: How Graphic Novels Work and What They Mean*, Boston: Da Capo Press.

Wood, R. (2002), 'The American Nightmare: Horror in the 70s', in M. Jancovich (ed.), *Horror, The Film Reader*, London: Routledge.

Wood, J. (2006a), *The Faber Book of Mexican Cinema*, London: Faber and Faber.

———. (2006b), *Talking Movies: Contemporary World Filmmakers in Interview*, London: Wallflower.

Yolcom, M. (2008), '*Pan's Labyrinth/El Laberinto del Fauno*: Review', *Marvels and Tales*, 22(2): 345–348.

Zalewski, D. (2011), 'Show the Monster', *New Yorker*, 86(47): 40–53.

Zhang, Y. (2012), *A Companion to Chinese Cinema*, Oxford: Wiley-Blackwell.

Zipes, J. (2008), 'Why Fantasy Matters Too Much', *CLCWeb: Comparative Literature and Culture*, 10(4): 3.

Index

Lightning Source UK Ltd.
Milton Keynes UK
UKHW050411301219
356097UK00007B/220/P